Charles Taylor

The Wisdom of Ben Sira

Portions of the Book of Ecclesiasticus from Hebrew manuscripts in the Cairo

Genizah collection presented to the University of Cambridge by the editors

Charles Taylor

The Wisdom of Ben Sira
Portions of the Book of Ecclesiasticus from Hebrew manuscripts in the Cairo Genizah collection presented to the University of Cambridge by the editors

ISBN/EAN: 9783337036362

Printed in Europe, USA, Canada, Australia, Japan

Cover: Foto ©ninafisch / pixelio.de

More available books at **www.hansebooks.com**

THE WISDOM OF BEN SIRA

PORTIONS OF

THE BOOK ECCLESIASTICUS

FROM HEBREW MANUSCRIPTS IN THE CAIRO
GENIZAH COLLECTION PRESENTED TO THE
UNIVERSITY OF CAMBRIDGE BY
THE EDITORS

EDITED FOR THE SYNDICS OF THE UNIVERSITY PRESS

BY

S. SCHECHTER M.A. Litt.D.
READER IN RABBINIC IN THE UNIVERSITY OF CAMBRIDGE AND
PROFESSOR OF HEBREW IN THE UNIVERSITY OF LONDON

AND

C. TAYLOR D.D.
MASTER OF ST JOHN'S COLLEGE CAMBRIDGE

CAMBRIDGE
AT THE UNIVERSITY PRESS
1899

All rights reserved

PREFACE.

BY a surprising series of discoveries in recent years much of the Hebrew of Ecclesiasticus, a book which had been known to the modern world only through Versions and some Rabbinic Quotations, has now again been brought to light.

The Revision of the Authorised Version of 1611, undertaken in 1870, having at length been accomplished, it was said in the Preface to the Apocrypha (1895), of the book Ecclesiasticus: "Considerable attention was paid to the text; but the materials available for correcting it were but scanty." On the 13th May in the following year, Dr Schechter at Cambridge observed in a bundle of fragments brought by Mrs Lewis and Mrs Gibson from Southern Palestine a time-worn leaf from a copy of the lost original Hebrew of Ben Sira's work.

The publication of this first fragment (ch. 39. 15—40. 8) of the WISDOM OF BEN SIRA in the *Expositor* led to the identification of the nine leaves following it (ch. 40. 9—49. 11), which had been acquired by the Bodleian Library through Professor Sayce "almost simultaneously" with the discovery of the leaf first found. The nine and the one, promptly edited by Messrs Cowley and Neubauer in Hebrew and English, with the Greek, Old Latin and Peshitto Syriac Versions, were published at the Clarendon Press early in 1897.

At Midsummer in that year Dr Schechter found in the Cairo Genizah collection at Cambridge another leaf of Ecclesiasticus from the same Codex, and afterwards from time to time six others, including the penultimate and last folios of the book, which were discovered together on the 27th August, 1897.

Two more leaves from this Codex, identified by Mr G. Margoliouth, are now in the British Museum, as announced in the *Times* of the 4th April, 1899. The one fits in between the first and the second in order of the seven leaves just mentioned, and the other between the third and the fourth.

In the same Genizah collection Dr Schechter had detected also two pairs of leaves from another manuscript of Ecclesiasticus, on the 2nd and the 24th of September, 1897, respectively. These four small leaves, which contain in close writing more than the seven from the other manuscript, could only have been singled out from a collection of so many thousands by a careful though necessarily rapid scrutiny. They altogether lack the striking Biblical and Masoretic appearance which distinguished the Ben Sira fragments previously found.

In this preliminary edition of the eleven new leaves found by Dr Schechter, the discoverer is responsible for the Text, the Notes on the Text, and the Introduction; and the present writer for the Translation and Footnotes and the Appendix, which contains discussions of some passages extracted from the folios edited by Messrs Cowley and Neubauer. For the defects of the first part of the volume I have to offer the apology that it had to be finished quickly after the completion of the Notes on the Text. Of the Text in manuscript I have as yet read only the ninth folio (ch. 49. 12—50. 22), which was published as the first of Dr Schechter's Genizah Specimens in no. 38 of the *Jewish Quarterly Review* (Jan. 1898).

Our cordial thanks are due to Mrs Lewis and Mrs Gibson for kind permission to give herewith, for the first time, facsimiles of the folio first discovered, a fragment second to none in interest to the decipherer.

Ben Sira's book is of unique interest to the scholar and the theologian as a Hebrew work of nearly known date, which forms a link between the Old Testament and the Rabbinic writings. The first step to its right appreciation is to note its discursive use of the ancient Scriptures, and the author's free way of adapting their thoughts and phrases to his purposes.

The Hebrew restores allusions which were lost or obscured in the Versions. A simple and good example of this is supplied by the first complete verse that we have of the original (ch. 3. 8), *My son, in word and in deed honour thy father; That all blessings may overtake thee.* The *Speaker's Commentary* corrects the rendering of the Authorised Version, "that a blessing may come upon thee from *them*," by substituting for *them* the singular *him*, "according to the better reading." The Hebrew, agreeing with neither, shews a reference to Deut. 28. 2, *and all these blessings shall come upon thee, and overtake thee, if thou shalt hearken unto the voice of the Lord thy God*, which is less clear in the Syriac, "that all his (?) blessings may come upon thee." Here, it will be noticed, Ben Sira does not quote exactly, but fits familiar words slightly disguised into a new context.

Again, the WISDOM OF BEN SIRA refers of course to the descriptions of Wisdom in the book of Proverbs. If, as an Eastern dame, she there says, *For at the window of my house I looked forth through my lattice*, the Son of Sirach must needs say of her votary that he looks in "through her window" (ch. 14. 23). And if the Paroemiast writes, *Say unto wisdom, Thou art my sister; and call understanding thy kinswoman*, it is for the later sage to represent her as "mother" and "wife of youth" (ch. 15. 2). And if she says in Solomon, *Come, eat of my bread, and drink of the wine which I have mingled*, it must be said in Ben Sira, "And she shall feed him with bread of wisdom; and give him water of understanding to drink" (ch. 15. 3).

In diction as in thought our author is a sedulous imitator of the Hebrew Scriptures. The words which he uses are not all his own, his work being more or less a tissue of old classical phrases, like a modern school composition in a dead language. Professor Israel Lévi in *L'Ecclésiastique* (p. XXIII.) remarks upon the strange misunderstandings of the Hebrew of Ecclesiasticus by its translator into Greek, and asks, "Mais quand le Siracide commet-il surtout ces bévues?" The answer is that it is in Bible passages that he most goes astray: "Quant aux néologismes, il les comprend toujours." The evidence for this strong statement will have to be well weighed. But manifestly some things in Ecclesiasticus are artificially reproduced from ancient sources, and are not necessarily expressed quite in the language of its day. The Greek translator stumbles at an archaism when in ch. 12. 5 he puts "loaves" for "war" (Jud. 5. 8).

Looking at the Prologue to Ecclesiasticus in the light of the new discoveries, we see now that it warned us to expect what we have found. Of his ancestor's work and his own the younger Siracide wrote: "my grandfather Jesus, having much given himself to the reading of the law, and the prophets, and the other books of our fathers, and having gained great familiarity therein, was drawn on also himself to write somewhat pertaining to instruction and wisdom; in order that those who love learning, and are addicted to these things, might make progress much more by living according to the law. Ye are intreated therefore to read with favour and attention, and to pardon us, if in any parts of what we have laboured to interpret, we may seem to fail in some of the phrases. For things originally spoken in Hebrew have not the same force in them, when they are translated into another tongue: and not only these, but the law itself, and the prophecies, and the rest of the books, have no small difference, when they are spoken in their original language. For having come into Egypt in the eight and thirtieth year of Euergetes the king, and having continued there some time, I found a copy (*or* a like work) affording no small instruction. I thought it therefore most necessary for me to apply some diligence and travail to interpret this book; applying indeed much watchfulness and skill in that space of time to bring the book to an end, and set it forth for them also, who in the land of their sojourning are desirous to learn, fashioning their manners beforehand, so as to live according to the law."

Our author "was drawn on also himself to write somewhat," after the manner of the Law, the Prophets, and the other Books, wherein he had "gained great familiarity" by much study. Ben Sira the younger, not having his ancestor's intimate acquaintance with the Hebrew Scriptures, naturally missed some of his allusions to them: as a translator he confesses his inability to give the "same force" in Greek to some things written in Hebrew: and he had to bring his arduous task to an end in a limited "space of time." Thus he prepares us for some of the remarkable errors which we find in his Version.

Its literary method, well described in Professor Cheyne's *Job and Solomon* (1887) before the discovery of the Cairo fragments, should perhaps be classed with the traces of Greek culture in Ecclesiasticus. Allusions after its manner occur in the book of Baruch and the Wisdom of Solomon ; but Sirach's work, which is on a larger scale, is also more systematic and comprehensive in its use and assimilation of the writings of the Fathers.

As regards his witness to Canonical Books, Ben Sira's Hebrew sometimes lightens our darkness, and sometimes only makes clearer what had been seen from the Versions before it was found. From the end of ch. 48 it was sufficiently obvious that he credited one author with the book of Isaiah as a whole ; but the Hebrew was wanted to shew that in speaking of "exactness of balance and weights" (ch. 42. 4) he appropriated a phrase from Isaiah 40. 15, "the nations are counted as the *small dust of the balance*." His reference to Ezekiel's mention of Job was not apparent in the Greek of Ecclus. 49. 9, "For verily he remembered the enemies in rain, And to do good to them that directed their ways aright." Commentators on Ecclesiastes had seen imitations of it in Ecclesiasticus : now we find a seeming play upon Koheleth's much discussed epilogue in a passage of Ben Sira (ch. 43. 27), of which in the Greek it had been said, "We have no hesitation in regarding this as a bold later addition by the younger Siracide."

It is remarkable that in the Greek of Ecclesiasticus the readings of a manuscript of inferior pretensions have now and again to be preferred to those of Codices which on received principles of criticism rank above it, as for example in ch. 51. 19, where "The best MSS. have 'and in the doing of hunger,' which is evidently impossible." Agreement of the great uncial MSS. in Ecclesiasticus is sometimes a consensus of error.

One Greek manuscript alone (248), which is followed by the Complutensian Polyglot, "preserves the right order of the chapters after ch. 30." It is one of the authorities for ch. 3. 25, *Without eyes thou shalt want light &c.* (A. V.), a verse thought to be spurious, but contained in the Hebrew. In ch. 43. 23, where "The most ancient authorities read *Jesus planted it*" (R. V. marg.), it reads, with the

Hebrew, *islands* for *Jesus*. In ch. 43. 26 it stands alone in its reading *angel*, which is clearly a rendering of a word in the Cairo text. These few examples will suffice to call attention to the excellence of this late cursive Codex, and by implication of the Versions and Editions which it has most influenced.

Extracts from the *Speaker's Commentary* given in the Notes to the Translation will enable the reader to confront more or less felicitous speculations about the vanished original with the Hebrew now in our hands. One sound critical deduction from the Versions scarcely needed further verification. Professor Bickell in 1882 announced his discovery of an alphabetic poem at the end of Ecclesiasticus; and our Genizah Text, while witnessing to the truth of his theory, has itself need to be emended in accordance with it. The true reading of the acrostic is discussed at the end of the Appendix.

The first section of our edition is intended to be read in connexion with the Notes on the Text, which were written before it. Some things in them are repeated in the Footnotes, which also occasionally throw out alternative suggestions for the reading or construction of the Text. In places where this is manifestly corrupt the attempt to give a coherent rendering is sometimes abandoned, and the English merely aims at representing the Hebrew as it is. Much more time than was available is required for the solution or adequate discussion of the numerous knotty problems which the Cairo Text presents.

C. TAYLOR.

CAMBRIDGE,
12th April, 1899.

CONTENTS.

I.

THE TRANSLATION.

Portions of Ecclesiasticus 3—16 and 30—51 translated from Cairo Genizah Hebrew Manuscripts with Footnotes.

II.

APPENDIX.

Notes on the Lewis-Gibson and Oxford Folios.
The Alphabetic Poem in Ecclesiasticus 51.
Facsimiles of the Lewis-Gibson Folio*.

III.

THE TEXT

WITH

PREFATORY NOTE.
INTRODUCTION.
NOTES ON THE TEXT.

* The verso to come first and face the preceding page.

I.
THE WISDOM OF BEN SIRA

PORTIONS OF ECCLESIASTICUS
3—7 11—16 30—33 35—38 49—51
TRANSLATED FROM THE HEBREW
WITH FOOTNOTES

ABBREVIATIONS.

The letters 𝔊 𝔐 𝔖 stand for Greek, Hebrew, and Syriac.
𝔐 is used of Ecclesiasticus only, and 𝔐ᵐ for the margin of 𝔐.
𝔊 in Ecclesiasticus is in general Fritzsche's text.
E refers to Edersheim on Ecclus. in the *Speaker's Commentary*.
A note of interrogation in brackets (?) means that the sense is doubtful, or that a conjectural reading of 𝔐 has been adopted.

THE WISDOM OF BEN SIRA.

3. 6 . . . . that honoureth his mother.
8 My son, in word' and in deed honour thy father;
   That all blessings may overtake thee.
9 The blessing of a father settleth the root;
   But the curse of a mother plucketh up the plant.
10 Take not honour to thyself by the shame of thy father;
   For it is no honour unto thee.
11 The honour of his father is a man's honour;
   And he that curseth his mother doth greatly sin.
12 My son, be stedfast in honouring thy father;
   And forsake him not all the days of thy life.
13 Yea, and though his mind fail, bear with (*or* help) him;
   And dishonour him not all the days of his life (鄕).
14 Benefaction to a father shall not be blotted out;
   But it shall be planted instead of sin.
15 In the day of affliction it shall be remembered unto thee,
   As heat upon hoar frost, to do away thine iniquities.

3. 6 מכבד] 𝔖 *qui matrem honorat.* Verse 4 also ends thus in the Versions.
8 וישינוך כל ברכות] Deut. xxviii. 2 *and all these blessings shall come upon thee and overtake thee.* See note on 鄕.
9 חיסד] Lit. *foundeth*, cf. Isaiah li. 16 *to plant heaven and found earth*. Prov. x. 25 *the righteous is an everlasting foundation*, xii. 3 *the root of the righteous shall not be moved*.
12 תעזבהו] 𝔖 (*it* for *him*) *ne desistas ab eo colendo.* 𝔊 καὶ μὴ λυπήσῃς αὐτόν, reading תעצבהו. See E, noting that 𝔖 (not 𝔊) agrees with 鄕.
13 עזוב] This may mean *help*, in contrast with עזב *forsake* (ver. 12). Compare Ex. xxiii. 5 *If thou see the ass of him that hateth thee lying under his burden, and wouldest forbear to* HELP *him, thou shalt surely* HELP *with him*, Neh. iii. 8 *and they* FORTIFIED *Jerusalem.* Or עזוב (𝔖 ܫܒܩ) may have the sense *remitte* debitum, cf. Neh. v. 10. See note on 鄕.
14—15 צדקת...תזכר] Ezek. xxxiii. 13 A. V. *all his righteousnesses shall not be remembered.*

16 For he that despiseth his father doeth presumptuously;
   And he that curseth his mother angereth his Creator.
17 My son, in thy wealth walk in meekness (𝕳 𝕊);
   And thou shalt be more beloved than he that giveth gifts.
18 Minish thy soul from all the great things of the world;
   And before God thou shalt find mercy.
20ᵃ For great is the mercy of God;
19ᵇ And he revealeth his secret to the meek.
21 Search not the things that are too wonderful for thee;
   And seek not that which is hid from thee.
22 What thou art permitted, think thereupon;
   But thou hast no business with the secret things.
23 And intrude not into that which is beyond thee;
   For thou hast been shewed that which is too great for thee.
24 For many are the conceits of the sons of men;
   And the imaginations of thoughts (𝕳) that make them to err.
26 A hard heart shall fare ill at the last;
   But he that loveth good things will guide himself therein.
27 Many are the sorrows of a hard heart;
   And he that is confident addeth iniquity to iniquity.
25 Without the apple of the eye light faileth;
   And without knowledge wisdom faileth.
28 Haste not to heal the stroke of the scorner;
   For there is no healing it: for he is a plant of evil planting.

17 בעשרך] R. V. *My son, go on with thy business in meekness; So shalt thou be beloved of an acceptable man.* 𝔊 suggests עשק (פסע).
18 מעם...עולם] The A. V. and R. V. make the *piel* of מעט intransitive (Eccl. xii. 3), but in Ben Sira as in neo-Hebrew it is transitive. He uses עולם (iii. 18, xvi. 7) for *world*, cf. Eccl. iii. 11 *also he hath set the world in their heart.* Cf. Sirac. xliv. *init.* Heb. שבח אבות עולם, 𝔊 πατέρων ὕμνος. Mishn. Ediyoth I. 4 אבות העולם. On *great things* see note on 𝕳, cf. Jer. xlv. 5 *And seekest thou great things for thyself? seek not.*

22 ואין לך עסק בנסתרות] From Deut. xxix. 28 (29) THE SECRET THINGS *belong unto the Lord our God: but the things that are revealed belong unto us and to our children for ever.*

23 חמר] See note on 𝕳. Rebel not (Ex. xxiii. 21) by intruding into (Col. ii. 18) things forbidden.

24 רעות] So 𝕳 with *daleth.* 𝔊 𝕊 רעות with *resh.* See note on 𝕳.

27 ומתחולל מוסיף עון על עון] Sirac. v. 5 להוסיף עון על עון, Psalm lxix. 28 תנה עון,על עונם. On מתחולל see note on 𝕳.

25 אישון] A. V. *Without eyes thou shalt want light.* "This verse must be omitted, as not supported by the best authorities. In the Syr. and Arab. Versions it follows after *v.* 27, and in the Arab. rather as a paraphrase" (E). Fritzsche, "addita sunt in (H) 248. 253. Co. Syr. Ar.: κόρας μὴ ἔχων ἀπορήσεις φωτός, γνώσεως δὲ ἀμοιρῶν (ἄμοιρος ὢν) μὴ ἐπαγγέλλου."

29 A wise heart will understand parables of the wise;
   And the ear that hearkeneth to wisdom shall rejoice.
30 Waters quench flaming fire;
   So righteousness maketh atonement for sin.
31 Whoso doeth good, it shall meet him in his ways (?);
   And in the time that he tottereth he shall find a stay.
4. 1 My son, mock not at the life of the poor (or of affliction);
   And make not the soul of him that is poor and bitter of soul (מר) to pine.
   2 Vex not the spirit (?) of the soul that lacketh;
     And hide not thyself from one that is crushed (?) in soul.
   3ª Trouble not the bowels of him that is humbled;
     And pain not the inward part of the poor.
   3ᵇ Withhold not a gift from thy needy;
   4ª And thou shalt not despise the supplications of the miserable;
   5ᵇ And thou shalt not give him place to curse thee.
   6 He that is bitter of spirit crieth in the anguish of his soul;
     And his Rock (צור) shall hear the voice of his cry.
   7 Make thyself (?) beloved of the congregation;
     And to a potentate moreover bow the head.
   8 Incline thine ear to the poor;
     And answer him Peace with meekness.
   9 Save the oppressed from his oppressors;
     And let not thy spirit loathe right judgement.
   10ª Be as a father to orphans;
       And instead of a husband to widows.
   10ᶜ And God shall call thee Son;   Fol. A 1 verso
       And shall be gracious to thee, and deliver thee from the pit.
   11 Wisdom teacheth (תו) her sons;
      And testifieth (תו) to all that attend to her.
   12 They that love her love life;
      And they that seek her shall obtain favour from the Lord.
   13 And they that retain her shall find honour from the Lord;
      And shall have grace shewed them by the blessing of the Lord.
   14 Ministers of holiness are her ministers;
      And God loveth them that love her (?).

31 ברכיו] Ϭ μέμνηται εἰς τὰ μετὰ ταῦτα. 𝔏 expeditus est in via sua, "reading ארחות for אחרית" (E), cf. ii. 3 (E), xxxii. 22 מ.

4. 3ª תחמר] Lam. i. 20 *my bowels are troubled.* See note on מ.

5ᵇ מקום] Compare τόπον διδόναι in the New Testament.

11 בניה...לכל] St Luke vii. 35 R. V. *wisdom is justified of all her children* (Matt. xi. 19 *works*). Compare the rabbinic expression *Sons of Torah.*

c

15 He that heareth me shall judge truth (𝔊 nations);
 And he that giveth ear to me shall dwell in my chamber within.
17ᵃ For I will go with him, making myself strange;
17ᶜ And at the first I (𝔐 he) will try him with temptations.
17ᵈ And what time his heart is filled with me;
18 I will turn and direct him,
 And reveal unto him of my secrets.
19 If he turn away and decline from me (?),
 I will train him with fetters (or restraints).
19⁽¹⁾ If he turn away from after me,
 I will cast him off, and deliver him to the spoilers.
20 My son, observe season and time (?);
 And fear evil, and be not shamefaced unto thyself.
21 For there is a shame (?) that ladeth with iniquity;
 And there is a shame that is honour and grace.
22 Have not respect of thine own person;
 And stumble (𝔐) not at thine offences.
23 Withhold not a word (or to speak) in season (?);
 Nor ever conceal thy wisdom.
24 For by speech wisdom is made known;
 And understanding by the answer of the tongue.
25ᵃ Gainsay not the truth (𝔐 God);
 And submit thyself unto God.
26 Be not ashamed to turn from iniquity;
 And stand not against a stream.
27 Lay not thyself down for a fool to tread upon;
 And be not contrary before rulers.
27⁽¹⁾ Sit not with one that judgeth unrighteously;
 For according to his pleasure (?) thou shalt judge with him.

15 נגדא ܠܓܐ ܘܚܕ 𝔖 [בחדרי סביח *intra me habitabit*.
21 [משאות עון] Lev. xxii. 16 והשיאו אותם עון אשמה. Zeph. iii. 18 מִשְׂאֵת
עליח חרפה, with variant עליך. See note on 𝔐.

23 [אל תמנע דבר] Cf. Prov. xi. 26 *He that withholdeth corn*, which is rabbinically applied to Torah. Sirac. xxxii. 3 ואל תמנע שיר. בעולם. It is doubtful how this should be emended. The translation assumes a reading בעת or בעתו followed by לעולם.

26 [שבלת] 𝔖 (reading *beth* as *kaf*) & *stulto ne resistas*, cf. Eccl. i. 17 שִׂכְלוּת *folly*. Sirac. v. 9 דרך שבולת. See in the Story of Ahikar, edited in Syriac by Dr Rendel Harris, no. 65 (p. 65) *My son, strive not with a man in his day, and stand not against a river in its flood*. See also in nos. 45—46 *My son, I have carried salt and removed lead; and I have not seen anything heavier than that a man should pay back a debt when he did not borrow. My son, I have carried iron and removed stones; and they were not heavier on me than a man who settles in the house of his father-in-law*, comparing Sirac. xxii. 14—15, and no. 6 of Dr Schechter's collection of Quotations from Ecclus. in Rabb. Lit. (*J. Q. R.* III. 691).

28 Unto death contend (?) for justice;
   And the Lord shall fight for thee.
28⁽¹⁾ Be not called a double dealer;
   And slander not with (?) thy tongue.
29 Be not boastful with thy tongue;
   And slack and negligent (?) in thy business.
30 Be not as a dog (𝕲 lion) in thine house;
   And strange and fearful in thy business.
31 Let not thine hand be opened to receive;
   And clenched in the midst of giving.
5. 1 Stay not upon thy strength (*or* wealth);
   And say not, It is in the power of my hand.
   1⁽¹⁾ Stay not upon thy force;
   To go after the desire of thy soul.
2 Go not after thy heart and thine eyes;
   To walk in the pleasures of wickedness.
3 Say not, Who can withstand my (𝕲 𝕾) strength?
   For the Lord avengeth (𝕭 seeketh) them that are persecuted.
4 Say not, I have sinned, and who (?) shall do aught unto me,
   For God is slow to anger?
4⁽¹⁾ Say not, The Lord is merciful;
   And he will blot out all mine iniquities.
5 Trust not to forgiveness;
   To add iniquity to iniquity.
6ᵃ Nor say, His mercy is great:
   He will forgive the multitude of mine iniquities.
6ᶜ For mercy and anger are with him;
   And his displeasure shall rest upon (?) the wicked.
7ᵃ Make no tarrying to turn unto him;
   And put not off (?) from day to day.
7ᶜ For suddenly shall his indignation go forth;
   And in the day of vengeance thou shalt perish.
8 Trust not on riches of falsehood;
   For they shall not profit in the day of wrath.
9 Be not winnowing with every wind,
   And turning the way of the stream (𝕭).
10 Be assured in thine own mind;
   And let thy word be one.
11 Be swift to give ear;
   And with patience of spirit return answer.

Fol. A 2 recto

28⁽¹⁾ בעל שתים בו] A doublet in the Hebrew. See ch. v. 14.

5. 8 נכסי שקר] 𝕲 ἐπὶ χρήμασιν ἀδίκοις. 𝕾 ܕܥܘܠܐ *iniquitatis* as in St Luke xvi. 9—11 ἐκ τοῦ μαμωνᾶ τῆς ἀδικίας...ἐν τῷ ἀδίκῳ μαμωνᾷ...τὸ ἀληθινὸν τίς ὑμῖν πιστεύσει; Sirac. xxxi. 8 ממון.

12 If it be in thee, answer thy neighbour;
  And if not, be thy hand upon thy mouth.
13 Honour and disgrace are in the hand (?) of talk;
  And the tongue of a man is his fall.
14ᵃ Be not called a double dealer;
  And with thy tongue slander not a neighbour.
14ᶜ For for the thief was created shame;
  And sore reproach for (𝔊 𝔖) the double dealer.
15 Little or much do not corruptly (𝔐);
6. 1ᵃ And instead of a friend become not an enemy.
  1ᵇ Reproach shall inherit (𝔐) an evil name and disgrace:
  So an evil man that is a double dealer.
  2 Fall not into the hand of thine appetite;
  That it should consume thy strength like an ox (?).
  3 It shall eat thy leaves and uproot thy fruit;
  And leave thee like a dry tree.
  4 For fierce appetite corrupteth them that have it;
  And the joy of an enemy overtaketh (𝔐) them.
  5 Many a friend doth a sweet palate make;
  And gracious lips that greet (?) with peace.
  6 Be they that are at peace with thee many;
  But he that hath thy secret one of a thousand.
  7 Hast thou gotten a friend? get him in trial (?);
  And be not in haste to trust on him.

14ᵃ (cf. vi. 1ᵇ) בעל שתים] A new phrase for the Hebrew Lexicon meaning *double*, lit. *dominus duarum* without specification as in δίγλωσσος, διπρόσωπος, διπλοκάρδιος of the part doubled. 𝔖 *ambulans in duabus*, cf. in the *perush* קב ונקי on *Mishlé* נתן נדר לאיש המסכסך והוא סיס לו לפעמים דרך איש ולפעמים דרך זר. See also Mayor's *St James* on ἀνὴρ δίψυχος, *Berachoth* 28 a שאין תובו כברו, Murray *New Eng. Dict.* on 'Double' and its compounds, Clem. R. ii. 12. 2 "Ὅταν ἔσται τὰ δύο ἕν, καὶ τὸ ἔξω ὡς τὸ ἔσω.

6. 1ᵇ תועבה חרפה] 𝔊 ὄνομα γὰρ πονηρὸν αἰσχύνην καὶ ὄνειδος κληρονομήσει, H. 253. Syr. κληρονομήσεις (Fritzsche).

2 ותעבה חילך עליך] Possibly this עליך is an accidental repetition of עליך *thy leaves* (ver. 3), in place of בשור *as an ox*. 𝔊 ἵνα μὴ διαρπαγῇ ὡς ταῦρος ἡ ψυχή σου. 𝔖 *ne quasi taurus robur tuum quaerat* (ܪܒܚܐ). Isaiah v. 5 לבער, LXX. εἰς διαρπαγήν. Thus 𝔊 may have read ותבער with *resh* for *hé*, the original Hebrew being perhaps ותבעה. Supposing 𝔖 to represent this reading, we have to find a suitable sense for בעה, on which see Kohut *Aruch Completum* ii. 138 a. For Numb. xxii. 4 *as the ox licketh up the grass* Targ. Jon. has היכמא דמבעי תורא ית עסבא. Compare the Greek βούλιμος, βουλιμία, *ox-hunger*. There is a Talmudic discussion about המבעה, and a Tosefta variant המבעיר with *yod*, *resh* for *hé*. On ותעבה as it stands see note on 𝔐. A. V. *Extol not thyself in the counsel of thine own heart; that thy soul be not torn in pieces as a bull* [*straying alone*].

4 בעליו] Prov. xxiii. 2 *if thou be a man given to appetite*.

THE WISDOM OF BEN SIRA.

8 For there is a friend that is for a season;
And that will not (?) continue in the day of affliction.
9 There is a friend that turneth to an enemy;
And he will make bare the strife to thy reproach.
10 There is a friend that is a companion at the table;
But he will not be found in the day of adversity.
11 In thy prosperity he is as thou art;
And in thine adversity he will remove away from thee.
12 If evil overtake thee, he will turn against thee;
And will hide himself from thy face.
13 Separate thyself from thine enemies;
And beware of thy friends.
14 A faithful friend is a firm friend;
And he that findeth him hath found a treasure.
15 There is no exchange for a faithful friend;
Nor price that can be weighed for his goodness.
16 A faithful friend is a balm (𝔊 𝔖) of life;
He that feareth God shall obtain it.
17^b For as he is, so is his neighbour;
17$^{bn)}$ And as his name, so are his works.
19^a As one that plougheth and as one that reapeth approach unto her;
And wait for the abundance of her increase.
19^c For in the tillage of her thou shalt toil a little;
And on the morrow (𝔚) thou shalt eat her fruit.
20 Rough is she to the fool;
And he that is void of understanding cannot bear her.
21 As a burdensome weight shall she be upon him;
And he will not tarry to cast her away.
22 For discipline is according to its (?) name;
And to the more part she is not plain (*or* right).

22 A. V. *For wisdom is according to her name.* "It seems impossible by any critical ingenuity to explain the first clause of this verse, since there is not any Hebrew or Greek word which would admit of a play upon the word *wisdom*" (E). מוסר (masc.) as a synonym for חכמה, cf. Prov. iv. 13 *Take fast hold of* INSTRUCTION *; let not go : keep her, for she is thy life,* החזק במוסר אל תרף נצרה כי היא חייך. In Ben Sira's מוסר, from the ambiguous יסר παιδεύειν (cf. xl. 29^c יסור, 𝔊 πεπαιδευμένος), there is a play also upon אסר *bind*, see vi. 25—30, passing over the two preceding misplaced verses, and cf. Sirac. xxxiii. 4 *bind up instruction*. iv. 19, where 𝔚 expresses with a threefold word-play that Wisdom's training is restraining. xxi. 19 𝔊 πέδαι ἐν ποσὶν ἀνοήτου παιδεία, 𝔖 *Instar carceris est sapientia stulto.* Compare Prov. vii. 22 מוסר אל מוסר אויל ובעכס, and see Dr Paul Ruben on מוסר in *Crit. Remarks on some Passages of the O. T.* (London, 1896). 𝔖 *her name is as her* ܐܒܓܕ, which means *doctrina, institutio* pueri. In Prov. iv. 13 𝔖 has *disciplinam meam,* 𝔊 ἐμῆς παιδείας for מוסר. With 𝔊 σοφία γὰρ κατὰ τὸ ὄνομα αὐτῆς cf. xliii. 8 μὴν κατὰ τὸ ὄνομα αὐτῆς (𝔥 כשמו והוא), and with ולא לרבים cf. Job xxxii. 9 יחכמו לא רבים. Prov. viii. 9 *plain* (נכחים)...*and right*.

XXII   THE WISDOM OF BEN SIRA.   [CH. 6

22[n] A potter's vessel is for the furnace to bake (?);
       And like unto it, a man is according to his thought.
22[m] Upon the bough (?) of a tree will be its fruit;
       So the thought of a man is according to his mind (?).
25   Incline thy shoulder, and carry her;
       And loathe not her cords (?).
27   Search and examine, seek and find;
       And hold her fast, and let her not go.
28   For afterward thou shalt find her rest;
       And she (?) shall turn to a delight unto thee.
29   And her net shall be to thee a strong defence;
       And her cordage robes of fine gold.
30   Her yoke (𝔊 Upon her) is an ornament (𝔊) of gold;
       And her bands are thread of purple.

Fol. A 2 verso   31   Thou shalt put her on as robes of honour;
       And crown thyself with her as a crown of beauty.
32   If thou be desirous, my son, thou mayest become wise;
       And if thou apply thy heart, thou shalt be prudent.
33   If thou art wishful to hear (𝔐);
       And incline thine ear (𝔐), thou shalt be instructed.
35   Be desirous to hear all discourse;
       And let no proverb of understanding escape thee.
36   See who (?) hath understanding, and seek him early;
       And let thy foot wear my (𝔐) threshold.
37a   And let thy mind be upon the fear of the Most High;
       And meditate (?) in his commandments continually.
37c   And he shall make thy heart discerning (𝔐);
       And make thee wise according as thou desirest.

7. 1   Do not evil to thyself, and evil shall not (?) overtake thee;
   2   Keep far from iniquity, and it shall turn aside from thee.
   3   Sow not upon the furrows of unrighteousness (?);
       Lest thou reap it sevenfold.

22[m] עברת] See note on 𝔐. 𝔊 xxvii. 6 γεώργιον ξύλου ἐκφαίνει ὁ καρπὸς αὐτοῦ, οὕτως λόγος (λογισμὸς 23. 248. 253. Co.) ἐνθυμήματος καρδίας ἀνθρώπου. 𝔖 Quemadmodum arboris cultura &c. The resemblance of עברת, בעברתה (vi. 19c) suggests an explanation of the disarrangement of the text.

27 והחוקתה ואל תרפה] See Prov. iv. 13 quoted above on verse 22.

29—30 ומוסרתיה כו׳] St Polycarp *Philippians* § 1, "those men encircled in saintly bonds, which are the diadems of them that be truly chosen of God and our Lord."

33 לשמע והט] The English represents 𝔐, which is defective.

37c יבין לבך] 1 Kings iii. 11—12 *Because thou...hast asked for thyself understanding to discern judgment...I have given thee* לב חכם ונבון.

7. 3 על און] As below in verse 12. In verse 3 און may be a corruption of און, i.e. און written with medial *nun* in an ancient MS. Cf. Hos. x. 4.

CH. 7]   THE WISDOM OF BEN SIRA.   XXIII

4   Seek not of God dominion;
    Nor likewise of a king a seat of honour.
5   Justify not thyself before God (𝔐 a king);
    And before a king profess not understanding.
6ᵃ Seek not to be a ruler;
    If thou hast not ability to quell pride.
6ᶜ Lest thou fear the person of the noble;
    And suffer lucre to corrupt thine integrity (?).
7   Condemn not thyself in the congregation at the gate (?);
    And cast not thyself down in the assembly.
8   Conspire not to commit a second sin;
    For in one thou shalt not be unpunished.
15 Loathe not appointed service of laborious work;
    For it hath been apportioned of God (?).
10 Be not impatient (𝔐 short) in prayer;
    And in almsgiving hesitate not (?).
11 Despise not a man that is in bitterness of spirit;
    Remember that there is one that lifteth up and casteth down.
12 Devise not injury against a brother;
    And likewise neither against a companion nor a neighbour.
13 Love not to make any manner of (?) lie;
    For the consequence (𝔐 hope) thereof shall not be pleasant.
14 Prate (?) not (*or* Be not familiar) in a congregation of princes;
    And repeat (?) not a word in prayer.
16 Esteem not thyself among the men of thy (?) people;
    Remember that wrath will not tarry (?).

6ᵃ חיל] The word is here translated *ability* with allusion to Ex. xviii. 21—25, *Moreover thou shalt provide out of all the people able men...hating covetousness* (בצע)...*And Moses chose able men* (אנשי חיל) *out of all Israel, and made them heads over the people, rulers* (שרי) *of thousands &c.* It would have been in the manner of Ben Sira to vary the word for ruler. He may have thought of חיל *wealth* as a qualification for a judge or ruler.

7 בעדת שערי אל ואל] Lit. *in the congregation of the gates of God.* 𝔊 𝔖 πόλεως (עיר). The translation omits שערי before ואל. Omitting שערי, we should get the familiar phrase בעדת אל, which may have been the source of error. 𝔐 xlii. 11ᶜ בעדת שער, 𝔊 ἐν πλήθει πολλῶν, "*lire πυλῶν des portes*" (Isr. Lévi).

15 בצבא] A metaphor from military service, see note on 𝔐. 𝔊 μὴ μισήσῃς ἐπίπονον ἐργασίαν καὶ γεωργίαν ὑπὸ ὑψίστου ἐκτισμένην.

13 על כחש] Read לכחש כל כחש with 𝔊 𝔖.

14 אל תסור] 𝔖 *Hide not thyself*, as if reading תְּפָתֵר with *resh* for *daleth*. 𝔊 may have read either תסוח (תשוח) or תסור, cf. xlii. 12 𝔐 ℳ. R. V. *Prate not in the multitude of elders.*

16 אל תחשבך] *Esteem not &c.*, cf. verse 17. 𝔖 *ne diligas teipsum plusquam populares tuos.* 𝔊 μὴ προσλογίζου σεαυτὸν ἐν πλήθει ἁμαρτωλῶν, with perhaps במרעים for עם במתי. See note on 𝔐.

17 Abase pride very exceedingly;
    For the hope of man is the worm (רִמָּה֯ אֱנוֹשׁ).
17[(1)] Be not in haste to say, A breach (?) *is upon me*;
    Commit thyself unto God, and delight in his way.
18 Exchange not a friend at a price;
    Neither a brother that is attached (*or* doubted) for gold of Ophir.
19 Despise (*or* Reject) not a wise wife;
    Seeing she is well-favoured above rubies.
20 Evil entreat not a servant that laboureth truly (?);
    Nor a hireling that giveth his soul (?).
21 Love a wise servant as thyself:
    Withhold not liberty from him.
22 Hast thou a beast? see that thine eye be upon it (?);
    And if it be trusty (?), keep it.
23 Hast thou sons? instruct them;
    And marry wives to them in their youth.
24 Hast thou daughters? guard their flesh;
    And make not thy face bright unto them.
25 Give away a daughter, and away with a trouble (?);
    But join her to a man of understanding.
26 Hast thou a wife? abominate (שְׂנָא) her not;
    Hast thou one that is hated? trust her not.
29 With all thy heart fear . . . .

* * * * * *

17[(1)] לֶאֱמֹר לִפְרֹץ] Or לאמר פרץ, פרץ *to say* (or עֲלֵי פִּי), cf. Gen. xxxviii. 29 *And she said...a breach upon thee.* Job xvi. 14 *He breaketh me breach upon breach.*

18 במחיר ואח תלוי] Ⓖ μὴ ἀλλάξῃς φίλον ἕνεκεν ἀδιαφόρου μηδ' ἀδελφὸν γνήσιον ἐν χρυσίῳ Σουφείρ, 𝔏 *et fratrem quem habes &c.* Read in Ⓖ διαφόρου, comparing xxvii. 1, xlii. 5 διαφ. al. ἀδιαφ., L. & S. *Lex.* διάφορον *price*, Hatch *Essays in Biblicai Greek* p. 261 (1889). תלוי *attached*, from תלה i.q. תלא *suspendit*, as Is. xxii. 23—24 *And I will fasten him as a nail in a sure place......And they shall hang upon him all the glory of his father's house.* Hos. xi. 7 וְעַמִּי תְלוּאִים לִמְשׁוּבָתִי *inhaerent aversioni a me.* So Rosenmüller, who quotes R. Tanchum تَابِض CONSTANTES *in declinando*, Kimchi on Hos. iv. 6 התלים בכהנים *adherents* of the priests, and in Greek an example of ἐξαρτάομαι *deditus* (lit. *suspensus*) *sum*. Compare Ex. xxviii. 7 וְחֻבָּר, LXX. ἐξηρτημέναι (al. -ισμέναι), Syr. *et cohaerebit*, cf. Prov. xviii. 24 אֹהֵב דָּבֵק מֵאָח. On תלוי *doubtful* see note on רֵעַ.

20 באמת] See the note on רֵעַ, where it is proposed to read *by a word* (iv. 24). Or read בְּעֶבֶד עוֹבֵד, supposing אמת to have been repeated accidentally.

22 ראה עיניך] Read עֵינְךָ עָלָיו, cf. Jer. xl. 4 עֵינַי עָלֶיךָ אֶת. Ⓖ κτῆνή σοί ἐστιν; ἐπισκέπτου αὐτά, καὶ εἰ ἔστι σοι χρήσιμα ἐμμενέτω σοι.

25 עסק] Ⓖ ἔργον μέγα. Compare in xl. 1 עֶסֶק גָּדוֹל, Ⓖ ἀσχολία μεγάλη, 𝔏 *negotia ingentia.* Or see note on רֵעַ.

11. 34^b And estrange thee to them that are dear to thee.   Fol. A 3 recto
12. 2 Do good to the righteous, and find recompense;
    If not from him, from the Lord.
  3 No good cometh of bestowing upon (?) him that is wicked;
    And (?) that hath not done righteousness.
  5^d A double portion of evil shalt thou obtain in time of need
    By all the good thou shalt have brought him.
  5^b Weapons of war (𝔐 𝔖) give not to him;
    Wherefore should he fight with them against thee?
  6 For God also hateth them that are evil;
    And to the wicked he will repay vengeance.
  7 Give to the good, and withhold from the evil;
  4 Honour the humble, and give not to the proud.
  8 A friend will not be known in prosperity;
    And an enemy will not be hid in adversity.
  9 In a man's prosperity even an enemy is a friend;
    And in his adversity even a friend separateth himself.
  10 Never trust an enemy;
    For like as brass his wickedness cankereth.
  11^a And even though he hearken to thee, and go crouching;
    Give thy heart to fear him.
  11^c Be to him as one that revealeth a mystery (𝔐 𝔖);
    And he shall not find opportunity to harm thee.
    And know thou the end of jealousy (𝔐 𝔖).

12. 3 למנוח רשע וגם] See note on 𝔐. 𝔊 οὐκ ἔσται (al. ἔστιν) ἀγαθὰ τῷ ἐνδελεχίζοντι εἰς κακά, καὶ τῷ ἐλεημοσύνην μὴ χαριζομένῳ. 𝔖 *to him that* HONOURETH *the evil,* cf. Prov. iii. 9 מֵחוֹנֶךָ. נָבֵר את ח'] In the next hemistich, reading וגוי for וגם, we should have the sense *and a* HEATHEN *that hath not done righteousness*, גוי ἔθνος standing for an individual, as often in the later Hebrew. So עם הארץ is used for one of the ὄχλος (*Jewish Fathers* ii. n. 13), cf. pl. עמי הארץ (Deut. xxviii. 10), מעמיה *from its people* (Lev. xxiii. 29), &c. There are cases in which צדקה means simply ἐλεημοσύνη, but we may sometimes use "righteousness" with that connotation, cf. Psalm cxii. 9 *He hath dispersed, he hath given to the poor; his righteousness endureth for ever.* In chap. iii. 14 צדקה is rendered "Benefaction."

5^b כלי לחם] Jud. v. 8 אז לחם שערים. 𝔊 ἐμπόδισον τοὺς ἄρτους αὐτοῦ καὶ μὴ δῷς αὐτῷ, reading כלי as a verb (i.q. כלא), which 𝔖 uses for *withhold* and *give not* in verse 7. See note on 𝔐.

8 לא יודע] 𝔊 οὐκ ἐπιγνωσθήσεται, "ἐπιγνωσθήσεται 106. 253., Vet. Lat. agnoscetur; ἐμφανήσεται H." (Fritzsche).

11^c כמנלה רו] A. V. *and thou shalt be unto him as if thou hadst wiped a lookingglass, and thou shalt know that his rust hath not been altogether wiped away.* "The Syr. has here some strange variants" (E). 𝔖 *Sis illi quasi secretum declarans, nec te poterit depravare; imo finem odii ejus deprehendes.* 𝔊 may have given מגלה the sense of Arab. جلا *polivit* gladium, speculum, or may possibly have read מגלה with *cheth.* 𝔊 at the end, reading קִנְאָה וֹדֵע אחרית חָלָאָה for וֹדֵע בּוֹ', καὶ γνώσῃ ὅτι οὐκ εἰς τέλος κατίωσε. 𝔖 ראוא for רו (Dan. רוא), cf. ראי *speculum.*

d

THE WISDOM OF BEN SIRA.   [CH. 12

12ᵃ Make him not to stand beside thee:
    Wherefore should he thrust thee away, and stand in thy place?
12ᶜ Set him not on thy right hand:
    Wherefore should he seek thy seat?
12ᵉ And afterwards thou shalt attain unto my words;
    And shalt lament at my lament.
13 Who will pity (?) a charmer that is stung;
    Or anyone that cometh nigh to a ravenous beast?
14 So is he that joineth himself to an impious man (𝔊 𝔖),
    And walloweth in his iniquities.
14⁽¹⁾ He shall not escape, until a fire be kindled in him.
14⁽¹⁾ When he cometh with thee, he will not bewray himself unto thee;
    And if thou fall, thou shalt not be able (𝔖) to deliver thyself (?).
15 So long as thou standest (?), he will not shew himself;
    And if thou (𝔊) totter, he will not bear up.
16ᵃ With his lips will an adversary speak sweetly (𝔊),
    While he deviseth deep pitfalls in his heart.
16ᶜ And even though an enemy weep with his eyes;
    When he hath found a season, he will not be satiated with blood.
17 If mischief hath befallen thee, he is found there;
    As a man that would help, he will seek reward (*or* to supplant).
18 He will shake his head, and wave his hand;
    And with much whispering (?) he will change his countenance.
13. 1 Whoso toucheth pitch, it shall cleave to his hand (?);
    And he that hath fellowship with a scorner will learn his way.
2ᵃ What is too heavy for thee wherefore shouldest thou lift?
    And wherefore have fellowship with one that is richer than thou?
2ᶜ What fellowship shall earthen pot have with kettle,
    When if this smite that, it is dashed in pieces?

13 חית שן] 𝔊 θηρίοις. Prof. Margoliouth conjectured rightly that Ben Sira wrote *beast of tooth* (𝔖). Cf. xxxix. 30 חית שן 𝔊, 𝔊 θηρίων ὀδόντες, Syro-hex. *teeth of beasts of tooth*. Deut. xxxii. 24 *teeth of beasts*.

17 ויחמש עקב] See note on 𝔐. 𝔊 καὶ ὡς βοηθῶν ὑποσχάσει πτέρναν σου, 𝔖 *calces tuos evellere studebit*. Schleusner, al. ὑποσκάψει pro ὑποσχάσει. Holmes and Parsons, υποσκαψει 23, 253. υποχαλαση 296, 308. υποσκελεσει 307. LXX. καὶ ἐσκαλε in Psalm lxxvii. 6 (7) וַיְחַפֵּשׂ רוּחִי. Aquila ἐσκαλλον for פרי in Ps. cxix. 85.

18 ולרובה לחש] For (?) ולרוב חלחיש. 𝔊 καὶ πολλὰ διαψιθυρίσει, so 𝔖 וסני מלחיש. 𝔊 for שְׂנֵא פנים (see Eccles. viii. 1) καὶ ἀλλοιώσει τὸ πρόσωπον αὐτοῦ, cf. xiii. 25, 𝔊 xxv. 16, xxxvii. 17. 𝔖 here ומסנא, reading שׂנא, and so in Eccles. viii. 1 נסתנא (LXX. μισηθήσεται).

13. 3 יענה הוא יתנוה] See note on 𝔐. Or read יענה (𝔐), and נענה דל נענה the poor is *oppressed*. In xliii. 21 ונוה כו', *It burneth up the produce like drought, and the* STATELINESS *of growing things as a flame* (C. & N.), read ובוה with *kaf* (𝔊 as if וכבה ἀποσβέσει) for *nun*, cf. Is. xliii. 2 תבוה לא *shalt not be burned*, Prov. vi. 28 תכוינה, Is. iii. 24 *brand* (כי) *for beauty*.

2c(1) What fellowship shall the rich have with the poor?
3 The rich doeth a wrong, and he boasteth himself of it (?):
The poor is wronged, and he must entreat withal (?).
4 If thou be right for him, he will make thee serve him;
And if thou be brought low, he will be sparing of thee.
5 If thou have substance (?), he will speak thee fair;
And he will impoverish thee, and will not be sorry.
6 Hath he need of thee? then he will toy with thee (?);
And he will smile upon thee, and encourage thee.
7 So long as it profiteth he will cajole thee.   Fol. A 3 verso
Twice or thrice he will shew thee reverence (?);
And then he will look at thee and pass thee by (?);
And will wag his head at thee.
8 Take heed that thou be not urgent (?) overmuch;
And be not like to them that lack intelligence.
9 Doth a noble draw near? be thou distant;
And so much the more he will approach thee.
10 Come not near, lest thou be put far off;
And stand not far off, lest thou be forgotten (𝔊).
11 Make not bold to be free (?) with him;
And mistrust thou his much talk.
11c For with his much talk maketh he trial of thee;
And he will smile upon thee, and search thee out.
12 He that is cruel will speak peace (?) and spare not;
While he plotteth a plot against the life of many.
13 Take heed and beware;
And go not with men of violence.

4 יחמל] Hor. *Od.* I. 34. I *Parcus deorum cultor et infrequens.* The note on 𝔐 suggests the emendation *he will* NOT *spare*, cf. verse 12 ולא יחמל. 𝔊 καὶ ἐὰν ὑστερήσῃς καταλείψει (al. -θλίψει) σε, 𝔖 *te deseret.*

6 והשיע לך] See note on 𝔐 observing that 𝔐 xliv. 8 has two readings, and cf. שעע, שעשע. 𝔊 ἀποπλανήσει σε. 𝔖 in verse 5 נשפר שועיתה for ייטב דבריו.

7 יחתל בך...יערצך] 1 Kings xviii. 27 *And it came to pass at noon, that Elijah mocked them* (ויהתל בהם), *and said, Cry aloud: for he is a god;* כי שיח וכי שיג לו, Sirac. xiii. 26 ושיג ושיח. Jer. ix. 3—4 *Take ye heed every one of his neighbour, and trust ye not in any brother: for...they will deceive* (יהתלו ב׳) *every one his neighbour.* Job xiii. 9 *Is it good that he should search you out?* or *as one man mocketh* (כהתל) *another, do ye so mock him?*, Sirac. xiii. 11c וחקרך. יעריצך ער״ץ *hif.* cum *acc.* "to fear, to reverence." 𝔊 ἀποκενώσει σε, see note on 𝔐. xliii. 8c 𝔐 מערץ. וחתעבר עבר *hithp.* has the sense *iratus fuit.* The translation makes it i.q. *kal* "pass by." 𝔊 καταλείψει σε, 𝔖 *a te delitescet.*

11 אל תבטח לחפש] 𝔊 μὴ ἔπεχε (al. πιστεύσῃς) ἰσηγορεῖσθαι μετ' αὐτοῦ. חפש is perhaps a verb related to חופש *freedom*, חפשי *free.*

12 מושל] The English is a translation of שלום, an anagram of מושל.

15 All flesh loveth its kind;
   And every man him that is like unto him.
16 The kind of all flesh consorteth therewith;
   And a man will have fellowship with his kind.
17 What fellowship shall wolf have with lamb?
   Such is the wicked to the righteous;
17ᵃˡ And so is the rich unto a man that is destitute.
18 How should there be (?) peace between hyena and dog?
   How should there be peace between rich and poor?
19 Wild asses of the wilderness are food for the lion:
   So the poor are the prey of the rich.
20 Lowliness is the abomination of pride;
   And the needy is the abomination of the rich.
21 A rich man when he is shaken is held up (?) of a friend;
   But the poor when he is shaken is thrust from evil to evil (?).
22ᵃ The rich speaketh, and his helpers are many;
   And his unseemly words are overlaid (?).
22ᶜ A poor man speaketh (𝔊 𝔖), and they hoot at him (?);
   Though he be wise that speaketh, there is no place for him.
23ᵃ When the rich speaketh, all keep silence;
   And (?) they extol his wisdom to the clouds.
23ᶜ When the poor speaketh, Who is this? say they;
   And if he stumble, they will help to overthrow him.
24 Good is wealth, if it be without iniquity;
   And evil is poverty in the mouth of arrogancy.
25 The heart of a man changeth his countenance;
   Whether for good or for evil.
26 A token of a merry heart is a bright countenance;
   And study and meditation is wearisome thought (?).
14. 1 Happy is the man whom his own mouth hath not troubled;
   And whose heart hath not condemned him (?).

21 מוט בסמך [Read (?) נמוט נסמך. רע means *evil* (𝔖), and *friend* (𝔊).

22ᵃ [מבועדיין] Aquila's rendering in Psalm xxii. 17 ἤσχυναν χεῖράς μου καὶ πόδας μου implies a reading באדו ידי ורגלי, which is explained by כישרו בו. Hitherto כער has been regarded as a neo-Hebrew word. Reading at the end of the verse מחופין with *cheth* from חפה *obduxit* auro, argento, we get the sense that his words are *veneered over* as base with precious metal. 𝔖 *they beautify his odious words*. Notice in 𝔐 the two plural terminations in *yod*, *nun*.

22ᶜ נע נע] *They raise* (ישאו) cries of נע נע. 𝔖 *they say to him* נע.

26 ושיג ושיח] See verse 7 n. 𝔊 καὶ εὕρεσις παραβολῶν διαλογισμὸς μετὰ κόπου (al. -μοί μ. κόπων). The Preacher *sought out...many parables...and much study is a weariness of the flesh* (Eccl. xii. 9—12).

14. 1 ולא אבה עליו דין לבו] A difficult or corrupt clause, translated above as if from some such reading as ולא בא עליו דין לבו. With אבל (note on 𝔐) for אבה

THE WISDOM OF BEN SIRA.

2 Happy is the man whose soul hath not reproached (💲 failed) him;
And whose expectation hath not ceased.
3 Wealth is not comely for a little heart;
And fine gold is not comely for one, whose eye is evil.
4 He that stinteth (?) himself gathereth for another;
And a stranger shall revel (?) in his goods.
5 He that is evil to himself, to whom will he be good?
And he will not enjoy (?) his own goods.
6 There is none more evil than he that is evil to himself;
And he hath with him the recompense of his wickedness.
9 In the eye of a fool (💲) his portion is small;
But he that taketh his neighbour's portion wasteth his own (?).
10 The eye of him that hath an evil eye (?) is grudging (𝔊) of bread;
And there is famine at his table.
10⁽¹⁾ An evil (💲) eye lavishing bread
Is as a fountain dried up that should well with water (?).
11 My son, if thou hast wherewithal, minister (💲) to thine own self;
And if thou hast, do good unto thyself;
And according to the power of ‖ thy hand, make thyself fat.   Fol. A 4 recto
12 Remember that there is no luxury in Sheol;
And death doth not tarry,
And the decree of Sheol (?) hath not been declared to thee.

---

we should scarcely want דין before לבו. 💲 *cujus oculis non est occultatum* (? אבד) *judicium*. "The Aethiop. somewhat boldly renders, or rather paraphrases: 'Happy is the sinner who is not troubled by grief.' The Syr. has for the second clause: 'from whose eyes justice is not hidden.' Probably the Greek read ולא התעצב מעוניו; the Syr. ולא התעצם מעיניו (E). 𝔊 λύπη for דין, cf. xxxviii. 17ᵉ n.

9 כושל] A. V. *covetous*. 💲 *stulti...qui autem usurpat quod proximi sui est perdit animam suam*, "evidently mispointing רע for רע" (E).

10 עין רע עון חטים] Reading עין רעה תחטא, we get the sense *An evil eye* EYES (scans, scrutinizes) *bread*. 1 Sam. xviii. 9 (עוין קרי) עון שאול עין את דוד *And Saul eyed David*. In ABOTH v. famine of a certain degree of intensity is called רעב של מהומה. See note on 💲.

10⁽¹⁾ עין טובה] 💲 *Oculus nequam multiplicat panem & siccum projicit super mensam*, omitting מעין and סים. The English represents a play upon the senses of the word for 'eye,' which also means 'fountain,' and omits על השלחן, cf. verse 10. Jer. li. 36 *and make her spring dry*. "Some misreading of the Hebrew must have caused the Syr. rendering: *Oculus nequam multiplicat panem*" (E). But on the other hand 💲 טובה may very well have crept in as an obvious correction of רעה before מרבה *multiplicans* (not -*at*) *panem*.

11 שָׂרֵת] The pointing suits שרת with *resh* for *daleth*.

12 כי לא בשאול] See note on 💲. Eccles. ix. 10—12 *Whatsoever thy hand findeth to do, do it with thy might; for there is no work, nor device, nor knowledge, nor wisdom, in Sheol....For man also knoweth not his time*. 𝔊 καὶ διαθήκη ᾅδου, cf. Isaiah xxviii. 15 ברית את מות כו (E).

xxx   THE WISDOM OF BEN SIRA.   [CH. 14

13 Do good to a friend before thou die;
    And as thy hand attaineth (?) give unto him.
14 Refuse not the day's good cheer.
    But encroach not upon a brother's portion (?);
    And covet not the desirable things of a neighbour.
15 Shalt thou not leave thy riches to another;
    And thy labour to them that cast lots?
16 Give to a brother (𝔅), and let thy soul fare delicately;
    For there is no seeking of luxury in Sheol.
16⁽¹⁾ And whatsoever thing is seemly to do;
    Do it before (?) God.
17 All flesh waxeth old as a garment;
    And the everlasting decree is, They shall surely perish.
18ᵃ As leaves grow upon a green tree,
    Whereof one withereth, and another springeth up;
18ᶜ So of the generations of flesh and blood,
    One perisheth, and another ripeneth (𝔅).
19 All his works shall surely rot;
    And his handywork shall draw after him.
20 Happy is the man that shall meditate in wisdom;
    And shall have respect to understanding.
21 That setteth his heart upon her ways;
    And considereth her paths (𝔖).
22 Going forth after her in search of her;
    And spying all her entries.
23 That prieth through her window;
    And will hearken at her doors.

16 ‎ופנק] 𝔊 καὶ ἀπάτησον (al. ἁγίασον) τὴν ψυχήν σου, "Vet. Lat. iustifica; Grotius legendum coniecit ἀγάπησον" (Fritzsche), but ἀπάτη and τρυφή are sometimes practically synonyms. See 2 Pet. ii. 13 ἐντρυφῶντες ἐν ταῖς ἀπάταις (al. ἀγάπαις) αὐτῶν, Hermae *Pastor* μνημονεύει τότε (?) τῆς τρυφῆς καὶ ἀπάτης...πᾶς οὖν ἄνθρωπος ὁ τρυφῶν καὶ ἀπατώμενος (*Sim.* vi. 5. 4), L. & S. *Lex.* ἀπάτη ΙΙ. *a beguiling* of time, *pastime*. 𝔊 𝔖 *Give and take &c.*, see note on 𝔅.

16⁽¹⁾ ‎וכל דבר שיפה] Eccles. iii. 11 ‎הכל עשה יפה v. 17 ‎טוב אשר יפה. 𝔖 "adds, probably as an apologetic corrective, *and whatever is fair to be done before the Lord, that do*" (E).

17 ‎נוע ינוע] 𝔊 θανάτῳ ἀποθανῇ. "*Dying thou shalt die* (‎מות תמות), here literally rendered from the Hebrew, as in LXX. Gen. ii. 17)" (E). But Ben Sira, after his manner, quotes with variations. Starting from ‎מות תמות, *dying thou shalt die*, he changes person and number, and the word for *die*, and writes *Expiring they shall expire*. 𝔊 ἀποθανῇ for ‎תמות sing., LXX. ἀποθανεῖσθε.

18ᶜ ‎כן דורות] Eccles. i. 4 ‎דור הולך ודור בא.

23—24 ‎בעד חלונה] He looks in at HER window, as she looks out at her window in Prov. vii. 6 *For at the window of my house I looked through my casement.* With *her wall* (𝔅 ‎בקירה) and *her window* cf. Cant. ii. 9 ‎בחלנו כו'. Prov. vii. 2—4

24 He that encampeth about her house;
   And driveth his pegs (?) into her wall.
25 And he pitcheth his tent by her side;
   And dwelleth in good neighbourhood.
26 And he will set his nest on her bough;
   And will lodge in her branches.
27 And he sheltereth in her shade from the heat;
   And will dwell in her habitations.
15. 1 For he that feareth the Lord shall do this;
   And he that layeth hold on the law shall attain unto her (?).
 2 And she shall meet him as mother;
   And receive him as wife of youth.
 3 And she shall feed him with bread of wisdom;
   And give him water of understanding to drink.
 4 And he shall be stayed upon her, and shall not be moved;
   And in her shall he trust, and he shall not be confounded.
 5 And she shall exalt him above his neighbour;
   And in the midst of the congregation shall she open his mouth.
 6 He shall find joy and gladness;
   And she shall cause him to inherit an everlasting name.
 7 Men of naught shall not attain unto her;
   And men of arrogancy shall not see her (𝔓 $).
 8 Far is she from scorners;
   And liars shall not remember her.
 9 Praise is not comely (𝔊 $) in the mouth of the wicked;
   For it was not apportioned him of God.
10 By the mouth of the wise shall praise be spoken;
   And he that mastereth her (𝔓 $) shall learn it.
11 Say not, My transgression was of God;
   For that which he hateth he made not (𝔓 $).

Keep my commandments, and live; and my law as the apple (באישון) *of thine eye.... Say unto wisdom, Thou art my sister; and call understanding thy kinswoman*, may have suggested to Ben Sira the verse באין אישון כי (iii. 25), and his comparisons כאם וכאישת (xv. 2), cf. Wisdom viii. 2 νύμφην.

15. 2 נעורים] See vii. 23 *wives in their youth*. A. V. here *and receive him as a wife married of a virgin*, R. V. *in her virginity*. "Comp. Prov. ii. 17. That γυνὴ παρθενίας means not virgin-wife, but wife of one's youth, seems established by LXX. Jer. iii. 4, where παρθενία is the translation of נְעוּרִים" (E).

10 ומשל בה] Verses 9—10 "are perhaps among the most difficult verses in Ecclus. The A. V. represents the Greek text with sufficient accuracy. Nothing can be learned from a comparison with the Syriac" (E). $ *Ore sapientum pronuntiabitur laus & qui potestatem habet in eam addiscet illam.*

11 לא עשה] So $ ܠܐ, cf. Wisdom xi. 24. Ὅ ἃ γὰρ ἐμίσησεν οὐ ποιήσεις. "It is not necessary to correct οὐ ποιήσεις into οὐ ποιήσει" (E).

12 Lest thou say, He it was that made me stumble;
For there is no need of men of violence.
13 Wickedness and an abomination the Lord hateth;
And will not let it befal them that fear him.
14 For (?) God created man from the beginning;
And put him into the hand of him that would spoil him;
And gave him into the hand of his inclination.
15 If thou choose, thou mayest keep the commandment;
And it is understanding (בינה) to do his will.
15⁽¹⁾ If thou trust in him, thou shalt even live.
16 Fire and water are poured out before thee:
Upon whichsoever thou choosest stretch forth thy hands.
17 Death and life are before a man:
That which he shall choose shall be given him.
18 The wisdom of the Lord aboundeth:
He is mighty in power, and beholdeth all.
19 The eyes of God see his works;
And he will take knowledge of (?) all a man's doing.
20 He commanded not a man to sin;
Neither did he make men of falsehood to dream.
20⁽¹⁾ And he hath no mercy on him that worketh vanity;
And on him that discloseth a secret.

16. 1 Desire not the shapeliness of vain youths;
And rejoice not in sons of wickedness.
2 Yea, and if they increase, delight (?) not in them;
If the fear of the Lord be not with them.
3ᵃ Trust not in their life, and rely not on their issues (?);
3ᵃ⁽¹⁾ For they shall not have a good end.
3ᶜ For better is one that doeth acceptably than a thousand;
And he that dieth childless than he that hath many sons of wickedness (?);
And than an ungodly posterity.
4 Of one that (?) feareth the Lord shall a city be peopled;
And by a family of transgressors it shall be made desolate.

16—17 [לפני אדם] Deut. xxx. 15 לפניך נתתי. Psalm lxvi. 12 באש ובמים. "The harsh Greek rendering of 16 *b* would represent what was elegant in the Hebrew original שלח ידך " (E).

16. 3ᵃ [בעקבותם] ⅏ *neque credas bonum fore finem illorum.* 𝔊 ἐπὶ τὸν τόπον αὐτῶν, al. πλῆθος. Vulg. *labores* (κόπον). "But from the usage in the LXX. there cannot be any doubt that the Hebrew original for τόπος was מקום " (E). עקב *finis*, as explained in the doublet 3ᵃ⁽¹⁾ by אחרית.

3ᶜ [עושה רצון] "The words *that is just* must be omitted as a later gloss" (E). ⅏ *voluntatem faciens.* Fritzsche εἰς with note, "εἰς δίκαιος 248. Co., Vet. Lat. unus timens deum." Cf. Wisdom iv. 1.

5 Many things like these hath mine eye seen;
And mighty things like these (𝔊) hath mine ear heard.
6 In the congregation of the wicked a fire burneth;
And in an ungodly nation wrath is kindled.
7 Seeing that he forgave not the princes of old time,
Who ruled (?) the world by their power.
8 And he spared not them that sojourned with Lot (?),
Who transgressed in their pride.
9 And he spared not the people of perdition,
That were dispossessed (?) in their iniquity.
10 So were the six hundred thousand footmen,
That were taken away in the arrogancy of their heart.
11ᵃ And if even one stiffen (*or* harden) his neck;
It were a marvel should he be unpunished.
11ᶜ For mercy and wrath are with him;
And he forgiveth and pardoneth;
But upon the wicked his indignation shall rest (?).
12 According to the greatness of his mercy, so is his correction;
He will judge each according to his doings.
13 He will not (𝔐) let the wrong-doer escape with plunder;
Neither will he frustrate the desire of the righteous for ever.
14 Whosoever doeth righteousness, there is a reward for him;
And according to his works shall every man go forth (𝔊)
before him.
15 The Lord hardened the heart of Pharaoh, who knew him not:
16 Whose works are manifest under heaven;
His mercies are seen of all his creatures;
And his light and his darkness (?) hath he apportioned to the
sons of men.
17ᵃ Say not, I am hidden from God;
And who shall remember me on high?
17ᶜ In the mass of people I shall not be known;
And what is my soul at the end of the spirits of all the sons
of men?

9 הנורשים] Or read *resh* for *daleth*, cf. xxxix. 23 גוים יורשים.
14 כל העושה צדקה] 𝔖 *Omni justitiam agenti est praemium.* 𝔊 πάσῃ ἐλεημοσύνῃ ποιήσει τόπον. With יצא cf. Psalm cix. 7 ישא יצא.
15—16 הקשה וי'] "Omit *vv.* 15, 16....It adds to our difficulties of interpretation that *vv.* 15, 16 are found in the Syr" (E). R. V. marg. "Verses 15 and 16 are omitted by the best authorities." Fritzsche on verse 14, "add. huic vs. 106. 248. Co. Syr. Ar. haec: κύριος ἐσκλήρυνε Φαραὼ μὴ εἰδέναι αὐτόν, ὅπως ἂν γνωσθῇ ἐνεργήματα αὐτοῦ τῇ ὑπ' οὐρανόν. πάσῃ τῇ κτίσει τὸ ἔλεος αὐτοῦ φανερόν, καὶ τὸ φῶς αὐτοῦ καὶ τὸ σκότος ἐμέρισε τῷ ΑΔΑΜΑΝΤΙ." A. V. *he hath separated his light from the darkness with an adamant.* 𝔖 *inter homines distribuit.* 𝔐 *to the sons of* אדם. For ושבתו read וחשבו. Ex. v. 2 *Pharaoh said...I know not the Lord.*

18 Behold, the heaven, and the heaven of heavens,
And the deep, and the earth;
When he descendeth upon them, they tremble (?),
At his visitation (?), and when he rageth.
19 The roots also of the mountains and the foundations of the world,
When he looketh upon them, quake exceedingly.
20 Surely upon me he will not set his heart;
And my ways who will consider?
20[b] If I have sinned, no eye shall see me;
Or if I deal falsely in any secret place (?), who shall know?
22 Work of right who shall declare unto him?
And of what is there hope, that I should be righteous (?)...?
23 They that want understanding will think such things;
And a perverse man (?) will imagine this.
24 Hearken unto me, and receive my proverbs (?);
And set your heart upon my words.
25 I will pour forth my spirit by weight;
And with carefulness will I declare my opinion.
26 When God created his works from the beginning;
According to their parts (𝕳 life) . . . .

* * * * *

18 עֲמוּדִים] Did Ben Sira use עָמַד for מָעַד? If the text is right, cf. Ezek. xxix. 7 *and madest all their loins to be at a stand* (R. V. marg. ...*shake*). See note on 𝕳.

20 לֹא יָשִׂים לֵב] A. V. *No heart can think upon these things worthily: and who is able to conceive his ways?*

20[(1)] R. V. *And there is a tempest which no man shall see; Yea, the more part of his works are among hidden things* (marg.). 𝔖 agrees with 𝕳.

22 כִּי אָצוּק] The translation suggests כִּי אֶצְדָּק, cf. Job xxii. 3 *Is it any pleasure to the Almighty* כִּי תִצְדָּק?, ib. xvii. 15 *where now is my hope?* Isaiah xxxii. 17 *work of* צְדָקָה.

25 וּבַחֲצַנְעַ] 𝔊 καὶ ἐν ἀκριβείᾳ ἀπαγγελῶ ἐπιστήμην. Prov. xi. 2 וְאֶת צְנוּעִים חָכְמָה, Symmachus παρὰ δὲ τοῖς ἐπιμελέσι σοφία. The word *careful* thus suggested for צָנוּעַ suits its parallelism with זָהִיר in xlii. 8c 𝕳 (xxxii. 3 n.). Eph. v. 15 βλέπετε οὖν πῶς ἀκριβῶς περιπατεῖτε, μὴ ὡς ἄσοφοι ἀλλ' ὡς σοφοί is according to the R. V. ἀκριβῶς πῶς κ.τ.λ., *Look therefore carefully how ye walk &c.*

30. 11 Let him not have rule in his youth;
   And bear not with his mischiefs.
11[a] Beat his shoulder while it is yet tender (?);
   Bruise (?) his loins while he is yet a youth.
12[a] Bow down his head in his youth;
   And smite through his loins when he is a little one.
12[c] Wherefore should he harden himself (𝔐), and rebel against thee;
   That thou shouldest have (?) faintness of spirit because of him?
13 Chastise (or Train) thy son, and make his yoke heavy;
   Lest in his folly he lift himself up (𝔐) against thee.
14 Better is one that is poor, and healthy in his body;
   Than a rich man that is plagued in his flesh.
15 Health of flesh (?) have I desired more than fine gold;
   And a joyful spirit more than rubies.
16 There is no wealth above wealth of sound flesh (?);
   And no good above goodness of heart.
17 Better is to die than a life of vanity;
   And eternal rest than continual pain.
17[b] Better is to die than life that is evil;
   And to go down to Sheol than lasting pain.
18 Goodness poured upon a mouth that is closed
   Is as an offering laid before a gravestone (?).
19 What can it profit idols of the nations,
   Which eat not, neither do they smell?
   So whoso hath wealth,
   And enjoyeth not of his substance (?).
20[a] With his eye   .   .   .   .   .

Fol. B 1 recto

30. 11[a] [כפתן בו חי על כפתן] See note on כפתן בו חי *as an adder &c.*, which it is there proposed to read בתפו עור חי, comparing Ezek. xxix. 7 תרוץ ובקעת להם כל כתף ובהשענם עליך תשבר והעמדת להם כל מתנים, cf. Sirac. xvi. 18 n. on עמד for מער. The parallelism would require חי to be a synonym for youthful, "of tender years." Below in verse 14 חי means *healthy*. Notice in 2 Sam. xxiii. 20 חיל קרי for חי, "And Benaiah the son of Jehoiada, the son of a *valiant* man." The use of חי as an epithet of "green" wood in Psalm lviii. 9, *Before your pots feel the thorns* כמו חי כמו חרון ישערנו, may have lead to a reading כפתן בו' (Schechter), "while his *branch* is yet tender," whence (by the simple error final *nun* for *vau*) the reading *as an adder*, cf. Psalm lviii. 3—4 *they go astray as soon as they be born...like a deaf adder &c.*

17] "After *a bitter life* H., the Syr., and Vet. Lat. insert *and eternal rest than*. This was undoubtedly in the original. Possibly the words were omitted for dogmatic reasons" (E).

19—20[a] [כן מי...לו עושר] See 𝔐. A. V. *so is he that is persecuted of the Lord.* 𝔊 ἐκδιωκόμενος κ.τ.λ. 𝔖 *ita se habet qui divitias possidet nec utitur illis.* In some MSS. the words οὕτως ὁ ποιῶν ἐν βίᾳ κρίματα are "ex 20. 3 desumpta et male hic addita" (Fritzsche).

20ᵇ   As an eunuch (?) embraceth a maiden and groaneth.
20ᵇ⁽¹⁾ So is he that doeth judgement with violence (?).
20ᵇ⁽²⁾ So is an eunuch (?) that lieth with a virgin.
        And the Lord requireth at his hand.
21   Give not thy soul to sorrow;
        And stumble not by thine iniquity (𝕳 counsel).
22   Joy of heart, that is the life of a man;
        And a man's cheerfulness lengthens his days (𝕲).
23ᵃ   Rejoice thy soul, and make thine heart joyful (?);
        And put vexation far from thee:
23ᵇ   For sorrow hath slain many;
        And there is no profit in vexation.
24   Envy and sorrow (𝕲 wrath) shorten days;
        And care maketh old untimely.

Fol. B 1 verso

25   The sleep of a good heart is instead of dainties;
        And his food is agreeable unto him.

31. 1 The wakefulness (𝕳) of the rich wasteth his flesh;
        His care (𝕳) dissipateth slumber.

20ᵇ—20ᵇ⁽¹¹⁾] Ecclus. xx. 4 A. V. *As is the lust of an eunuch to deflower a virgin.* The Hebrew runs together two passages in which 𝕾 𝕲 have ܪ̈ܒܝܐ ܡܗܝܡܢܐ, εὐνοῦχος. This Syriac word means נאמן *faithful*, and conversely the Cairo text has סרים (for סריס) and נאמן in the two passages respectively, where the Versions have *eunuch*. 𝔐 נאמן might be thought to be a translation from 𝕾 as נאמן is not found elsewhere in the sense εὐνοῦχος, but compare the uses of אמון, אומן, אומנת for *guardian*, and cf. note on 𝔐. At the beginning of *Bereshith Rabbah* the words of Wisdom ואהיה אצלו אמון (Prov. viii. 30) are quoted, and it is said אמון פדגוג כו' . Thus *Torah* (which is Wisdom) is made to be παιδαγωγός (Gal. iii. 24), as I have pointed out in *Sayings of the Jewish Fathers* Addit. Note 55 (p. 173, 1897). For אמון the Targum has מהימנא, fem. of מהימנא. Cf. Esther i. 10 מהומן.

21—24] [רון] Read DAVON a synonym of דאגה, see notes on 𝔐. In the unpublished Appendix to *Sayings of the Jewish Fathers* a note on chap. 11. begins thus, "מרבה דווֹן [דווֹן =] דאגה . 𝕭 רוי ודאבון נפש שמפתר תמיד כו' . M. Shelom. דווֹן כן הוא הנרפא בעדוך תרגום ינון דווֹנא," 𝕭 being the commentary on Aboth in so-called "Machsor Vitry," which has now been edited by Rabbiner S. Hurwitz with an Introduction by Dr A. Berliner for the מקיצי נרדמים. Verse 24 𝔐 ורין, 𝔐 (?) וחרון (𝕲 𝕾), or ורון which might have been misread וחרון. Ben Sira expatiates on the idea of or suggested by Eccles. xi. 10 *Therefore remove vexation* (כעס) *from thy heart, and put away evil from thy flesh* (Targ. ולא תרום ביש על בסרך), *for childhood and youth are vanity*, Ps. xxxix. 12, lxii. 10 הבל (xli. 11 𝔐 הבל אדם בני, 𝔐 בנויתו). In verse 22 read האריך ימיו, 𝕲 μακροημέρευσις.

25 יעלה] His food agrees with him, cf. note on 𝔐. 𝕲 li. 17 προκοπή, 𝔐 עלה *her yoke*. See Fritzsche's note on the disorder of the Greek text in most codices. "The Greek MSS. (with the exception of 248, the *unus vetustus codex* cited by Nobilius) proceed from ch. xxx. 24 to ch. xxxiii. 16" (E).

31. 1 [שקד 𝔐 שקד. In xlii. 9 𝔐 שקד מטמנת לאב בת, 𝔐 מטמון, 𝕲 (reading שקר with *daleth*) gives θυγάτηρ πατρὶ ἀπόκρυφος ἀγρυπνία, thus making מטמון (or

CH. 31]   THE WISDOM OF BEN SIRA.   XXXVII

2 Care for sustenance breaketh off slumber;
   And sore sickness (𝔐) dissipateth slumber.
2ᵇ⁾ Reproach putteth to flight a faithful friend;
   But he that hideth a secret is beloved (?) as one's soul.
3 The labour (𝔐) of the rich is to gather (𝔊 𝔖) wealth;
   And if he rest, it is to take pleasure.
4 The poor toileth for the lack of his house;
   And if he rest, he becometh needy.
4⁽¹⁾ The labour of the poor is for the lack of his means (?);
   And if he rest, it is to his lamentation (or he is distressed).
5 He that pursueth after gold shall not be innocent;
   And he that loveth hire shall err thereby.
6 Many are there that have been given in pledge (?) to gold;
   And that trusted (?) on rubies.
6⁽¹⁾ And they found not how to escape from evil;
   Neither to save themselves in the day of wrath.
7 For it is a stumblingblock to the fool;
   And whoso is simple is enticed thereby.
8 Blessed is the man (𝔐) that hath been found perfect;
   And that hath not gone aside after mammon.
9 Who is he? and we will call him blessed:
   For he hath done wonderously among his people.
10ᵃ Who is he? that we may cleave (𝔐) unto him;
   And he shall have peace, and he shall have glory.
10⁽¹⁾ For when as the peace of his life multiplieth,
   I will be a glory unto thee (?).

ת—) an adjective to a noun placed after it, as remarked in *L'Ecclésiastique*. See in the next hemistich 𝔐 וראגתה, 𝔓... דאגה חם, where Smend (quoted by Lévi p. 50) reads תפריע. Cf. xliii. 22 טל פורע, 𝔊 ἀπανῶσα (? פוגע). Note that מחיה, which the translation omits here, is an anagram of ימחה.

2 ראגת מחיה] 𝔊 μέριμνα ἀγρυπνίας ἀποστήσει νυσταγμόν. 𝔖 *Alimenti cura*. "The Syriac rendering for ἀγρυπνία, 'food,' seems difficult to account for, except as a corruption of *māmūn*, 'wealth'" (E).

2⁽¹⁾ אוהב כנפש] See note on 𝔓, or read אהוב, cf. 𝔐 verse 8 מצוא. Scandal spread to one's "reproach" (vi. 9) destroys friendship, which reticence would preserve. Compare also ch. xli. 22ᶜ מאוהב כו׳.

4⁽¹⁾ לא נחה לו] Comparing xli. 9 𝔓 we may read with a word-play ואם ינוח לאנחה לו. It would seem that כחו is a doublet of כיתו (ver. 4).

5 יינה] 𝔊 πλησθήσεται. E conjectured that 𝔊 had ישבע, "a false reading for יינה, of which perhaps the last letter was lost in the Greek translator's copy."

6 חבולי] See note on 𝔓. Wisdom i. 4 *a body that is held in pledge by sin*.

7 יוקש] Allured as by a *bait*. See *Journal of Philology* vol. II. 130 (1869) art. Note on the Hebrew root יקש.

9 ונאשרינו] 𝔐 תאשרינו, with ת for *vau*, *nun*.

10ᵃ—10⁽¹⁾ תפארת...ברבוח...ברכו כו׳] A chaos of variants.

10⁽ⁿ⁾ Who hath blessed it (?), and made his life perfect?
I will be a glory unto thee (?).
10ᶜ Who was able to stray, and strayed not?
And to do evil to a neighbour, and would not?
11 Therefore his good is sure;
And the congregation shall declare his praise.

* * * * * * *

Fol. B 2 recto   **32.** 1ᵇᶜ Be to them as one of them;
Take thought for them, and afterward be seated:
2ᵇᶜ Supply their want, and afterward recline.
That thou mayest rejoice in their honour;
And receive favour at the table (?).
3 Speak, O elder, for it pertaineth to thee;
And be carefully wise (?), and hinder not song.
4 In a place for wine pour not forth talk;
And in a place for music (?) pour not forth talk:
And wherefore shouldest thou be always (𝔖) wise?

11 ותהלתו] 𝔖 *laudes ejus.* "Here more probably *his righteousness*" (E).

32. 1ᵇᶜ חרבין] So 𝔖 ܩܝܢܐ. רבין *proprie de quadrupedibus.*

2ᵇᶜ ועל מוסר] See note on 𝔐. The sense may be paraphrased τότε ἔσται σοι δόξα ἐνώπιον πάντων τῶν συνανακειμένων σοι (Luke xiv. 10).

3 והצנע שכל] 𝔐ᵃ לכת (Mic. vi. 8), thus attesting the reading והצנע. 𝔊 ἐν ἀκριβεῖ ἐπιστήμῃ. Compare xvi. 25 𝔐 ובהצנע אתווה רעי, 𝔊 καὶ ἐν ἀκριβείᾳ ἀπαγγελῶ ἐπιστήμην, 𝔖 *et in sapientia.* xlii. 8ᶜ 𝔐 והיית זהיר באמת ואיש צנוע לפני כל חי, 𝔊 καὶ δεδοκιμασμένος ἔναντι παντὸς ζῶντος. Field's *Hexapla* on Micah's לכת והצנע gives, "Ο᾽. καὶ ἕτοιμον εἶναι τοῦ πορεύεσθαι...Θ. καὶ ἀσφαλίζου τοῦ πορεύεσθαι...Ε᾽. καὶ φροντίζειν...," and from St Jerome, with reference to these renderings, "et nos diximus, *sollicitum ambulare.*" Compare the Arabic ܢܝܥ which *maxime de rebus adhibetur in quibus peragendis arte opus est* (Freytag). 𝔊 in Ecclus. suggests a comparison of הצנע לכת with ἀκριβῶς περιπατεῖτε (xvi. 25 n.). צנע in rabbinic has the sense *hide*, with which might be connected צנוע *modest*, cf. Prof. Driver's Glossary in the Oxford *Original Hebrew* of Ecclus., and Prof. Israel Lévi *L'Ecclésiastique* p. 48. With והצנע שכל in this sense cf. St James iii. 13 ἐν πραΰτητι σοφίας. The reference to Eccles. vii. 16 in verse 4, Why be always wise?, *dulce est Desipere in loco,* suggests that at a festivity the sage is to be not obtrusive in his wisdom. ואל תמנע שיר. "It is remarkable that Chrysostom cites this passage (xii. 395, Ben.) with the word 'not' expressly omitted: τί ἐστιν Καὶ ἐμποδίσεις μουσικά; ...The same reading is found in 248, Co." So E, giving a reference to Clem. *Paed.* ii. 7 (Potter p. 203), where the verses 3, 7, 8 (which 𝔖 omits) are quoted in the form, Λάλησον, πρεσβύτερε, ἐν συμποσίῳ· πρέπει γάρ σοι· ἀλλ᾽ ἀπαραποδίστως λάλησον, καὶ ἐν ἀκριβείᾳ ἐπιστήμης. Νεανίσκε, καί σοι ἐπιτρέπει ἡ Σοφία, λάλησον, εἰ χρεία σου, μόλις δὶς ἐπερωτηθείς· κεφαλαίωσον λόγον ἐν ὀλίγοις.

4 ובלא מוזמר סח] 𝔊 ὅπου ἀκρόαμα μὴ ἐκχέῃς λαλιάν, ἀκρόαμα being "*anything heard*, esp. *with pleasure*...as *a play, musical piece*" (L. & S.). By transpositions we get במ' תמנע שיח with בם' for במקום ὅπου. 𝔖 translates only the clause ובמ' המזמור אל תשפך שיח

CH. 32]   THE WISDOM OF BEN SIRA.   XXXIX

4[1] As a seal upon a purse of gold,
   Is a hymn to God at a banquet of wine.
5 As a boss (?) of ruby on a circlet (𐤇𐤋) of gold,
   Is a concert of music (?) at a banquet of wine.
5[1] As a collar of gold wherein are emerald and sapphire;
   So are fine words comely at a banquet of wine.
6 As settings of fine gold and a seal of carbuncle,
   Is the voice of music with the pleasance of mead.
7 Speak, O young man, if thou be wanted;
   With compulsion if one ask thee twice or thrice.
8 Restrain speaking, and diminish it exceedingly;
   And be like to one that knoweth and holdeth his tongue.
9 Among elders set not thyself up;
   And press not (?) much on princes.
9[1] Before hail (𐤇𐤋) speedeth (?) lightning;
   And before one that is downcast speedeth favour.
10 Before hail (𐤇𐤋) speedeth (?) lightning;
   And before one that is shamefast favour.
11 At the appointed time tarry not;
   Get thee home and do pleasure (?).
11[1] At table time multiply not words;
   Even though a thing hath come into thy mind.
12 .   . in thy heart (?), and do pleasure;
   In the fear of God, and not with lack of understanding (𐤇𐤋 all).

בט׳ היין כו׳. Evidently מומור is a doublet of יין. R. V. *Pour not out talk where there is a performance of music*, A. V. *a musician.* "Rather *an entertainment*....The Latin version 'where there is *no* attention' is characteristic; one Greek MS. has the same mistake; the Arm. also renders 'attention,' but is otherwise faithful" (E). For ובל עת read with 𝔖 ובכל עת.

9 בין זקנים] G ἐν μέσῳ μεγιστάνων μὴ ἐξισάζου (X. ἐξουσιάζου), καὶ ἑτέρου λέγοντος μὴ πολλὰ ἀδολέσχει, "ὅπου γέροντες (λέγοντες 248.) 248. Co. Vet.Lat. Syr. Ar." (Fritzsche). A. V. *and when ancient men are in place use not many words*, R. V. *And when another is speaking make not much babbling.* "The better MSS. read: *when another is speaking*...248 and Arm. represent a middle stage, 'where there are speakers.' To us it seems evident that the received reading is correct; and a miswriting of the Greek will probably be the simplest account of the variant" (E). G 𝔖 transpose 𝐏 thus, בין שרים אל תקומם וזקנים כו׳. Starting with 𝐏 we may suppose the corruption of γέροντες to ἑτέρου λέγοντος to have occasioned the transposition of μὴ πολλὰ ἀδολέσχει (𝔖 *noli contumelia afficere*). Cf. vii. 14 אל תמור בעדת שרים. Jud. xvi. 16 *she pressed him daily with her words*.

11[1] שלחן] 𝔖 *Tempore mensae ne multum garrias, dumque memoria polles domum tuam proficiscere*, thus ending with פטר לביתך from verse 11. For 'table' compare Clem. *Paed.* II. 1, where ἡ τράπεζα τῆς ἀληθείας is contrasted with other ἐδύσματα.

12 בחסר כל] 𝔖 as if רצונך, and apparently בחסר without כל, which may have fallen out before כל. The translation suggests לב for כל.

13 And for all these things (?) bless thy Maker;
   Which satisfieth thee with his goodness.
13(1) He that seeketh God may expect favour (?);
   And he that is a madman shall be snared thereby (?).
14 He that seeketh God will receive discipline;
   And he that seeketh him diligently shall obtain an answer.
14(1) He that seeketh things pleasing to God shall receive instruction;
   And he will answer him in his prayer.
15 He that seeketh the law shall obtain her;
   And he that is a madman shall be snared thereby.
16 He that feareth the Lord shall discern judgement;
   And shall bring forth counsels from twilight (𝕴).
16(1) They that fear the Lord shall discern his judgement;
   And they shall bring forth much wisdom (𝕸) from their heart.
17 A man of violence (𝕸) will wrest reproofs;
   And will draw the law (?) after his need.
17(1) A wise man will not conceal wisdom (𝕸);
   And a scorner will not keep his tongue.
18ª A wise man will not take a bribe (𝕴):
   One that is proud and a scorner will not keep the law.
19 Without counsel do not anything;
   And after thy doings vex not thyself.
20 Go not in a way set with snares;
   And stumble not at an offence twice.
21 Trust not in the way of the spoiler (?);
22 And be watchful of thy latter end.
22(1) Trust not in the way of the wicked;
   And be ware in thy paths.
22(b) In all thy ways keep thy soul;
   For whoso doeth these things keepeth a commandment.
23 In all thy doings keep thy soul;
   For he that doeth this keepeth a commandment.

13 הַמּוּרך] G τὸν μεθύσκοντά σε. "Lit. *inebriateth thee*....Drusius cites an observation of Jerome that the Hebrew language puts '*ebrietas* pro *satietate*'" (E).

16 מנשף] See note on 𝕴. By transposition we get מנשש ἀπὸ ψυχῆς, agreeing with 𝔖 and 16(1) מלבם. G ὡς φῶς as a paraphrase, perhaps seeing a reference to Psalm xxxvii. 6 והוציא באור צדקך which is not in 𝕴.

18ª וליץ זר..חכם] See 𝕸 and note on 𝕴. Gaab's correction διανόημα ἀλλοτρίου (Fritzsche) is not confirmed by the Cairo text.

22 וּבַאֲחֲרִיתְךָ] G καὶ ἀπὸ τῶν τέκνων σου φύλαξαι. A sentiment "here so unnatural and inappropriate that we incline to the Syriac text, *and be of good heed in thy paths*, supposing the Greek to represent the corruption of אֲרְחוֹתֶיךָ into אַחֲרִיתְךָ, which has occurred already" (E), cf. iii. 31 n. See in 22(1) וּבְאָרְחֹתֶיךָ *and in thy paths*, and compare Job viii. 13 LXX. τὰ ἔσχατα for אָרְחוֹת.

24 He that observeth the law keepeth his soul;
   And he that trusteth in the Lord shall not be ashamed.
33. 1 Evil shall not befall him that feareth the Lord;
   But in temptation even again he shall be delivered (?).
  2 He that hateth the law shall not be wise;
   And he is moved as...tossed with tempest (?).
  3 A man of discernment discerneth a matter;
   And his law   .   .   .   .   .

  *   *   *   *   *   *   *

35. 9 In all thy works (𝔐) shew a bright countenance;   Fol. B 3 recto
   And dedicate thy tithe with gladness.
  10 Give to God (?) according as he hath given to thee;
   With goodness of eye, and as thy hand hath found (?).
  11 For he is a God that recompenseth;
   And sevenfold will he return unto thee.
   He that giveth to the poor lendeth to the Lord;
   And who is a rewarder but he (𝔐 𝔖)?
  12ᵃ Bribe (𝔖 Hesitate) not, for he will not receive;
   And trust not upon a sacrifice of oppression.
  12ᶜ For he is a God of judgement;
   And with him is no respect of persons.
  13 He will not shew favour toward the poor;
   And he will hear the supplication of the afflicted.
  14 He will not reject the cry of the fatherless;
   And of the widow, when she maketh much complaint (𝔐).
  15 Do not tears run down the cheek?
   Doth she not sigh because of her miseries?
  16 Bitterness that is well-pleasing (𝔐) is her lamentation (?):
   Her (𝔊 His) cry hasteth to the clouds.
  17ᵃ The crying of the poor passeth through thick clouds (𝔐);
   And resteth not until it come nigh.
  17ᶜ It will not remove till God shall visit;
   And till he that judgeth righteously shall do judgement.
  18ᵃ Yea, and God will not tarry;
   And as a mighty man he will not refrain himself:

35. 9 בכל מעשיך] See E on 𝔖 *illi qui non est redditurus &c.*

11 אלוה] See 12ᶜ אלהי, xxxvi. 1 אלהי הכל, xlv. 23ᵉ אלוה כל but with a small *yod* above the line and dots (..) underneath, as may be seen in the facsimile of the Oxford fol. 6 verso. In xlvi. 14 it is proposed in *L'Ecclésiastique* (p. 116) to read ישׁב 𝔐 (Ps. lxxix. 12 וחשב), 𝔐 ישׁלם (Prov. vi. 31). אלהי כי' for רפקד אהלי יעקב.

16 תמרורי רצון הנחת] See note on 𝔐. Or with רצון read אנחתת. 𝔊 θεραπευων ἐν εὐδοκίᾳ, cf. Esth. ii. 12 מרוקיהן (LXX. θεραπείας) and תמדוקי.

f

XLII   THE WISDOM OF BEN SIRA.   [CH. 35

18ᶜ   Till he smite the loins of the unmerciful;
      And repay vengeance to the heathen:
18ᵉ   Till he dispossess the sceptre of pride;
      And quite cut down the rod of the wicked:
19ᵃ   Till he render to a man his due;
      And a man's recompense according to his devising:
19ᶜ   Till he plead (?) the cause of his people;
      And make them joyful (𝔐) with his salvation.
20   Mercy from the Lord in time (?) of affliction
      Is as cloud (?) of rains in season of drought.
20⁽¹⁾   .   .   .   .

Fol. B 3 verso **36.** 1ᵃ Save us, O God of all;
       2   And exalt thy fear over all the nations.
       3   Shake thy hand (𝔐) over the strange people;
            And let them see thy mighty acts.
       4   As thou hast been sanctified in their eyes over us;
            So in our eyes get thee honour over them.
       5   And let them know as we have known,
            That there is no God but thou.
       6   Renew signs, and repeat wonders;
            Glorify thy hand, and strengthen arm and right hand.
       7   Wake up indignation, and pour out wrath;
            And subdue the foe, and drive away (?) the enemy.
       8ᵃ   Hasten the end, and visit (𝔓) the appointed time (?);
       8⁽¹⁾ For who shall say unto thee, What doest thou?
      10   Make an end of the head of the princes of Moab (𝔓);
            That saith, There is none but me.
      11   Gather all the tribes of Jacob;
            And let them inherit as in the days of old.
      12   Have mercy upon the people that is called by thy name;
            Israel, whom thou didst surname Firstborn.

---

20 בעת חויים] Read בענן, that is בעןן with medial *nun* at the end, cf. xxxi. 9 𝔐 ן for *vau, nun*. 𝔊 ὡς νεφέλαι. 𝔖 *Et erubescat osor in tempore afflictionis veluti nubes pluviae tempore quo requiritur*. "Mr Douce has pointed out the resemblance" to this verse of Portia's *The quality of mercy is not strained: It droppeth, as the gentle rain, &c*. See Bp Charles Wordsworth on Shakespeare and the Bible (p. 112, 1892). Ecclus. xiii. 1 *He that toucheth pitch shall be defiled therewith*, cf. *Henry IV*. Pt I (*ib*. p. 340). For another allusion to the *Apocrypha* in the *Merchant of Venice* see "A Daniel come to judgment" (*ib*. p. 87). חויים. It is remarked on xl. 13 𝔐 בחזי קולות in *L'Ecclésiastique* that 𝔖, misunderstanding the words from Job xxxviii. 25, reads 'כ קלות, *et quasi flumina levibus plena nubibus &c*. "Sa traduction de חזיו par *nuées* est conforme à la tradition, entre autres au Targoum." 𝔖 קלות *light* is a misreading (*ib*. p. L.) which points to a Hebrew original. For בעת Dr Schechter suggests also בעב (Is. xviii. 4), בעתר (Ezek. viii. 11).

13 Have mercy upon thy holy city;
    Jerusalem, the place of thy dwelling.
14 Fill Sion with thy majesty;
    And thy temple from thy glory.
15 Give testimony to the firstling of thy works;
    And establish the vision spoken in thy name.
16 Give their reward to them that wait for thee;
    And let thy prophets be true.
17ª Hear the prayer of thy servants;
    According to thy good pleasure (?) unto thy people.
17ᶜ And let all the ends of the earth know (𝕳),
    That thou art our God for ever (?).
18 The throat eateth every meat;
    Yet is one meat more pleasant than another (𝕸).
21 A woman will receive every man (?);
    Yet is one woman beautiful (𝕸).
    *   *   *   *   *   *

37. 27 My son, prove thy soul in thy life (𝕸 in wine);   Fol. B 4 recto
    And see thou give it not that which is bad for it.
28 For not all is good for all:
    Not every soul chooseth every sort.
29 Be not insatiable (𝔊) for every luxury;
    And be not effuse on all dainties.
30 For in much luxury (𝕸 food)·nesteth sickness;
    And he that surfeiteth shall come nigh to loathing.
31 By intemperance many perish utterly (?);
    But he that taketh heed shall add to life.
38. 1 Honour a physician before need of him (𝕳):
    Him also hath God apportioned.

36. 14 [הודך..היכלך] A. V. *Fill Sion with thine unspeakable oracles.* R. V. *Fill Sion; exalt· thine oracles.* "The passage has been admirably restored by Tischendorf from the Vat. ἀρεταλογίας. The former editions had ἄραι τὰ λόγιά σου.... See Mayor on Juvenal xv. 16" (E). 𝔊 (Swete) πλῆσον Σιὼν ἀρεταλογίας σου, καὶ ἀπὸ τῆς δόξης σου τὸν λαόν σου. 𝕳 𝕾 ναόν σου, cf. xlix. 12 קדש היכל, 𝔊 ναὸν ἅγιον—"vulgo legitur λαόν" (Fritzsche), and see Hatch & Redpath's *Concordance.* A. V. *an holy temple.* R. V. *a people holy,* marg., "Some ancient authorities read *temple.*" See note on 𝕳 l. 5.

17ª [ברצונך עמך 𝕾 עמך על ברצון]. 𝔊 *according to the blessing of Aaron על עמך.* See Numbers vi. 23.

37. 31 [בלא מוסר] Through lack of self-*restraint*, cf. vi. 22 n. On ינועו וענעו, 𝕸 נועו see note on 𝕳, cf. xiv. 17 ינועו נוע, xxxv. 18ᵉ ינדע נדוע.

38. 1 [לפני צרכו] On רעי see note on 𝕳. A. V. *Honour a physician with the honour due unto him for the uses which ye may have of him.* The words *which &c.* "must be omitted as not in the Greek...we must emend πρὸ τῆς χρείας αὐτοῦ for πρὸς τὰς χρείας" (E), but cf. 𝕸 *according to thy need.* 𝕾 xviii. 19 quoted by E, "before thou fightest procure for thyself an helper, and before thou art sick a physician."

f 2

2 From God a physician getteth wisdom;
   And from a king he shall receive gifts.
3 The skill of a physician shall lift up his head;
   And he shall stand before nobles.
4 God bringeth out medicines from the earth;
   And let a prudent man not refuse them.
5 Was not water made sweet with wood,
   For to acquaint every man with his (𝔊 their) power?
6 And he gave man understanding;
   To glory in his (𝔊 their) might.
7ᵃ By them doth the physician assuage pain;
8ᵃ And likewise the apothecary maketh a confection:
8ᵇ That his work may not fail (?);
   Nor health from among the sons of men (𝔊 his earth).
9 My son, in sickness be not negligent (?):
   Pray unto God, for he will heal.
10 Flee from iniquity, and from respect of persons;
   And from all transgressions cleanse thy heart.
11 Offer a sweet savour (?) as a memorial;
   And fatness estimated according to thy substance (?).
12 And to the physician also give (?) a place;
   And he shall not remove, for there is need of him likewise.

Fol. B₄ verso

13 For there is a time when in his hand is good success (?):
14ᵃ For he too will supplicate unto God,
14ᵇ That he will prosper (𝔊) to him the treatment (*or* draught),
   And the healing, for the sake of his (?) living.
15 He that sinneth against his Maker
   Will behave himself proudly (𝔊) against a physician.
16ᵃ My son, let tears fall over the dead:
   Be in bitterness, and wail with lamentation.

2 יחכם רופא] E תמארת...רפאות, an ingenious word-play not in 𝔐. But in verses 6—7ᵃ we find להתפאר and רופא.

9 אל תתעבר] Or (?) תתעבר with *kaf.* 𝔊 μὴ παράβλεπε, A. V. and R. V. *be not negligent.* The word is parallel to תאוך *tarry* in ch. v. 7ᵃ, where the note on 𝔐 suggests *kaf* for *beth*.

12 ואל ישמש מאה בנב צרביך] So 𝔐, on which see the note on 𝔐. Supposing מאתכ to have been written in an old MS. for מאתך, the one *kaf* would easily have been lost before the other, leaving מאת, afterwards corrupted into מאה. Note that we have here an example of abbreviations, which, as is well remarked in *L'Ecclésiastique* (p. XLVII), may have occasioned some of the corruptions in extant Hebrew MSS. In a margin it is quite natural to abbreviate, and anything in a margin may creep into the text of a later copy.

14ᵇ משרה] 𝔊 ἀνάπαυσιν. 𝔖 *sanitatem*. See note on 𝔐.

THE WISDOM OF BEN SIRA.

16ᶜ According to the manner of each, bury his (ℳ their) flesh;
   And hide not thyself when they die (?).
17ᵃ Weep bitterly, and make grievous wailing;
   And appoint mourning accordingly (?):
17ᶜ A day or two because of hearsay (?);
   And be comforted for the sake of health (?).
18 Out of sorrow (?) cometh harm;
   So the sad of heart buildeth up trouble (?).
20 Set not the heart upon him (ℳ) any more;
   Dismiss his remembrance, and remember the end.
22 Remember his sentence, for it is thy sentence;
   His yesterday, and thine to day.
21 Remember him not, for there is no hope for him;
   What shalt thou profit him (?)? and thou shalt hurt thyself.
23 When the dead is at rest, let his remembrance rest;
   And be comforted when his soul departeth.
24 The wisdom of the scribe increaseth wisdom (𝕳);
   And he that hath little business shall become wise.
25ᵃ How shall he get wisdom that holdeth the plough (or goad),
   And glorieth in the stimulant (?) spear?
25ᶜ He is busied with oxen, and leadeth about cattle (?);
   And his discourses are with bullocks.
26 And his wakefulness is to victual (?) the stall:
   He setteth his heart to plough furrows.
27 Likewise the artificer . . . .
   Which by night is busied (ℳ) . .
   *   *   *   *   *
49. 12 And they erected the holy temple;   Fol. B 5 recto
   Which was prepared for everlasting glory.
13ᵃ Nehemiah, glorious is his memory;
   Who raised up our ruins:
13ᶜ And healed our breaches;
   And set up gates and bars.

16ᶜ ואל תתעלם] Deut. xxii. 1—4, Is. lviii. 7 ומבשרך אל תתעלם.
17ᵃ בכי וההם] So ℳ, rightly as to בכי. 𝔊 θέρμανον, see note on 𝕳.
17ᶜ בעבור דמעה...עון] 𝔊 χάριν διαβολῆς, 𝔖 propter homines. דמעה being possibly a repetition from verse 16ᵃ, the English suggests שמעה. 𝔊 for עון בעבור ἕνεκεν λύπης, 𝔖 vitae causa. The note on 𝕳 suggests בעבור עונה when the time has passed. The English follows 𝔖, "health" standing for חיים as "healthy." in ch. xxx. 14 for חי. Arab. tum successorem ejus confortare, with perhaps חיים in the sense living ones. A reading חיין with nun (xiii. 22ᵃ n.) corrupted into דוון (cf. xxx. 21 n.) would account for 𝔊 λύπης, cf. in verse 18 מדין for מדוון, 𝔊 ἀπὸ λύπης. Isaiah i. 5 LXX. εἰς λύπην for די. 𝕳 xiv. 1 רין, 𝔊 λύπῃ.
25ᵃ מהעיר] Or (?) המעיר, cf. Job xli. 2 (10) בו' יעירנו. חניה for goad.
49. 12 ויריםו] See Shabbath 11a on Ezra ix. 9 לרומם את בית אלהינו.

14 Few have been created upon the earth like Enoch (?);
And he also was taken within (?).
15 Like Joseph was ever a man born?
And also his body was visited.
16 And Shem and Seth and Enosh were visited (𝔐);
And above every living thing was the glory of Adam.
50. 1ª Great one of his brethren, and glory of his people,
Was Simon, son of Johanan (𝔐), the priest;
1ᵇᶜ In whose generation the house was repaired (?);
And in whose days the temple was fortified.
3 In whose generation a cistern was digged (𝔐);
A pit (or store) like the sea (?) in its abundance.
2 In whose days a wall was built;
A bulwark of refuge (?) in the temple of the King.
4 Who took thought for his people against the spoiler;
And fortified his city against the besieger.
5 How glorious was he when he looked forth from the tent;
And when he went out from the house of the veil!
6 As the morning star from amid thick clouds;
And as the full moon in the days of (?) the solemn feast.

14 מעט] 𝔊 οὐδὲ εἷς. "Syr. 'few'; doubtless an intentional alteration, perhaps from a Christian hand" (E).
50. 1ª יוחנן] 𝔖 Syro-hex. *Nethanya*, 𝔊 *Onias* with variants (𝒥. *Q. R.* x. 473). הכהן as in Vet. Test. *Zadok the priest*. 𝔊 adds ὁ μέγας, omitting *Great one &c.* 𝔐 xlv. 24ᶜ בכהונה גדולה.
1ᵇᶜ נפקד] 𝔊 ὑπέρραψεν (? נתפר), Syro-hex. ܣܢܝ, cf. Eccles. iii. 7 ועת לתפור, Ezra iv. 12 וְאֻשַּׁיָּא יָחִיטוּ.

3 אשיח בם] A. V. *In his days the cistern to receive water, being in compass as the sea, was covered with plates of brass*. R. V. *the cistern of waters was diminished*, with note "The text here seems to be corrupt." 𝔖 ܘܚܦܪ *and he digged*. Arab. وحفر *was digged*. 𝔊 ἐν ἡμέραις αὐτοῦ ἐλατομήθη ἀποδοχεῖον ὑδάτων, χαλκὸς ὡσεὶ θαλάσσης τὸ περίμετρον. So Fritzsche, with note "scripsi ἐλατομήθη, חָצַב, ex coniectura; libri ἠλαττώθη... χαλκὸς] λάκκος III. 55. 155. 254. 296. 308," wrongly preferring χαλκός to λάκκος and not divining the Hebrew for his ἐλατομήθη (Ex. xxi. 33 LXX. ἢ λατομήσῃ λάκκον, Heb. יכרה). For בם read with 𝔊 בים, and for אשיח read שיחה or שוחה or אשוח as suggested in the note on 𝔐. The sense of the verse had been made out approximately from the Versions (E), but 𝔐 מקוה from Gen. i. 10 was wanted to account for the comparison בים *as a sea*. On the extensive cisterns and aqueduct of ancient Carthage see Dr Thomas Shaw on Barbary and the Levant (Oxf. 1738), and Mr R. Bosworth Smith's *Carthage and the Carthaginians*. In illustration of the hyperbole בים cf. Ammianus Marcellinus XVI. 10. 14 *lavacra in modum 'provinciarum exstructa: amphitheatri molem solidatam lapidis Tiburtini compage, ad cuius summitatem aegre visio humana conscendit.*

5 מח נהדר] 𝔐 xlvi. 2 יד בנטותו נחדר סח.
6—8ª בימי מועד] See 𝔊 𝔖 A. V. and R. V. Nisan in uncials may have become ΝΕωΝ.

THE WISDOM OF BEN SIRA.

7 And as the sun dawning upon (?) the temple of the King;
And as rainbow seen in the cloud.
8ᵃ As budding branch (?) in the days of the solemn feast;
And as the lotus by the watercourses.
8ᶜ As flower of Lebanon in the days of summer;
9ᵇᶜ And as fire of incense upon the meal-offering:
In (or As) a gold plated vessel, and a chalice (or weighty),
That is set with pleasant stones.
10 As a green olive full of berries;
And as a wild olive tree with branches full of sap.
11ᵃ When he put on robes of honour;   Fol. B 5 verso
And clothed himself with robes of beauty.

9ᵇᶜ א,יל......זהב בבלי] Next after וזהב in the MS. (fol. B 5 r.) are traces not of any ordinary letter, but of something like a *cheth* (or *hé*) of exceptional form with the first stroke sloping down to the right. The smallness of the letter suggests that it is to be read as *cheth*. For a *hé* of like form see in the last complete hemistich of the Lewis-Gibson folio, recto, בן לרעים לרעה נהפכו. Passing over two letters, we come to the faded point of a *yod*. Between this and the *cheth* is what might at first be taken for a *mem*, but that in this script that letter ends with a slope to the left, and the stroke before the *yod* is upright. Reading it as *vau*, we see before it what looks most like a *beth*, but may have been a *pé*. Thus after וזהב would have been חפוי, or possibly by clerical error תבוי. Before the *alef* are the feet of two strokes, which may have belonged to ח or נו. For examples of the flat-footed *tau* of this script see in the Lewis-Gibson folio, recto, at the end of line 1, בתרועה; and in the verso, col. 2, line 4 from the end, שינת לילה, where *nun* precedes *tau*. After the *alef* is what I take to be the nearly complete outer rim of a *teth*, round a hole in the paper. It ends in a point below to the left, and has two slight protuberances above, such as would be shewn by the *teth* of מעם in line 4 if all of it but a hair's breadth along the top were covered up. Thus, reading *vau*, *nun* at the beginning of the word, we get ונאטיל. As favouring חפוי (thus read in 1897), it may now be added that a word from חפח occurs in xiii. 22ᵃ 𝔐 (fol. A 3 v.), where מופין is wrongly corrected by a *hé* (for *cheth*) written above the line. After חפוי there was doubtless an unusual word, as the letters א.יל alone suggest. Supposing it to have been ונאטיל, what can this mean? (1) Kohut in *Aruch Completum* explains אָנְטָל (I. 146 a) by the Arabic ناطل, the Greek ἀντλίον &c., and the German *Weinmass, Schöpfeimer*. Again, under נטל (v. 334 a) he gives 𝔖 נָטְלָא, and from Talmud Babli also נטלא, meaning דלי לשאוב "a vessel to draw with," as in *Chullin* 107a נטלא בת רביעתא. Accordingly in the translation NATIL is rendered *chalice*. (2) For the sense *weighty* cf. Prov. xxvii. 3 וְגֶטֶל חוֹל *A stone is heavy, and the sand weighty*. The discordance of the Versions points to a *crux*. 𝔖 reads רמפתך שפיר..., "Quasi torques aureus *eleganter distinctus*," which may have come out of the reading suggested, with חפח changed to פתח. From טיל... *minus* the top of ל may have come טוב (שפיר). 𝔊 gives ὡς σκεῦος χρυσίου ὁλοσφύρητον, *as a vessel of gold whole-hammered* or "made of solid beaten metal," which may very well include the sense of חפוי *overlaid* as with gold beaten out. 𝔊 perhaps read ונאטיל as from נטל in the sense *massive*. Syro-hex. טמימא.

11ᶜ When he ascended the altar of majesty;
And made glorious the precinct of the sanctuary.
12ᵃ When he received the pieces out of the hand of his brethren;
While himself standing by the altar-fires:
12ᶜ Round him a crown of sons,
Like cedar plants in Lebanon.
12ᵉ And they compassed him about like willows of the brook:
13ᵃ All the sons of Aaron in their glory:
13ᵇᶜ With the fire-offerings of the Lord in their hand,
Before all the congregation of Israel.
14 Until he finished serving the altar,
And arranging the fires of the Most High.
16ᵃ Then sounded the sons of Aaron, the priests,
With trumpets of turnery.
16ᶜ And they sounded, and made their glorious voice heard;
To bring to remembrance (?) before the Most High.
17ᵃ All flesh together hasted,
And fell down upon their faces to the earth:
17ᶜ To worship before the Most High;
Before the Holy One of Israel.
18 And the choir uttered its voice;
And over the multitude they made sweet melody (?).
19ᵃ And all the people of the land chanted,
In prayer before the Merciful.
19ᶜ Until he finished serving the altar;
And had brought its customary offerings unto it.
20ᵃ Then he came down, and lifted up his hands
Over all the congregation of Israel.
20ᶜ And the blessing of the Lord was on his lips;
And in the name of the Lord he gloried.
21 And they bowed down again a second time,
The people all of them, before him.
22ᵃ Now bless ye the Lord, the God of Israel,
Which doeth wonderously in the land.
22ᶜ That bringeth up man from the womb;
And maketh him according to his will.
23 May he give you wisdom of heart;
And may there be (?) peace among you.

14 עד כלותו לשרת] Fritzsche on 𝔊, "καὶ συντέλειαν λειτουργῶν, ובלה משרת, sed videtur scriptum fuisse [sic] וּבְכַלֹּה לְשָׁרֵת."

16ᵃ מקשה] Ex. xxv. 18, 31 *beaten work*, R. V. marg. *turned*.

18 המון כו׳] 𝔊 ἐν πλείστῳ οἴκῳ ἐγλυκάνθη μέλος, better ἐν πλ. ἤχῳ with "106. 157. 248. Co." (Fritzsche), Syro-hex. ܩܝܢܬܐ בסניאא יובבא חלית קינתא. Payne Smith under ܡܒܣ (1. 1537 α) has the misprint "Sir. 4, 18."

24 May his mercy stand fast with Simon;
   And may he confirm to him the covenant of Phinehas,
24[b] Which he executed (?) unto him and unto his seed,
   As the days of heaven.
25 Two nations my soul abhorreth;
   And the third is no people:
26 The inhabitants of Seir and Philistia;
   And the foolish nation that dwelleth in Sichem.
27ª The instruction of understanding and proverbs fitly spoken (?)
   Of Simon, son of Jesus, son of Eleazar, son of Sira.
27ᶜ Whose heart prophesied as with a harp (?);
   And who poured forth understanding.
28 Happy is the man that meditateth on these;
   And he that layeth them to his heart shall be wise.
29ᵇ For the fear of the Lord is life.
51. 1ᵇ I will praise thee, O God of my salvation;
1ª I will give thanks unto thee (?), my God, my Father;
1ᶜ I will declare thy name, O stronghold of my life.
2ª For thou hast redeemed my soul from death.
2ᵇ Thou hast kept back my flesh from corruption;
2ʰᵇ¹ And hast delivered my foot from the hand of Sheol.
2ᵈ Thou hast delivered me from the evil report of the people;
   From the scourge of (?) the tongue, and from the lip of them
   that go aside to lies.
2ᵉ Thou wast with me against them that rose up against me;
3ª Thou hast holpen me according to thy great mercy:
3ᵇ Out of the snare of them that watched for my halting (?);
   And from the hand of them that sought my life.
3ᵈ From many troubles thou hast saved me;
4ª And from chokings of flaming fire
4ᵇ From flames of a fire not blown (?);
5ª From the womb of the deep
5ᵈ From cunning lips, and weavers of lies;

26 שעיר] 𝔊 (Fritzsche) Σηείρ "ex Vet. Lat., qui praebet Seir, et conveniunt cum eo Syr. et Ar....pro ὁ μωρός versio aethiopica praebet Ἀμωραῖος."

27ᶜ אשר ניבע במחור] 1 Chron. xxv. 1—3 *who should prophesy with harps... with the harp, who prophesied &c.* Read (?) נבא בכינור or בבנור (Ps. xlix. 5), *nun* and part of *tau* being interchanged in variants. See note on 𝔐.

51. 3ᵇ סלע] Read צופי צלעי, comparing Jer. xx. 10 R. V. *For I have heard the defaming* (דבת) *of many, terror on every side. Denounce, and we will denounce him, say all my familiar friends* (כל אנוש שלמי), *they that watch for my halting* (שמרי צלעי), cf. 𝔐 שלומך אנשי (vi. 6), דבת *bis* (li. 2ᶜ). 𝔊 ἐκ βρυγμῶν ἑτοίμων εἰς βρῶμα, cf. *Aruch Compl.* v. 49 a לעס *kauen, mit den Zähnen zerbeissen*. With Vet. Lat. *de portis* (𝔊 πλειόνων) *tribulationum* in 3ᵈ cf. vii. 7 n.

Fol. B 6 verso

5ᵇ And the arrows of a deceitful tongue.
6 And my soul drew near unto death;
And my life to Sheol beneath.
7ᶜ And I turned around, and there was none that helped me;
And I looked for one that would succour, and there was none.
8ᵃ And I remembered the mercies of the Lord;
And his lovingkindnesses which are from everlasting.
8ᶜ He that delivereth them that trust in him;
And redeemeth them from all evil.
9 And I lifted up my voice from the earth;
And from the gates of Sheol I cried.
10ᵃ And I exalted the Lord, *saying*, Thou art my Father;
10ᵃ⁽¹⁾ For thou art the mighty one of my salvation.
10ᵇ Leave me not in the day of trouble;
In the day of wasteness and desolation.
11ᵃ I will praise thy name continually;
And I will remember thee with prayer.
11ᶜ Then the Lord heard my voice;
11ᶜ⁽¹⁾ And gave ear unto my supplication.
12ᵃ And he ransomed me from all evil;
And freed me in the day of trouble.
12ᶜ Therefore I gave thanks, and I will sing praise;
And I will bless the name of the Lord.
12ᶜ⁽¹⁾ O give thanks unto the Lord, for he is good;
For his mercy endureth for ever.
⁽²⁾ O give thanks unto the God of praises;
For his mercy endureth for ever.
⁽³⁾ O give thanks unto him that keepeth Israel;
For his mercy endureth for ever.
⁽⁴⁾ O give thanks unto him that formeth all;
For his mercy endureth for ever.
⁽⁵⁾ O give thanks unto him that redeemeth Israel;
For his mercy endureth for ever.
⁽⁶⁾ O give thanks unto him that gathereth the outcasts of Israel;
For his mercy endureth for ever.
⁽⁷⁾ O give thanks unto him that buildeth his city and his sanctuary;
For his mercy endureth for ever.

5ᵇ וחצי לשון] See the Versions. Reading καὶ βολῆς (or βολίδος) for 𝔊 διαβολῆς (?), we might suppose βασιλεῖ to be a doublet.

8ᵃ וחסדיו] 𝔊 ἐργασίας, (?) εὐεργεσίας (𝔖).

8ᶜ (12ᵃ) מכל רע] A. V. *out of the hands of the enemies*. "The better MSS. have
hands of the Gentiles" (E). Fritzsche "πονηρῶν 23.; vulgo *ἐθνῶν*."

10ᵃ—10ᵃ⁽¹⁾ ישעי...אבי אתה] Ps. lxxxix. 27. The Versions ארני for אתה.

CH. 51]   THE WISDOM OF BEN SIRA.   LI

(9) O give thanks unto him that maketh the horn of the house of
David to bud;
For his mercy endureth for ever.
12c(9) O give thanks unto him that chose the sons of Zadok to be priests;   Fol. B 7 recto
For his mercy endureth for ever.
(10) O give thanks unto the Shield of Abraham;
For his mercy endureth for ever.
(11) O give thanks unto the Rock of Isaac;
For his mercy endureth for ever.
(12) O give thanks unto the Mighty One of Jacob;
For his mercy endureth for ever.
(13) O give thanks unto him that chose Zion;
For his mercy endureth for ever.
(14) O give thanks unto the King of the kings of kings;
For his mercy endureth for ever.
(15) And he will lift up the horn of his people:
A praise for all his saints;
Even for the children of Israel, a people near unto him.
Praise ye the Lord.
13 I was a youth;
And I delighted in her, and sought her.
13(b) My foot trod in her truth;
O my Lord, from my youth I learned wisdom.

13—29] Clear traces of Bickell's acrostic (E, note on 𝔐) are found in these verses, and some of the missing letters are perhaps still discoverable. In 20bcd read with 𝔊 לב קניתי without *vau*, as the beginning of a line; in 23 read (?) with a transposition סכלים פנו אלי; in 26a צואריכם (𝔊 τὸν τράχηλον ὑμῶν) without *vau*; and in 28 begin with שמעו. Thus we get all the letters from *lamed* to *tau*, and verse 20a(1) ידי פתחה שעריה gives *yod*. I had written thus far without looking at Bickell's form of the acrostic, which is given in the Appendix. To get the *kaf*, read בוננתי נפשי for נפשי נתתי (ver. 20a). Some of the letters between *alef* and *yod* require most discussion. The first Prologue to Ecclus. in the A. V. ends thus: "This Jesus did imitate Solomon, and was no less famous for wisdom and learning, both being indeed a man of great learning, and so reputed also." The book of Proverbs ending with an "Alphabet" on the virtuous woman, it was *a priori* not unlikely that Ben Sira would end with one on Wisdom. If he did so, this would account for the title of the midrashic "Alphabet of Ben Sira." Conversely this title is testimony to the genuineness of ch. li. 13—29.

13 נער] Solomon says in Wisdom viii. *I loved her, and sought her out from my youth, I desired to make her my spouse...I prayed unto the Lord &c.* See Dr F. W. Farrar's note on viii. 2 in the *Speaker's Commentary*, and cf. Sirac. xv. 2 *And she shall...receive him as wife of youth.*

13(1) חכמה למדתי] To this verse corresponds 𝔊 15 ἐπέβη ὁ πούς μου ἐν εὐθύτητι, ἐκ νεότητός μου ἰχνευον αὐτήν. Comparing 𝔐 𝔖 with 𝔊 13—15 to ἰχνευον αὐτήν, we see that either 𝔊 is an expansion or 𝔐 𝔖 are defective. The latter

g 2

14ᵃ And I prayed a prayer in my youth;
16ᵇ And I found knowledge abundantly.
17 Her yoke (?) was a glory to me;
   And to my teacher will I give thanks.
18 I thought to benefit;
   And I would not turn when I found it (?).
18ᵇ⁽¹⁾ My soul longed for her;
   And I would not turn my face from her.
20ᵃ I gave my soul after her;
20ᵃ⁽¹⁾ And for ever and ever I will not swerve...
20ᵃ⁽²⁾ My hand opened her gates;
   And I looked for her (?), and beheld her (𝔖);
20ᵇᶜᵈ And in pureness I found her.
   And I gat me (?) understanding from her beginning;
   Therefore . . . .
21 My inward parts were hot (?) as an oven for her, to behold her;
   Therefore I possessed her as a good possession.
22 The Lord gave me the reward of my lips;
   And with my tongue will I give him thanks.
23 Turn unto me, O foolish ones;
   And lodge in my house of learning.
24 How long shall ye lack these things,
   And your soul be very thirsty?
25 I opened my mouth and spake of her,
   Get ye wisdom in possession without money.
26ᵃ And (?) bring your necks into her yoke;
   And let your soul take up her burden.
26ᶜ She is nigh to them that seek her;
   And he that giveth his soul findeth her.
27 See with your eyes that I was a little one;
   And I laboured (𝔊 𝔖) in her and found her.

Fol. B 7 verso

view seems to be the right one. 𝔐 𝔖 13 begin about "her" without mention of Wisdom, and in 13⁽¹⁾ wisdom is not personified. 𝔊 on Wisdom begins naturally with ἐζήτησα σοφίαν, and goes on to speak of "her." באמתה דרכה is well illustrated in the note on 𝔐 by Psalm xxv. 5 הדריכני באמתך. In accordance with this and with 𝔖 we should perhaps, if באמתה be right, read with a transposition דרכה רגלי באמתה. See Appendix.

17 עלה] 𝔊 προκοπὴ κ.τ.λ., cf. vi. 30, xxx. 25 n., li. 26ᵃ. Compare the rabbinic *Yoke of Torah*, and in the New Testament "My yoke."

18 לחיטיב ולא אחפך] 𝔊 (Fritzsche) τοῦ ποιῆσαι αὐτήν, "ποιῆσαι με lll. 157." Nearer to 𝔐 would be τοῦ εὖ ποιῆσαι. ולא אחפך bis in 18—18⁽¹⁾. For the former אחפך we might read ארפה, cf. vi. 27 *find...let not go*. See note on 𝔐.

18ᵇ⁽¹⁾ חישקה] Or (?) מרדה, to suit the acrostic. See Appendix.

20ᵃ⁽¹⁾—20ᵃᶜᵈ ידי בו] The former verse, ending at מצאתיה (𝔖), is too long. For ולב read with 𝔊 לב, an initial word of the acrostic.

28 Hear, ye many (?), my teaching in my youth;
    And ye shall get silver and gold by me.
29 My soul shall rejoice in my age (*or* his praise);
    And ye shall not be ashamed of my song.
30 Work your works in righteousness;
    And he shall give you your reward in his season.
30[2] Blessed is the Lord for ever;
    And praised be his name to generation and generation.
30[3] Hitherto are the words of Simon, son of Jesus, who is called
    Ben Sira.
30[3] The Wisdom of Simon, son of Jesus, son of Eleazar, son of Sira.
30[4] Be the name of the Lord blessed henceforth and for ever.

29 בישיבתי] Or בשבתי as suggested in the note on 𝔐. 𝔊 ἐν τῷ ἐλέει αὐτοῦ... ἐν τῷ αἰνέσει αὐτοῦ. 𝔖 *Laetetur anima vestra de poenitentia mea, & ne pudeat vos canticorum meorum.* Schleusner, "Cant. Tr. Puer. 14 ἔλεος est *venia peccatorum.*" The translation presupposes as an alternative תשמח ב׳ בשבחו, cf. 30⁽¹⁾ ומשובח, Dan. ii. 23, iv. 31—34 Heb. *I thank thee, and praise thee, O thou God of my fathers, who hast given me wisdom &c.* 𝔐 xvi. 16 by error ושבחו.

30⁽³⁾ בר אסירא שנקרא בן סירא] 𝔖. Dr Samuel Krauss has a good discussion of the name Sira in "Notes on Sirach" in no. 41 of the *Jewish Quarterly Review* (Oct. 1898), where it is said, "I regard the word סירא as an abbreviation of אסירא.... This אסירא Fritzsche... regards as a participle of the verb אסר, and it would mean *vinctus,* bound.... I however see in this word more than a mere participle; it seems to me to be the Aramaic form of the Hebrew proper name אָסִיר, without vowels אסיר, in Aramaic אסִירָא not אסִירָא. The name is first met with in Exod. vi. 24 as one of Korah's children, and consequently also in the similar list in 1 Chron. vi. 7, 8, 22. In Exod. vi. 24 and Chron. vi. 7, 22 the Peshita has אָסִיר.... The LXX, ed. van Ess, has Exod. vi. 24 'Ασείρ (like Σιράχ), but in Chron. vi. 22, 23, 27 'Ασήρ." Dr Krauss compares עוּר, עוּרָא, and notices Eliezer for Eliezer, and "the same shortness" in Eccles. iv. 13 הסוּרים מבית as in Sira. If the full form of the name was אסיר or אסירא, this gives additional interest to Ben Sira's play upon אסר *bind* (vi. 22 n.). In the book of Ben Sira it was אסור למקרי (Schechter in *J. Q. R.* III. 691). Was it (Sanhedr. 100 *b*) because it says in ch. xlii. 9—10 *A daughter is for her father a vain treasure &c.?* Perhaps here it was originally a word-play, which was afterwards taken too seriously. Some ancient authority having pronounced the book of Ben אסירא אסור *forbidden,* in the sense that it was not of the Hagiographa, men of later generations felt bound to prove it unfit to be read. With Sira cf. Ḥiḳar for Aḥiḳar (ch. iv. 26 n.).

II.
APPENDIX

NOTES ON
ECCLESIASTICUS 39—51
WITH TWO FACSIMILES

APPENDIX.

In the parts (A) and (B) of this Appendix the subsections begin with lines of text from Messrs Cowley and Neubauer's *The Original Hebrew of a portion of Ecclesiasticus* (Clarendon Press, 1897), the editors' translation being also given in each case. (C) contains a notice of Professor D. S. Margoliouth's recent publication *The Origin of the 'Original Hebrew' of Ecclesiasticus*, of which I received a copy (21st May, 1899) when on the point of revising the first proof of a portion of the Appendix. (D) is on the acrostic at the end of the book Ecclesiasticus.

(A).

The following notes on some difficult passages in the Lewis-Gibson folio (of which facsimiles are given at the end of the Appendix) are chiefly extracts from the writer's *Studies in Ben Sira* published in no. 39 of the *Jewish Quarterly Review* (vol. x. 470—488, 1898), an article which contains also the suggestion on ch. xliii. 20 וברקב in (B).

CHAPTER 39.

15ᵃ [בש]ירות נבל וכלי מינֹיֿ   וכן תאמר בתרועה :
17ᶜ ..... יעריך נ .   ומוצא פיו אוצרו :
18 תהֹהֹתֹ[יו] רצונו יצליח   ואין מעצור לתשועתו :

Verse 15. [*With s*]*ongs of the harp and of stringed instruments, and thus with a shout shalt thou say.* Dr Smend reads נֶבֶל with two *segols*, perhaps rightly. In *L'Ecclésiastique* the hemistich is read [בש]ירות נבל ודבריו מבועריןֿ פֶ֜ן מִינִי שָׁיֹּר]. Perhaps it ended וכלי מינין, cf. xiii. 22ᵃ מחופין. Could כ' מינין have meant instruments *of* all *kinds* (Dan. iii. 5 (וכל זני זמרא) ?

Verse 17ᶜ. ...... *appraise* ...... *and the utterance of his mouth is his treasure.* The first word of the line seems to be בדברו (Smend, 𝔊 ﷼): a fragment of its second *beth* is, I think, clear, and the word fits in and is appropriate. If the text of the first hemistich means something like, "By

h

His word He ordereth all things" (*J. Q. R.*), we may compare Wisdom xv. 1 R.V., Sirac. xliii. 26 𝔊. It is scarcely possible to make the text of 𝔐 agree with 𝔊 ἐν λόγῳ αὐτοῦ ἔστη ὡς θημωνία ὕδωρ, which may however correspond to a different reading in the Hebrew. Under and a little to the right of עָרִיךְ is apparently a faint trace of a variant, which may belong to the text translated by 𝔊.

Verse 18. *In* [*his*] *place he maketh his pleasure to prosper, and there is no restraint to his salvation.* The beginning of the line has been read in a variety of ways. The Oxford editors well remark that the first word seems to have been altered, and its three letters as they stand seem to me to spell nothing at all. After it, and just before a slight crease across the line, is a faded stroke of exceptional form, which may be part of ל, i.e. *alef* and *lamed* joined together, of which examples varying in form may be seen in the Oxford facsimiles and in chapters iii.—xvi., cf. iii. 18 ולפני תמצא רחמים. In the margin it seemed to me that there was a slight trace of a variant, which might be read חפץ, with which the whole line would be,

.חפץ א׳ ורצונו יצליח   ואין מעצור לתשועתו :

Fritzsche gives the Greek as,

ἐν προστάγματι αὐτοῦ πᾶσα ἡ εὐδοκία,
καὶ οὐκ ἔστιν ὃς ἐλαττώσει τὸ σωτήριον αὐτοῦ,

with the note, "Clem. Alex. *Paed.* II. 8 ὅτι ἐν προστάγματι αὐτοῦ εὐδοκία γίνεται, καὶ οὐκ ἔστιν ἐλάττωσις εἰς σωτήριον αὐτοῦ. ita etiam Vet. Lat." But in Potter (II. 4, p. 194) and also in Dindorf (Oxon. 1869) I find πᾶσα εὐδοκία γίνεται. St Clement's ἐλάττωσις εἰς represents the construction of 𝔐, but the word ἐλάττωσις implies an auricular corruption of מעצור (1 Sam. xiv. 6) to מחסור (𝔐 xl. 26ᶜ), or possibly a transposition מצעור, ἐλαττοῦν LXX. being used for both חסר and צער.

CHAPTER 40.

6   מעט לחזק כרגע ישקוט   ומבין בהל[ות] . . . ש :

6ᶜ   מעט טע מחזון נפשו   כשריר ד׳ . . . . . רודף :

Verse 6. *A little...for a moment he is quiet, and from the midst of terror*[*s he is perturbed* ?]. "Reading יִשָׁגֵּשׁ; or ? יִרְגַּשׁ is disquieted." 𝔊 ὀλίγον ὡς οὐδὲν ἐν ἀναπαύσει, καὶ ἀπ᾽ ἐκείνου ἐν ὕπνοις ὡς ἐν ἡμέρᾳ σκοπιᾶς.

Although the word before כרגע had been read לחיק, לחוק, לרוק, it seemed to me to be obviously לריק εἰς κενόν, of which לרוח (Eccles. v. 15) is a synonym. 𝔐 קָה may be read as רוח with *resh, vau* run together, cf. xliii. 20 מְקוֹרוֹ, מְקוֹה. In 𝕲a read ὀλίγον ὡς οὐδὲν ἀναπαύσεται (Margoliouth), supposing ΕΝ to have been dittographed, and ΤΑΙ to have dropped out before ΚΑΙ.

In 𝕲b "The Armenian Version gives two very satisfactory emendations, ἐνυπνίοις and κοπιᾷ"(E). Supposing ἐκείνου, a corruption of εἰς κενόν, to have been also misplaced, we may conjecture that 𝕲 read καὶ ἀπ' ἐνυπνίων for ומבין בהלות, or that מֽ read or was understood by the translator to read ומבין חלומות.

ש ....] The line ends with an isolated ש, before which must have stood *resh* or *daleth*, since the paper is torn in such a way that a portion of any other possible letter would have remained where there is now nothing visible. A not unsuitable word to end the line is נגרש or יגרש, before which may have stood ים' *sea* (𝕲 יום ἡμέρᾳ, 248. Co. ἡμέραις). The sense would then be, that the man assays to rest a little but in vain, on account of dream-terrors by which he is *troubled as the sea*, as it is said in Isaiah lvii. 20, with the same contrast of the words גרש and שקט,

הרשעים כים נגרש כי השקט לא יוכל וינרשו מימיו רפש וטיט:

The simile from the sea has a parallel in ch. xxxiii. 2 ὡς ἐν καταιγίδι πλοῖον; and the supposed rendering "he labours as by day," (?) ὡς ἡμέρας κοπιᾷ instead of ὡς ἐν ἡμέρᾳ σκοπιᾶς, is illustrated by ch. xxxviii. 27 ὅστις νύκτωρ ὡς ἡμέρας διάγει.

Verse 6ᶜ .... *from the vision of his soul, (he is) as a fugitive [hurrying on before] the pursuer.* 𝕲 τεθορυβημένος ἐν ὁράσει καρδίας αὐτοῦ, ὡς ἐκπεφευγὼς (248. Co. ἐκφυγὼν) ἀπὸ προσώπου πολέμου, ܒܥܠܕܪܐ, πολεμίου.

מעט טע] The scribe has repeated מעט from the previous line. Read מטעטע, a participle of the form מתטעטע (cf. 2 Chron. xxxvi. 16 וּמִתַּעְתְּעִים, Payne Smith *Thesaurus Syriacus* ܬܠܠ), and for the whole line read,

מטעטע מחזון נפשו   כשריד הנס מפני רודף:

So also *L'Ecclésiastique*, and in verse 6 לריק, but not לרוח.

(B).

On the subjects of this section also see the above-mentioned very valuable commentary *L'Ecclésiastique* by Professor Israel Lévi (Paris, 1898), a French edition of the Lewis-Gibson and Oxford folios with introductory essays on the *Description du manuscrit, Langue et style de l'auteur, L'Ecclésiastique et la Bible, La version grecque, Version syriaque, &c.*

CHAPTER 42.

וישׂ   ‏: וְעַל מַחֲלֹקוּת נַחֲלָה וְיֵשׁ   3 עַל חֶשְׁבּוֹן חוֹבֵר וְאָרוֹן   שׁוּתָף
חמורת
אפה ואפה   ‏: 5ᵃ וְעַל תְּמָחוּת אֵיפָה וָאֶבֶן   4ᵃ וְעַל שַׁחַק מֹאזְנַיִם וָפֶלֶס
מוסר   ‏: 5ᶜ וְעַל מַמְחִיו עֲבַד בְּנֵר   4ᵇ עַל מִקְנֶה בֵּין רַב לִמְעָט   חשבון

Fritzsche's Greek is,

3 περὶ λόγου κοινωνοῦ καὶ ὁδοιπόρων,
  καὶ περὶ δόσεως κληρονομίας ἑταίρων·
4 περὶ ἀκριβείας ζυγοῦ καὶ σταθμίων,
  καὶ περὶ κτήσεως πολλῶν καὶ ὀλίγων·
5 περὶ ἀδιαφόρου πράσεως καὶ ἐμπόρων,
  καὶ περὶ παιδείας τέκνων πολλῆς,
  καὶ οἰκέτῃ πονηρῷ πλευρὰν αἱμάξαι.

Fritzsche's notes on these verses are as follows : " 3. κοινωνῶν X. CH., Vet. Lat. sociorum—καὶ ante περὶ δόσεως om. III. 106. 155. al.—ἑτέρων III. X. C. 106. 155. 307.—4. περὶ ἀκρ.] καὶ ἀκρ. 248. Co.—σταθμῶν 106. 157. Co.—recepi καὶ ante περὶ κτήσεως ex III. X. C. 106. 155. al.; vulgo om.— 5. διαφόρου III. X. C. 155. 157. 307. Co.—καὶ ante ἐμπόρων (ἐμπόρου C.) om. III. X. C. 23. 106. 155. al. Co.—ἐμπόρων, סחר."

Verse 3. *Of reckoning with a partner and a master, and of the division of an inheritance and a property.* So C. & N. with the note on *master*, " Marg. (fellow-)traveller," וארח being written above וארון. 𝔊 κοινωνοῦ ... ἑταίρων, the former word for שותף, and the latter apparently for חובר transposed to the end of the line. Also 𝔊 καὶ ὁδοιπόρων for וארח, which resembles וארון, i.e. וארון written with medial *nun*. The word ארח *wayfarer, guest* may have been suggested to Ben Sira by ארח *way* in Is. xl. 14, on which see below. A.V. *Of reckoning with thy* (R.V. *a*) *partner and travellers.* מחלקות may mean *discussions* (ABOTH V. 'ש מחלוקת והלל), not *divisions* (𝔊 δόσεως).

Verse 4ᵃ—5ᵃ. *Of the small dust of the scales and balance, and of exchange by ephah and stone (weight)*, with reference (C. & N.) to Is. xl. 15 ‏וכשחק מאזנים נחשבו. פלס may very well have been suggested by the preceding במאזנים ... כפלס (ver. 12), and וארח by the intermediate את מי נועץ ויבינהו וילמדהו בארח משפט (ver. 14), cf. 2 משפט, 21*d* לכל מבין (Lévi, p. 59). Only פלס could shew the reference to Isaiah's "small dust of the balance," a phrase which Ben Sira characteristically uses without regard to its original context, except that this may have suggested other words to him, including possibly חשבון (Is. נחשבו). Wisdom xi. 22 A.V. *For the whole world before thee is as a little grain of the balance*, with marginal reference "Isai. 40. 15."

APPENDIX. LXI

Verse 4ᵇ—5ᶜ. *Of buying* (marg. *reckoning*) *between much and little, and of smiting* (marg. *the correction of*) *a deceitful* [*servant*].

Dr Smend reads this line as below, adding in a footnote (p. 13) "המחיר (Gr. διάφορον = מחיר) oder תמהיר (= feilschen)?," and in a subsequent note (p. 30), "Der letzte Buchstabe in ממהיר kann des Raumes wegen kein ו sein,"—

חשבון   עַל מִקְנֶה בֵּין רַב לִמְעַט   וְעַל ממהיר [מ]מכר חֹנֵר :   סופר

Lévi adopts Smend's reading, with *cheth* for *hé*, remarking (p. 47) that in the MS. *le* ח *est généralement plus large que le* ה, and supposing a *mem* of ממחיר to be *de trop*. Leaving a word doubtful, I would read וְעַל ממחיר ... סוחר with ממחיר for מחיר διαφόρου, comparing vii. 18 𝔐 במחיר, 𝔊 ἕνεκεν διαφόρου (al. ἀδιαφ.). In ch. xxvii. 1 𝔊 (Swete) reads,

χάριν ἀδιαφόρου (א* διαφόρου) πολλοὶ ἥμαρτον,
καὶ ὁ ζητῶν πληθῦναι ἀποστρέψει ὀφθαλμόν.

If here too we read διαφόρου, the word ἀδιάφορος vanishes from the LXX. If before סוחר came ממכר, this would account for ממחיר.

In *L'Ecclésiastique* (p. 47) כו׳ (𝔐 תמורת) וְעַל תמהות is translated *Et de l'équivalence des éphas*, and 𝔊 περὶ ἀδιαφόρου by *de la non-différence*, sc. *de la vente des commerçants*, 𝔊 being supposed to have rendered whatever stood for תמהות by ἀδιαφόρου. According to this view the Greek text is in disorder. But I think it is quite unnecessary to assume this; for either with 𝔐 תמורת, or with Lévi's תמות or תמהות for תמהות, the hemistich 5ᵃ is well enough represented by 𝔊 περὶ ἀκριβείας ζυγοῦ καὶ σταθμ. (Is. xl. 12 σταθμῷ ... ζυγῷ), which may or may not have served originally for both clauses of the line שחק כו׳ (or עַל כו׳). Keeping the order of 𝔊 we may read after περὶ ἀκριβείας κ.τ.λ., as the rendering of the next line in 𝔐,

περὶ κτήσεως πολλῶν καὶ ὀλίγων,
καὶ περὶ διαφόρου (מחיר) πράσεως ἐμπόρων.

In 𝔐 5ᵃ תמהות may very well be a corruption of 𝔐 תמורת which, after 𝔊 and Lévi jointly, might be rendered "exact equivalence," cf. iii. 14, iv. 10ᵃ ותמור *and instead of*.

There remains in 𝔊 καὶ περὶ παιδείας τέκνων πολλῆς, with only 𝔐 מוסר παιδεία corresponding to it in the MS. This accounts for the conjectural reading ממחיר כו׳ in the Oxford edition, the tops of the letters to the beginning of סוחר (?) being torn away. Something preserved in 𝔊 has disappeared from 𝔐, and a marginal survival מוסר from the missing line of text now stands opposite to a line to which it does not belong. This exemplifies one of the ways in which strange dislocations may occur. A later scribe might have put מוסר into the text of a wrong verse.

CHAPTER 43.

מופיע בצאתו	2 שמש מביע° בצדרתו חמה	: מה נורא מעשי יייָ	
	13 גבורתו תתוה ברק	ותנצח זיקות.....	ותנצח זיקים
כר׳	17c [בר]שף יניף שלגו	וכארבה ישכון רדתו :	רד
	20 צינת רוח צפון ישב	וכרקב יקפיא מקורו :	מקוה
	20c על כל מעמד מים יקרים	וכשריון ילבש מקוה :	
	21 יבול כחרב ישיק	ונוה צמחים כלהבה :	וצור
טל פורע	22 מרפא כל מערף ענן טל	פורע לדשן שרב : .	רטב
משובתו	23 מחשבתו . . שיק רבה	ויט בתהם איים :	אוצר
	24 יורדי הים יספרו קצהו	לשמע אזננו נשתומם :	
מעשיו	25 שם פלאות תמהי מעשהו	מין כל חי וגבורות רבה :	
למעניהו למען	26 למענו יצלח מלאך	ובדבריו יפעל רצון :	
	27 עוד כאלה לא נוסף	וקץ דבר הוא הכל :	

Verse 2. [מה נורא] *The sun, when he goeth forth* (marg.), *poureth out warmth: how terrible are the works of the Lord!* The Greek (Fritzsche) is,

ἥλιος ἐν ὀπτασίᾳ διαγγέλλων,
ἐν ἐξόδῳ σκεῦος θαυμαστόν, ἔργον ὑψίστου.

In the latter hemistich and in verse 8 𝔐 has the Biblical מה נורא, which in verse 2 is followed by *works* (pl.), perhaps wrongly, but cf. Ps. lxvi. 3 מה נורא מעשיך. 𝔊 ⅏ make the sun *a terrible* (נורא) *vessel*, cf. 𝔐 8ᵉ כלי צבא, 𝔊 σκεῦος παραβολῶν (C. & N., Swete with v. l.) an obvious corruption of παρεμβολῶν (Fritzsche), ⅏ מכבשא. In retranslating σκεῦος θαυμαστόν we accordingly think first of כלי נורא. But as this does not at once account for מה, and 𝔊 varies its renderings (cf. xii. 5ᵇ כלי מה, 𝔊 ἐμπόδισον), we may reasonably try another word for σκεῦος. Lévi suggests מנה as a slip of the pen for מה. What had occurred to me was that the error was auricular, and that 𝔊 read rightly *mannora*, but rendered this wrongly as if מן נורא. In reply to the objection that 𝔊 would not have understood מן, see the remark of Lévi quoted on p. VII.

In the former part of the verse 𝔐 בצאתו (𝔊 ἐν ἐξόδῳ) may be right, and 𝔐 בצרתו with *resh* for *alef* is accounted for by the occurrence of בהצהירו nearly under it (ver. 3). If מביע and מופיע are variants, this illustrates the suggestion in ch. l. 9ᵇᶜ n. that the scribe may have written חבוי there for חפוי. 𝔊 (rightly as Lévi judges) takes in the two verbs and has nothing for חמה, which he explains as a dittograph of מה, "ou une

APPENDIX. LXIII

variante de שמש." But, this being sometimes feminine (ch. l. 7), there may have been a reading with מביעה or בצאתה before מה. The superfluous חמה would then obviously be המה dittographed. Finally, Psalm xix. יביע אומר כו' having suggested מביע διαγγέλλων, חמה *heat* (usually *sun*), &c., the sense would be that the sun shining in his course proclaims, "How awful are the works of the Lord," שמש מופיע מביע בצאתו מה כו'.

Verse 13. [ברק] *His might marketh out the lightning, and maketh brilliant the flashes* [*in judgement*]. A corrupt marginal reading is rendered by C. & N., "His rebuke marketh out the morning, and casteth off the living substance in [judgement]." The Greek of the verse is

προστάγματι αὐτοῦ κατέσπευσε (-παυσεν) χιόνα,
καὶ ταχύνει ἀστραπὰς κρίματος αὐτοῦ.

Neither reading gives appropriate sense. Snow does not move with speed, like lightning, and stopping the snow is not what is wanted here. The place for χιόνα is verse 17ᶜ, שלגו. Comparing ch. xxxii. 9⁽¹⁾—10 ינצח ברק *speedeth lightning*, and rendering תתוה "marketh" (C. & N.), or "dessine" (Lévi), we get the sense that the Creator first forms the lightning, and then hurls the flashes in judgement. H. & R. *Concordance* s.v. κατασπεύδειν (נחץ), 1 Ki. 21. 8 (9) A κατασπεῦδον, B κατὰ σπουδήν.

Verse 17ᶜ. [כרשף] *Like* (marg.) *darting flashes he sheddeth abroad his snow, and like locusts* (*when*) *they settle is the falling down thereof* (marg.). 𝔊 ὡς πετεινὰ καθιπτάμενα, reading perhaps עיף.

Lévi, "Le mot רשף signifie ici *oiseau* comme dans Job. 5. 7, et peut-être Deut. 32. 24", see Gesen. *Thesaur.* Job v. 7 ובני רשף ינבירו עוף, LXX. νεοσσοὶ δὲ γυπὸς τὰ ὑψηλὰ πέτονται. Add from Field's HEXAPLA, Aquila καὶ υἱοὶ πτηνοῦ..., Symmachus τὰ τέκνα τῶν πετεινῶν ὑψοῦσι πτερά. Whatever רשף means in Job, Ben Sira may have taken it to mean *oiseau*, as in verse 20 he may have written רקב for ἀσκός.

Verses 20—20ᶜ. [וברקב] *The cold of the north wind he causeth to blow, and congealeth his spring* (marg. *the pond*) LIKE ROTTENNESS (?). *Over every standing water he spreadeth a crust, and a pond putteth on as it were a breastplate.* 𝔊 ψυχρὸς ἄνεμος βορέης πνεύσει, καὶ παγήσεται κρύσταλλος ἀφ' (al. ἐφ') ὕδατος κ.τ.λ.

The difficulty is in the word rendered *as rottenness*, but with a query. The Greek states the fact that ice is formed in cold weather; but the context seems to desiderate a simile, to stand in parallelism with כשריון, "as it were a breastplate."

Various emendations of ברקב have been thought of, but "A better solution is suggested by Job xiii. 28 (Sept.) ὃ παλαιοῦται ἴσα ἀσκῷ ἢ ὥσπερ ἱμάτιον σητόβρωτον, where ἀσκῷ is for רקב (A. V. & R. V. *a rotten thing*), in the sense *leather bottle*. This is a sense of the Targumic רוקבא (Syr. רקבא as in Job l. c.), on which see Kohut *Aruch Completum* s. v. רקב (1); and it gives a parallelism which is illustrated by the story of the Gibeonites, who went to Joshua with old bottles and old garments, saying, *These bottles of wine, which we filled, were new; and, behold, they be rent: and these our garments and our shoes are become old by reason of the very long journey*," cf. Psalm xxxii. 7 LXX. ὡσεὶ ἀσκὸν ὕδατα, Joshua iii. 16 Symm. ἄσκωμα for נֵד *heap* of waters. The LXX. rendering in Job was adopted by Abraham Geiger, see also Schleusner s. v. ἀσκός. Whatever ברקב meant in the Hebrew of Job, Ben Sira may have used it in the sense there given to it by the Septuagint. See *J. Q. R.* x. 471—2.

On רקב in this sense it has been remarked, that "it is an Aramaic word which Sirach would not have used because it does not occur in holy writ. But apart from this, the possibility of the word having been used by Sirach in that sense is disproved by the incongruity of the expression. You can collect liquids in a skin-bottle, but you cannot make them freeze to it" (*J. Q. R.* XI. 159). Freezing to the bottle was however not thought of in the *Studies in Ben Sira*. Ice on water being compared in the next line to a breastplate, it was suggested that in verse 20 it is compared to the skin of a leather bottle. A writer accustomed to glass bottles might have compared it to the glass of such a bottle with water in it.

Verse 21. ונוה] *It burneth up the produce like drought, and the* STATE-LINESS *of growing things as a flame.* "Above בחרב is written הרים (see Job 40. 20)." See xiii. 3 n., comparing on 𝔊 in *L'Ecclésiastique* (p. 75), "ayant lu וכבה, il n'a pas hésité à rendre exactement le sens de ce verbe," cf. iii. 30 יכבו 𝔐, 𝔊 ἀποσβέσει.

Verse 22. פורע] *The dropping of a cloud healeth all things, (even) dew releasing the parched young grass*, so C. & N. with query and notes.

As care or sickness "dissipateth" slumber (xxxi. 1—2 תפריע), so dew or moisture may be said to dissipate scorching drought. Comparing Ps. lxv. 12—13 'ירעפון דשן כו we get the sense for this verse, that clouds drop dissipating (?) moisture to fertilise parched land, שרב in Isaiah xxxv. 7 being parallel to צמאון. Probably רטב was meant to explain or replace טל, which belongs to the left column.

Verse 23. איים] *His counsel burneth up (?) the great (deep), and he planteth islands in the ocean.* "Reading וימע as 𝔊." The Greek is given in the form λογισμῷ αὐτοῦ ἐκόπασεν ἄβυσσον, καὶ ἐφύτευσεν αὐτὴν Ἰησοῦς, so Swete (vol. II. 735) with the note "αβυσσος א^{c.a} | Ιησους] Ιϛ ΒΧ Ιησους AC." Fritzsche for ἐφύτευσεν αὐτὴν IHCOYC gives ἐφύτευσεν ἐν αὐτῇ NHCOYC (𝔐 איים), with the MS. 248 and other authorities, remarking "insipidam lectionem αὐτὴν Ἰησοῦς vulgo receptam haud defuerunt, ut par erat, theologi qui probarent et defenderent." Vet. Lat. *et plantavit illum* DOMINUS IESUS (Fritzsche, C. & N. p. xli.).

Verses 24—26. *They that go down to the sea &c. By reason of him* (marg. *for his own purpose*, Prov. xvi. 4) [*his*] *messenger prospereth, and by his words he performeth (his) pleasure.* C. & N. conjecture in a note, יצליח מלאכה *he maketh (his) business to prosper.* 𝔊 26 (Swete),

δι' αὐτὸν εὐοδία τέλος αὐτοῦ,
καὶ ἐν λόγῳ αὐτοῦ σύνκειται πάντα.

APPENDIX.   LXV

For this Fritzsche has

δι' αὐτὸν εὐοδία τέλος αὐτοῦ,
καὶ ἐν λόγῳ αὐτοῦ σύγκειται τὰ πάντα,

with the note "καὶ δι' αὐτὸν εὐοδοῖ ὁ ἄγγελος αὐτοῦ καὶ ἐν 248. Co.—ευδοκια III.—recepi τὰ πάντα ex III. X. C. 55. 106. al. Co.; vulgo πάντα."

The immediately preceding verses being on the experiences of seafarers, one is tempted to read מַלָּח *mariner* for מלאך in verse 26, but Lévi (p. 77), taking a suggestion from Ps. cvii. 23 *They that go down to the sea in ships, that* DO BUSINESS *in great waters*, to which Ben Sira alludes, makes מלאך in 𝔅 mean "*travailleur* de la mer." Whether original or not, מלאך is clearly an old reading and ὁ ἄγγελος αὐτοῦ (248.) a rendering of it with the pronoun added rightly or wrongly. With מלאך explained as in *L'Ecclésiastique* the sense would be that mariners "font ce qu'ils veulent," by the grace of God, who *bringeth them unto their desired haven* (Ps. cvii. 30). It remains to account for the reading in 𝔊.

ΔΙΑΥΤΟΝΕΥΟΔΙΑΤΕΛΟϹΑΥΤΟΥ·

Change the second Τ to Γ and break up the line thus,

ΔΙ ΑΥΤΟΝ ΕΥΟΔΙ ΑΓΕΛΟϹ ΑΥΤΟΥ·

We have then only to write ΟΙ for the second Ι and ΓΓ for Γ, and to insert Ο the article, and we get

ΔΙ ΑΥΤΟΝ ΕΥΟΔΟΙ Ο ΑΓΓΕΛΟϹ ΑΥΤΟΥ,

from which, conversely, we can work back to τέλος αὐτοῦ κ.τ.λ. as a corruption of the reading of 248. Notice the accidental correspondence of τέλος αὐτοῦ with 24 𝔅 קצהו.

[רצון] To account for 𝔊 καὶ ἐν λόγῳ αὐτοῦ σύγκειται τὰ πάντα, I can only suggest that it is due to ocular aberration, τὰ πάντα being a rendering of the word הכל under רצון, and σύγκειται a verb added for completeness.

Verse 27. *More like this we will not add, and the conclusion of the matter is, He is all.*

Mr Thomas Tyler, the author of a well known commentary on Ecclesiastes, has called attention in the *Guardian* (1897) to the correspondence of 𝔅 with the penultimate verse of Ecclesiastes,

סוֹף דבר הכל נשמע את האלהים ירא ואת מצותיו שמור כי
זה כל האדם :

See also in *Sayings of the Jewish Fathers* Addit. Note 51,

"With Eccl. xii. 13 (p. 96 n.) compare Ecclus. xliii. 27 καὶ συντέλεια λόγων Τὸ πᾶν ἐστιν αὐτός [1 Cor. xv. 28 ἵνα ᾖ ὁ θεὸς πάντα ἐν πᾶσιν], on

i

which it is remarked in the *Speaker's Commentary* 'This clause is evidently a spurious Hellenistic addition by the younger Siracide.' The verse runs thus in the *Original Hebrew* of Ecclus. (p. 18 ed. Cowley & Neubauer):

"עוד כאלה לא נוסף   וקץ דבר הוא הכל :

Compare E § VII. *The Greek Version of Ecclesiasticus* (pp. 14 n., 23), and notice xlii. 25ᵃ הכל נשמע וה. The preceding clause has been read הוא חי עומד לעד (Smend, Lévi p. 60), וקים וה. ⅏ πάντα ταῦτα ζῇ καὶ μένει εἰς τὸν αἰῶνα, cf. Eccles. iii. 14 *whatsoever God doeth it shall be for ever: nothing can be put to it, nor anything taken from it* (xlii. 21ᶜ ולא נאצל כו נצ).

CHAPTER 44.

שבח אבות עולם :

16 חנוך [נמ]צא תמים והתהלך עם ייי ו[נ׳]לקח אות דעת לדור ודור :

ועולם כו'] ⅏ Πατέρων ὕμνος, C. & N. *Praise of the Patriarchs*. Lévi (p. 80), "On serait tenté de traduire עולם par 'monde,' 'les pères du monde'; mais ce mot n'a pas encore, dans l'Ecclésiastique, l'acception qu'il a reçue plus tard; en outre, il ne s'agit ici que des ancêtres des Israélites," but see ch. iii. 18 n. Rabbinically Ps. lxxxix. 3 עולם חסד יבנה is made a Scripture proof that the world is built upon "the bestowal of kindnesses" (*Jewish Fathers* 1. n. 6).

Verse 16 [אות דעת] Cf. xlvi. 10 למען דעת. *Enoch [was f]ound perfect, and walked with the Lord, and was taken, being an example* (lit. *sign*) *of knowledge to all generations.* ⅏ ὑπόδειγμα μετανοίας ταῖς γενεαῖς. On this much discussed μετανοίας see *L'Ecclésiastique*, which suggests that the word here perhaps does not mean *pénitence*. "Peut-être aussi faut-il le corriger en ἐπινοίας *réflexion*. M. Noeldeke propose ἐννοίας. *La Sapience*, 4. 15, commente assez bien ces mots en disant…οἱ δὲ λαοὶ ἰδόντες καὶ μὴ νοήσαντες…." On Wisd. iv. 10—14 see the *Speaker's Commentary*. A meaning of μετανοέω is to change one's *opinion*. For אות כו' the Latin has *ut det gentibus poenitentiam*. E adds, "The versions all alter this sentiment (except Aeth.)…Copt. *an example of wisdom* (διανοίας ?); .S. H. *to be an everlasting example* (with MS. 253)." ⅏ notwithstanding, Enoch must somehow come under the rule that God ἀπ' ἀρχῆς ἑκάστην γενεὰν ἐπὶ μετάνοιαν καλεῖ διὰ τῶν δικαίων, see *Apost. Const.* ii. 55 quoted by Dr J. B. Lightfoot on Clem. R. VII. Enoch was a notable or instructive sign γενεᾷ καὶ γενεᾷ (Luke xi. 30 'I. τοῖς N. σημεῖον).

APPENDIX.   LXVII

CHAPTER 45.

22ᶜ אך ...... לא ינחל   ובתוכם לא יחלק נחלה :
22ᶜ אשי יון] . ל .... ל .... ישראל :
24ᶜ אשר תהיה לו ולזרעו   כהונה גדולה עד עולם :
25ᶜ נחלת אש לפני כבודו   נחלת אהרן לכל זרעו :

Verses 22—22ᶜ. *Only [in the land of his people] he should not inherit, and amongst them he should not divide an inheritance; The fire-offerings of the Lord [should be their portion and their inheritance]........Israel.*

In the former verse Lévi reads אך בארצם (𝔖), and explains 𝔊 ἐν γῇ λαοῦ by auricular corruption of אַרְצָם into עַם אֶרֶץ. This implies the pronunciation ܐܪܥ for what would now be אֶרֶץ, as in the HEXAPLA, or (for example) in *Arsareth* (אֶרֶץ אַחֶרֶת).

In verse 22ᶜ Lévi supposes אשי ייי *fire-offerings of the Lord* to have been written by mistake for אני ייי *I the Lord.* But it may be suggested that the line began with אשר, cf. 𝔊 αὐτὸς γὰρ μερίς σου, 𝔖 ܡܛܠ ܕܗܘܝܘ.

Verse 24ᶜ. *Which should be to him and to his seed, an high priesthood for ever.*

ܥܕ ܥܠܡ וכהונה גדולה A title "inconnu à la Bible" (Lévi). 𝔊 ἱερωσύνης μεγαλεῖον, a peculiar rendering which gives a Greek construction to the Hebrew. Lat. *sacerdotii dignitas. L'Ecclésiastique* on xxxix. 30 θηρίων ὀδόντες (Deut. xxxii. 24) for שן חית, "G. a traité חית à *l'état construit,* 'bête de,' comme un génitif grec."

Verse 25ᶜ. *An inheritance of fire in the presence of his glory was the inheritance of Aaron unto all his seed.*

Perhaps we should read in the first hemistich נחלת איש לבנו בכורו, *The inheritance of a man* (𝔊 βασιλέως) *is to his firstborn son,* cf. Gen. xliii. 33 *the firstborn according to his birth-right.* The inheritance of Aaron is to *all his seed:* they are all consecrated. In Num. iii. 12 the Levites are "instead of all the firstborn."

CHAPTER 46.

19ᶜ כופר ונעלם ממ]י לקח[תי וכל אדם לא ענה בו :

Verse 19ᶜ [ונעלם] *From [whom] have I [taken] a ransom or a secret gift* [perhaps נעלים a pair of sandals]? *and no man answered against him.* 𝔊 χρήματα καὶ ἕως ὑποδημάτων, cf. Gen. xiv. 23.

1 Sam. xii. 3 כופר ואעלים כו, LXX. ἐξίλασμα καὶ ὑπόδημα. "Notre texte confirme donc la leçon des Septante... S. a pour נעלים 'une offrande' קורבנא, traduction fantaisiste. Il met aussi, '*Il* ne prit pas'" (Lévi). But the meaning may be that he neither exacted 'ransom' openly nor accepted a secret 'offrande.' Eccles. xii. 14 במשפט על כל נעלם.

i 2

CHAPTER 47.

3 לכפירים שחק כגדי   ולדובים כבני בשן :

Verse 3. *He mocked at lions as at a kid, and at bears as at the herds of Bashan.* 𝔊 ὡς ἐν ἄρνασι προβάτων. 𝔖 ܐܪܒܐ. Arab. ملان.
Lévi on 𝔊, "Dans les Septante ces mos traduisent כבני צאן." As David was keeping צאן (1 Sam. xvii. 34), the word would come in naturally here. If it was ever pronounced ⲤⲀⲚ, it might easily after בני have been converted into ⲂⲀⲤⲀⲚ.

CHAPTER 48.

24 ברוח גבורה חזה אחרית   וינחם אבלי ציון :
25 עד עולם הגיד נהיות   ונסתרות לפני בואן :

Verses 24—25. *By a spirit of might he saw the end, and comforted the mourners of Sion. For ever he declared the things that should be, and hidden things before they came.*

"By a spirit *of might*" (רָ֫בּ ֵל, 𝔊 μεγάλῳ), from Is. xi. 2. Ben Sira ascribes the book of Isaiah, including chaps. xl. sq., to Isaiah, cf. xl. 1 נַחֲמוּ כו', lxi. 2—3 לַאֲבֵלֵי צִיּוֹן...לְנַחֵם. Is. xl. 15 *small dust of the balance* was referred to in xlii. 4ᵃ רָ֫בּ (p. LX).

CHAPTER 49.

7ᵇ לנתוש ולנתוץ ולהאביד להרס   וכן לבנת לנטע ולהעז :
8 יחזקאל ראה מראה   ויגד זני מרכבה :
9 וגם הזכיר את איוב   המכלכל כל ד[ר]כי צ[ד]ק :
10 וגם שנים עשר הנביאים   תהי עצמתם פר[חת ממקומו]תם :

Verse 7ᵇ. *To pluck up and to break down, &c.* L'*Ecclés.* q.v., "Passage intéressant pour la critique du texte biblique et l'histoire des versions." See the facsimile facing p. xxxvii. in the Oxford edition.

Verses 8—9. *Ezekiel saw the vision, and declared divers kinds of chariot. Also he made mention of Job, who maintained all the w[ays of righ]teousness.*

The Greek of the latter verse is given by Fritzsche as,

καὶ γὰρ ἐμνήσθη τῶν ἐχθρῶν ἐν ὄμβρῳ,
καὶ ἀγαθῶσαι τοὺς εὐθύνοντας ὁδούς,

with καὶ κατώρθωσε (H. 106. 157. 248. 253.) as a variant.

APPENDIX.   LXIX

A. V. *For he made mention of the enemies under* the figure of *the rain, and directed* (marg. *did good) them that went right.*

R. V. *For verily he remembered the enemies in storm* (Gr. *rain*), *And to do good to them that directed their ways aright.*

"...*under the figure of the rain*] Lit. *in rain*.... But the whole verse is so difficult and unsatisfactory that it cannot be supposed to represent the original faithfully. The Aeth. renders: 'and he mentioned the enemy with wrath,' anticipating Fritzsche's conjecture that the Hebrew עֲזוֹ *wrath* was corrupted into זֶרֶם *flooding rain* in the translator's copy. The Syr., 'and even concerning Job he said,' clearly reading אִיֹּב for אוֹיֵב, as Arnaldus and Geiger observed. Accepting this correction ('Job' for 'the enemy'), both these scholars imagine the reference to be to Ezekiel's mention of Job (xiv. 14). But it is improbable that so unimportant a fact would be alluded to here....We suggest that the Greek translator misread בִּשְׂעִירִם *in rain-shower* (Deut. xxxii. 2, which the LXX. render by ὄμβρος as in our verse), instead of בִּשְׂעָרָה *in storm*—or else 'He remembered the enemy in wrath,' if he misread זֶרֶם for עֲזוֹ. Either of these corrections would make clause 1 correspond with clause 2, which would not be the case if we were to correct 'enemy' into 'Job,' the introduction of that name being also unsuited to the context" (E).

In *L'Ecclésiastique* (p. 147) it is noticed that a blot in the MS. (see the Plate facing p. xxxvii. in the Oxford edition) makes the latter part of the clause 9a illegible; the true reading is taken to be to the effect that he (the prophet) mentioned Job בְזָרִים *parmi les étrangers*; and it is remarked "C'est une transition pour dire un mot de ce personnage, connu de l'auteur par l'ouvrage qui raconte son histoire et qu'il a beaucoup utilisé."

When Ezekiel writes. "Though these three men, Noah, Daniel, and Job were in it &c.," the thing that would strike Ben Sira, who had relations with the outer world, is that Job should have been mentioned on equal terms with Noah and Daniel, who were not strangers, as a pattern of rectitude. With בְּ for בֵּן as in the בְּרַבִּי, פֵּן may have run, as Lévi suggests, וְגַם הֹזְכִּיר אֵת אִיּוֹב בְּזָרִים כוּ, he made mention of Job, *son of strangers*, as one who fulfilled all righteousness. From בְּזָרִים easily comes בּוֹעֵם *in wrath* (Aeth.); and with slight change *or none at all* the sense ἐν ὄμβρῳ (LXX.), for "זָרִים pro זֶרֶם dictum esse statuebant nonnulli intpp., ut SAADIAS (الرسول), ABEN ESRA, MICHAELIS, LOWTHUS al. in verbis Jes. I. 7 כְּמַהְפֵּכַת זָרִים." (Gesen. *Thesaur.*).

𝔊 may have read [ὃς] κατώρθωσε κ.τ.λ., for המכלכל דרכי צדק, whence with ר for ד.

ΚΑΤΑΘΩϹΑΙ.

Verse 10. The minor prophets, quoted in rabbinic as "The Twelve," are here referred to by Ben Sira as "the twelve prophets."

(C).

Professor Margoliouth's *The Origin of the 'Original Hebrew' of Ecclesiasticus* (p. LVII) is referred to in this section by the letter M. The thesis maintained in it is that the Cairo Text is a retranslation, partly from the Syriac, and partly from a Persian translation of the Greek; and it is suggested that "the Hebrew translator worked with some form of *both primary versions before him*" (M p. 7).

On the relation of 𝔖 to 𝔓 something will be said at the end of (D). That 𝔓 is partly a retranslation from 𝔊 through the Persian was suggested by a Persian gloss in the Oxford fol. 1, recto. "Literally translated it means 'it is probable that this was not in the original copy, but was said by the translator,...'copyist,' 'reporter,' or 'narrator'" (M p. 4). "The suggestion that the Hebrew is made from a Persian translation leads to more conjectures than one cares to make" (M p. 10); for Persian is a language in which words may be freely metamorphosed by such slight change as the addition or omission or shifting of a dot. The change from برف *snow* to برق *lightning* (p. LXXII) is of this nature. The argument of M in this case is too artificial to be convincing; but with its steps reversed it would be simple and natural, and would go to prove that the Greek came from the Hebrew through the Persian.

The following subsections touch upon what I take to be the principal details in the argument of M, in the course of which it is said, "I attach little importance to several of the Persian conjectures; but some three, I think, are certain" (M p. 12). In such of them as are hereinafter discussed I do not find any that is, so far as I can judge, sound.

I.

M p. 14 sq. (1) "We shall now collect some cases of mistranslation which the 'Original Hebrew' offers; and of these the clearest and most distinct is that in xli. 12, where the Syriac has 'take care of thy name, for that will accompany thee more than thousands of treasures of *wickedness*,' ܐܠܦܐ ܕܣܝܡܬܐ ܕܒܫܐ; (Hebrew) 'more than thousands of treasures of *wisdom*.' Our friend was not a good enough scholar to know that דעתא must in Syriac be ידעתא, and that 'treasures' ought to be in the construct state." Afterwards it is allowed that he must have known better, "for on the margin he has suggested 'treasures of desire,' i.e. *precious treasures*." (2) "Now we know from the usage of the Peshiṭta that the word used here often stands for און; and the Greek 'coin' may well represent הון 'wealth.' Between these two readings...there is little to choose." (3) "The marginal reading חמדה is a correction such as without the history of the error that the ancient versions furnish us with *we should naturally approve*. It is, however, a correction which displays a kind of critical acumen which in scribes is a dangerous gift. Unless, therefore, we can trace these marginal variants to the Greek or Syriac, we must regard them with suspicion." The Hebrew under discussion is,

מאלפי אוצרות חכמה :   חמדה

APPENDIX.

Here "treasures of חֶמְדָּה" seems to me to be the right reading, and חָכְמָה *wisdom* a previous scribe's error, what is meant being that the best and most desirable (Prov. iii. 15) of material things are not comparable to a good name. In (1) it is assumed that the translator first ignorantly or carelessly rendered דַעְתָּא (as if דִידַעְתָּא) by חָכְמָה, which he knew to be inappropriate, and then invented the suitable reading חֶמְדָּה. If *wisdom* had been the right word (Col. ii. 3) in the Hebrew, a translator might have kept it in spite of the Syriac. Knowing that it was not, he would have looked back to the Syriac and corrected his rendering.

For 𝔐 חֶמְדָּה there is good ancient authority. M does not notice in the Greek the reading *great treasures &c.* (H. & P., Syro-hex.), which looks like a paraphrase rather than a rendering *verbum verbo*. In the Old Latin we find *quam mille thesauri* PRETIOSI *et magni*, al. *magni* PRETIOSI (C. & N. p. xxxix.). Thus the reading "precious treasures" (M p. 14), which "we should naturally approve" (M p. 15) if it had support in the Versions, is found in the Latin, where it is possibly a survival from an earlier form of the Greek. 𝔐 חָכְמָה is best explained as a clerical error, which may be illustrated by the three consecutive lines from ch. xxxii.,

	ירְאֵי יְיָ יָבִינוּ מִשְׁפָּטוֹ	וְכָחְמוֹת רַבּוֹת יוֹצִיאוּ מִלִּבָּם׃	וַחֲכָמוֹת
חמס	17 אִישׁ חָכָם יִטֶּה יָטָה תוֹכָחוֹת	וְאַחַר צַרְכּוֹ יִמְשֹׁךְ תּוֹחָה׃	וְיֹאחֵר לִמְשׁוֹךְ
חכמה	17⁽¹⁾ אִישׁ חָכָם לֹא יְכַסֶּה כְּחֵמָה	וְלִיץ לֹא יִשְׁמָר לְשׁוֹנוֹ׃	

2.

M p. 9. "xliii. 2 (Greek) 'The sun by appearing proclaiming when he cometh forth,' a terse sentence which in itself contains much of the xixth Psalm. His appearance is a sermon; he preaches without using words....Hebrew text, 'The sun discharging in his affliction heat' (שֶׁמֶשׁ מַבִּיעַ בְּצָרָתוֹ חֵמָה): the margin suggests, 'shining at his going forth' (מוֹפִיעַ בְּצֵאתוֹ)....We first observe that the Greek says the sun *proclaims*, that is gives voice: whereas the Hebrew says he discharges *warmth*. Is there any language within reach in which the ideas of *speech* and *warmth* are likely to be confused?...In Persian *sukhn afshāndan* naturally means 'to utter speech,' 'to speak.' But the same words are exceedingly likely to be rendered 'to discharge heat,' if there is anything in the context to suggest it. Between the Persian word for 'speech' (سخن) and the Arabic word for 'heat' (سخن), which a Persian may use if he likes, there is nothing but the context to distinguish." It might have been added that Psalm xix. 3 יַבִּיעַ אֹמֶר *uttereth speech* would help to explain the insertion of the word 'speech' (which is not in 𝔊) in the supposed Persian translation, cf. 𝔐 xvi. 25 אֲבִיעָה בְּמִשְׁקַל רוּחִי. To account for 𝔐 בְּצָרָתוֹ it is suggested that the translator derived 𝔊 ὀπτασίᾳ from ὀπτᾶν *to roast* (p. 9 sq.), and then "softened" his expression "by the substitution of *affliction* for *roasting*."

THE WISDOM OF BEN SIRĀ.

𝕲 ἐν ἐξόδῳ supports הן בצאתו against 𝕳 בצרתו, and the simplest explanation of חמה is to explain it away (p. LXII sq.). M p. 16 on 𝕳 מה נורא, 𝕲 ⅏ σκεῦος θαυμαστόν, remarks that "there are only two possible explanations; either the author used the Aramaic *mān* for 'vessel,' or the Hebrew translator of the Syriac mistook the Syriac *mānā* for 'what'." Two other explanations are given above on p. LXII.

3.

M p. 10. "xliii. 13 (Greek) 'By his command he hurried down [v. l. 'stopped'] the snow.' (Orig. Hebrew) 'His might marketh out the lightning.' Leaving the question of the verbs alone for a moment, and confining ourselves to 'snow' and 'lightning,' it is clear that it will be difficult to find any language *other than Persian* in which the names of these objects are likely to be confused. *In Persian they differ by one dot.* Their names are برف and برق, *barf* and *bark*....I believe, however, that the Greek is corrupt, and that χειμῶνα 'storm' should be restored for χιόνα in this place; the context seems to render this change necessary. *The 'Original Hebrew' is, therefore, a translation* (if this explanation be right) *of a corruption of a Persian translation of a corrupt reading in the Greek.*" This chain of errors leads by a marvel to a right result, for ברק is the obvious parallel to ויקות (p. LXIII). Tracing the chain backwards we get ברק, ברق, برف, χιόνα, a wrong reading, by the omission of a dot, from a right one. This, as far as it goes, is a simple and good proof that 𝕲 came from 𝕳 through the Persian; and no doubt many more such arguments could be invented.

κατέσπευσε χιόνα] On נצח (? נחץ) in verses of Ben Sira see the note on 𝕳 xxxii. 9⁽¹⁾—10. 𝕳 𝕱 𝕲 suggest that χιόνα came in after κατέσπευσε as a variant for ברק (κεραυνόν). Lightning and hail come together in the Old Testament, cf. Sirac. xxxix. 29 πῦρ καὶ χάλαζα (ברד).

4.

M p. 10 sq. "xliii. 6 (Greek) 'And the moon in all things to her season, showing of times and a sign of eternity.' (Syriac) 'And the moon abides to its time, a showing of times and a sign from everlasting.'...The Hebrew text is

וגם ירח ירח עתות שבות   ממשלת קץ ואות עולם :

... In the first place we see why the word *moon* is doubled. The corrupt Greek 'in all' has been literally rendered باهر, and that word sometimes means 'the moon.'...'Unto its time' [marg.] is probably rendered by the words بار بار, &c....Having traced at any rate most of this infelicitous restoration to its home, we may now leave it there."

ירח ירח] These two words are the key to the passage. M takes them for *moon, moon*; but Ben Sira's habit of word-play suggests that he

APPENDIX.

meant to say *Luna lunat*. In the next line but one, transposing text and margin, we get

בחרישו הוא　　　חדש כשׁמו והוא יתחדש

with a play upon חֹרֶשׁ *month* and a verb *renovavit se* (Ps. ciii. 5) from חָדָשׁ *new*, 𝔊 μὴν κατὰ τὸ ὄνομα αὐτῆς κ.τ.λ. The corrupt variant חרש בחדשו illustrates the rendering *moon, moon* in verse 6. Taking ירח רח as noun and verb, we get the sense that the *moon measures returning seasons, being a rule of time and an everlasting sign*, the word "returning" being possibly a doublet.

Gesen. *Thesaur.*, "יָרֵחַ rad. inusit....ירח m. *luna...mensis*...Apud Arabes inde derivatum est ورخ II. diem mensis adscripsit epistolae, et cogn. أَرَخَ I. II. IV. id., تَأْرِيخ diei adscriptio, chronicon, cui dies adscripti sunt."

With ירח cf. 𝔓 xiii. 11 לחפש. A Hebrew word may have been used as a verb by Ben Sira although we have not found it so used elsewhere. If to "moon" in Arabic means to *date* a letter, it may mean in Ecclus. to date or measure (cf. *mensis*) seasons. The words ממשלת and אות are used of sun and moon in Gen. i. 14—16, and the moon is made the measurer of seasons in Psalm civ. 19 ἐποίησε σελήνην εἰς καιρούς.

The Greek of ch. xliii. 6 ירח בו' ירח in the form,

καὶ ἡ σελήνη ἐν πᾶσιν εἰς καιρὸν αὐτῆς,
ἀνάδειξιν χρόνων καὶ σημεῖον αἰῶνος,

is obviously not all accurate. The reading of "the remarkable MS. 248 which gives some Greek that closely resembles the Syriac" (M p. 11) is καὶ σελήνην ἐποίησεν εἰς στάσιν εἰς κ.τ.λ., where εἰς στάσιν may be for ἔστησεν, a doublet of ἐποίησεν. M however goes on to say, that no. 248 "is a guide to the original; so that it seems fairly safe to render, 'The moon too maintains the indication of dates in accordance with her time, and business in general.' Business (ēth 'ōlām, misread ōth) could not be maintained without the fixing of dates; and this is rightly put before all other services that the moon renders. The word *ta'rīkh*, which seems to have been used in Carthage, and is the ordinary Arabic for 'date,' is connected with the Hebrew name for 'the moon'; but we need not suppose any reference to it here, as the passage is clear without it." For "business in general" M might have quoted Ecclus. xxxviii. 24 *they will maintain the state of the world*, but 𝔓 𝔊 𝔖 אות is against any such rendering of עולם here.

קץ] 𝔊 χρόνων, 𝔖 ܘܙܒܢܐ, Lévi " Pour présider aux *temps*." Kohut *Aruch Compl.* VII. 173 *b* קץ...עת קבוע... *bestimmte Frist, festgesetzte Zeit*. קץ is parallel to מועד in 𝔓 xxxvi. 8ᵃ, and the moon is למועדים (Ps. civ. 19). From קץ it is but a step to עת־קץ (Dan. viii. 17), and thence to עת. Thus 𝔓 קץ may mean "times" (𝔊 𝔖), but a retranslator would not have used it in that sense.

k

5.

M p. 11. "xliii. 17c (Greek) 'Like birds flying he sprinkles snow.' (Hebrew) 'Like a flame he waves his snow,' כרשף יניף שלגו. Here as before the 'original' is a long way behind the translation. The poetical comparison of the snow to a flight of birds is made to give way to a poor comparison of it to flame, which is not in the least like. Here our excursion into Persia will be very short. Of the meanings given to the Persian *parwāz* the first is 'flight, flying,' the second '*light, splendour*'; *shikastan* is an ordinary word, and sometimes it means 'scatter,' sometimes 'shake'."

While there is ample authority for רשף in the sense *oiseau* (p. LXIII), it is not a word which a retranslator would have used in that sense. M by an oversight testifies to the fact that we have here a verse from the original Hebrew of Ecclesiasticus.

6.

M p. 12. "xliii. 22 (Greek) 'Dew confronting from the hot wind will cheer,' i.e. will refresh from the hot wind. (Hebrew) 'Dew paying (?) to the fat of the hot wind.' δρόσος ἀπαντῶσα ἀπὸ καύσωνος ἱλαρώσει. טל פורע לדשן שרב. The same as usual. The translation fine and clear, the Hebrew 'original' ludicrous. One point we see at a glance: the original has mistaken ἱλαρώσει, which is the 3rd person future active, for the dative singular of the verbal noun. Now 'the refreshingness' of the *hot wind* is too much for our translators to take in; and in the change from that word to 'fat' we see their attempt at criticism. I am inclined to think the Persian translator used چرى in its secondary sense of 'mildness, softness,' somewhat as the Latin translator says 'humilem efficiet eum' for the same word; the Hebrew translator takes it in its primary sense of 'fat.' What the first word in this sentence means is far from clear; the variant for 'hot wind,' i.e. 'moist,' perhaps refers to a suggestion that *sarāb* might be read *sharāb* 'drink'."

פורע] In a literal retranslation of xliii. 22 𝔊,

ἴασις πάντων κατὰ σπουδὴν ὁμίχλῃ,
δρόσος ἀπαντῶσα ἀπὸ καύσωνος ἱλαρώσει,

we should naturally put פוגע for ἀπαντῶσα (H. & R. *Concordance*). A comparison of 𝔊 with 𝔐 (p. LXII) then suggests that פורע was misread פוגע. For פרע *kal* in Ben Sira see xxxviii. 20 𝔐 זברו פרע, 𝔊 ἀπόστησον αὐτήν (λύπην).

מעורף...טל] Deut. xxxiii. 28 טל יערפו. 𝔊 κατὰ σπουδήν is best accounted for as an early corruption in the Greek. Apart from 𝔐 we might think of κατασπεύδει (ver. 13), but 𝔐 suggests ἴασιν κατασπεύδει.

לדשן] This is best pointed as a verb לְדַשֵּׁן, cf. Isaiah xxxiv. 7 הדשן 𝔐 xiv. 11, ועפרם מחלב ידשן. The argument from the Persian assumes a pointing לְדֶשֶׁן which the context makes "ludicrous." In Vet. Lat. read *hilarem* for *humilem*.

APPENDIX.

7.

M p. 7. "One more illustration may be taken from Professor Smend's edition. In xl. 26c the equivalent for the Greek 'help' and Syriac 'helper' is מעין. That word (unknown in this sense in Hebrew, Chaldee, or Syriac) is the Arabic translation of the very Syriac word used here that is given in the Syro-Arabic glossaries (Payne Smith, col. 2815), &c." Here it may be remarked that מעין (a conjectural reading across a hole in the paper) is given as doubtful in the edition quoted (p. 29). Lévi ignores it in his note, "M. Bacher nous semble avoir deviné juste: מושען, qui convient bien mieux au contexte et aux versions que מטמון 'trésor,' supposé par les éditeurs"; and the verse as he reads it is (p. 28),

אין (ב)יראת ייי מחסור ‚ ואין לבקש עמה מ(ו)שע(ן):

Ben Sira writes of Wisdom in ch. xv. 3—4 והאכלתהו כו' ונשען עליה, cf. iii. 31 משען, v. 1 אל תשען. Arabisms may have been introduced into 𝔓 and 𝔐 by Arab scribes and glossators. מעין is Dr Smend's retranslation from ܡܥܕܪܢܐ (C. & N., p. 8).

It will be for Persian scholars to criticise the Persian of M. In other matters some of its statements are questionable or incomplete.

ἐν ὀπτασίᾳ] See pp. LXII, LXXI. "For the rendering 'by his affliction' to correspond with ὀπτασίᾳ 'appearance' it is not perhaps possible to give as satisfactory an account....One thing that may be reasonably inferred is that the translator did not know the meaning of the word ὀπτασίᾳ. For this he is not to be blamed, as it is *recherché* and rare" (M p. 9). But (1) Hatch and Redpath's *Concordance* gives the following references for ὀπτασία, "Es. 4. 17. Si. 43. 2, 16. Ma. 3. 2. Da. TH. 9. 23 & 10. 1, 7 *bis*, 8, 16. [AQ. Ez. 1. 1; SM. Ge. 22. 2. Ez. 1. 1, 5; TH. Ez. 1. 1. Da. 9. 23 & 10. 1, 16]." (2) M seems to connect 𝔊 ἐν ὀπτασίᾳ with a wrong word in the Hebrew. It gives the sense of 𝔐 מופיע (𝔓 xii. 15 יופיע, Gesen. *Thesaur.* יפע); and 𝔊 translates 𝔐 בצאתו by ἐν ἐξόδῳ, rejecting 𝔓 בצרתו which M renders 'by his affliction.'

מעין] In § 7 we should have been informed that the reading is doubtful, and that Dr Smend himself writes, "In מעין fehlt von מ die obere linke Spitze und die Nase. Nicht ausgeschlossen sind כ oder auch ב. Von ע is das (linke) Fussende, die linke und die rechte Spitze da. Letztere kann kaum ein ' sein" (p. 29), the only distinct letter of the word being the *nun*. Was מעין suggested to the decipherer by "Payne Smith, col. 2815," or 2816? A possible reading is מעון (l. 2) *habitatio, refugium*, cf. 𝔓 xiv. 27 ובמעונותיה. Hence (?) 𝔊 מעון βοήθειαν, ܡܥܕܪܢܐ *helper* (Jer. xvi. 19).

מקוה...כים] A derivation of 𝔓 l. 3 *b* from 𝔊 through the Persian privately communicated (29th May) does not account for בם (כים), and is open to criticism in other respects.

(D)

CHAPTER 51.

In the *Zeitschrift für katholische Theologie* (1882) Professor G. Bickell reconstructs Ben Sira's *Alphabetisches Lied* from the Versions as follows:

13 **א**ני בעוד נער לפני טעותי	בקשתי חכמה לנוכח :
בתפלתי שאלתיה	וער קין אדרשה :
גמלה כענב בושל	ישמח לבי עליה :
דרכה רגלי במישור	מנעורותי הקרתיה :
הטיתי כמעט אזני	
16ᵇ **ו**רב מצאתי לי מוסר :	
17 **ז**את היתה לי לכשרון	למחכמי אתן כבוד :
18 **ח**שבתי לעבור אתה	ואקנא טוב ולא אבושה :
טבועה נפשי בתוכה	ופני אל עבודתה שמתי :
ידי פרשתי למרום	ואשגה ואדעה :
20ᵃ **כ**וננתי נפשי אליה	ובטוהר מצאתיה :
20ᵇ לב קניתי בה מראשית	על כן לא איעזבה :
21 **מ**עי נכמרו לנוצרה	על כן קניתי קנין טוב :
22 **נ**תן יה ללשוני שכר	ובשפתי אשבחנו :
23 **ס**ורו אלי כסילים	והתלוננו בבית מוסר :
24 **ע**ד מתי תחסרו הגה	ונפשכם צמאה מאד :
25 **פ**תחתי פי ואדבר	קנו לכם חכמה בלא כסף :
26ᵃ **צ**ואריכם תנו בעולה	ותקח נפשכם מוסר :
26ᶜ **ק**רובה היא למשחרה	וטכוגן נפשו מוצאה :
27 **ר**או בעיניכם מעט עמלתי	ואשכח לי רב מנוחה :
28 **ש**מעו מוסר כמספר	וכסף וזהב רב תקנו בה :
29 **ת**שמח נפשכם בהסדו	ואל תחפרו בתהלתו :
30 **פ**עלו פעלכם לפני עת	ויותן שכרכם בעתו :

APPENDIX. LXXVII

Σοφια Ιησου LI. 13—30 from Fritzsche's *Libri Apocryphi Veteris Testamenti Graece*.

13 ἔτι ὢν νεώτερος,
πρὶν ἢ πλανηθῆναί με,
ἐζήτησα σοφίαν προφανῶς ἐν προσευχῇ μου·
14 ἔναντι ναοῦ ἠξίουν περὶ αὐτῆς,
καὶ ἕως ἐσχάτων ἐκζητήσω αὐτήν.
15 ἐξ ἄνθους ὡς περκαζούσης σταφυλῆς εὐφράνθη ἡ καρδία μου,
ἐν αὐτῇ ἐπέβη ὁ πούς μου ἐν εὐθύτητι,
ἐκ νεότητός μου ἴχνευον αὐτήν.
16 ἔκλινα ὀλίγον τὸ οὖς μου καὶ ἐδεξάμην,
καὶ πολλὴν εὗρον ἐμαυτῷ παιδείαν.
17 προκοπὴ ἐγένετό μοι ἐν αὐτῇ·
τῷ διδόντι μοι σοφίαν δώσω δόξαν.
18 διενοήθην γὰρ τοῦ ποιῆσαι αὐτήν,
καὶ ἐζήλωσα τὸ ἀγαθόν,
καὶ οὐ μὴ αἰσχυνθῶ.
19 διαμεμάχηται ἡ ψυχή μου ἐν αὐτῇ,
καὶ ἐν ποιήσει νόμου διηκριβωσάμην·
τὰς χεῖράς μου ἐξεπέτασα πρὸς ὕψος,
καὶ τὰ ἀγνοήματα αὐτῆς ἐπένθησα.
20 τὴν ψυχήν μου κατεύθυνα εἰς αὐτήν,
καὶ ἐν καθαρισμῷ εὗρον αὐτήν·
καρδίαν ἐκτησάμην μετ' αὐτῆς ἀπ' ἀρχῆς,
διὰ τοῦτο οὐ μὴ ἐγκαταλειφθῶ·
21 καὶ ἡ κοιλία μου ἐταράχθη τοῦ ἐκζητῆσαι αὐτήν,
διὰ τοῦτο ἐκτησάμην ἀγαθὸν κτῆμα.
22 ἔδωκε κύριος γλῶσσάν μοι μισθόν μου,
καὶ ἐν αὐτῇ αἰνέσω αὐτόν.
23 ἐγγίσατε πρός με ἀπαίδευτοι,
καὶ αὐλίσθητε ἐν οἴκῳ παιδείας,
24 διότι ὑστερεῖτε ἐν τούτοις,
καὶ αἱ ψυχαὶ ὑμῶν διψῶσι σφόδρα.
25 ἤνοιξα τὸ στόμα μου καὶ ἐλάλησα,
κτήσασθε ἑαυτοῖς ἄνευ ἀργυρίου·
26 τὸν τράχηλον ὑμῶν ὑπόθετε ὑπὸ ζυγόν,
καὶ ἐπιδεξάσθω ἡ ψυχὴ ὑμῶν παιδείαν,
ἐγγύς ἐστιν εὑρεῖν αὐτήν.
27 ἴδετε ἐν ὀφθαλμοῖς ὑμῶν, ὅτι ὀλίγον ἐκοπίασα,
καὶ εὗρον ἐμαυτῷ πολλὴν ἀνάπαυσιν.
28 μετάσχετε παιδείας ἐν πολλῷ ἀριθμῷ ἀργυρίου,
καὶ πολὺν χρυσὸν κτήσασθε ἐν αὐτῇ.
29 εὐφρανθείη ἡ ψυχὴ ὑμῶν ἐν τῷ ἐλέει αὐτοῦ,
καὶ μὴ αἰσχυνθείητε ἐν αἰνέσει αὐτοῦ.
30 ἐργάζεσθε τὸ ἔργον ὑμῶν πρὸ καιροῦ,
καὶ δώσει τὸν μισθὸν ὑμῶν ἐν καιρῷ αὐτοῦ.

THE WISDOM OF BEN SIRA.

Bar Sira l.l. 13—30 from De Lagarde's *Libri Apocryphi Veteris Testamenti Syriace.*

APPENDIX.   LXXIX

The Cairo Text of ch. li. 13—30, shewing the letters of Ben Sira's Alphabet which remain and the places of missing letters.

¹³**א**ני נער הייתי וחפצתי בה ובקשתיה :
¹³⁽¹⁾**ב**אמתה דרכה רגלי אדני מנעורי הכמה למדתי :
¹⁴**ו**אתפלל תפלה בנערותי ¹⁵והרבה מצאתי דעה :
¹⁷**ע**לה היה לי לכבוד ולמלמדי אתן הודאה :
¹⁸**ח**שבתי להיטיב ולא אהפך כי אמצאנו :
¹⁸⁽¹⁾**ה**שקה נפשי בה ופני לא אהפך ממנה :
^{20a}נפשי **נ**תתי אחריה ⁽¹⁾ולנצח נצחים לא אטה... :
²⁰⁽²⁾ידי **פ**תחה שעריה ולה אחוז ואביט ב.. :
^{20bcd}ובטהרה מצאתיה ולב קניתי לה מתחלתה בעבור כ... :
²¹**מ**עי יהמו כתנור לה להביט בה בעבור כן קניתיה קנין טוב :
²²**נ**תן יי' לי שכר שפתותי ובלשוני אהודנו :
²³**פ**נו אלי סכלים ולינו בבית מדרשי :
²⁴**ע**ד מתי תחסרון מן אילו ואילו ונפשכם צמאה. מאד תהיה :
²⁵**פ**י פתחתי ודברתי בה קנו לכם הכמה בלא כסף :
^{26a}וצואריכם בעלה הביאו ומשאה תשא נפשכם :
^{26c}**ק**רובה היא למבקשיה ונותן נפשו מוצא אתה :
²⁷**ר**או בעיניכם כי קטן הייתי ועמדתי בה ומצאתיה :
²⁸רבים[**ש**מעו למורי בנערותי וכסף וזהב תקנו בי :
²⁹**ת**שמח נפשי בישיבתי ולא תבושו בשירתי :
³⁰מעשיכם עשו בצדקה והוא נותן לכם שכרכם בעתו :

א

The acrostic evidently begins with אני, although Lagarde's Syriac has ܐܠܐ for ܐܢܐ. In the first line of it the writer says that he was נער, and afterwards he says that he was קטן (ver. 27). As he was an imitator of Solomon, he may have had in mind the wise king's choice of wisdom in I Kings iii. 7—15 ואנכי נער קטן לא ארע צאת ובא כו׳. 𝔊 πρὶν ἢ πλανηθῆναί με is judiciously rendered *or ever I went abroad* (A. V. with marg. *astray*, R. V.), which suits the context and the parallel. It is doubtful what stood in the Hebrew, this as we have it being defective at the beginning of the acrostic.

ב

The *beth* of באמתה דרכה is a spurious initial, פן דרכה belonging to the fourth line of the acrostic. The Greek

ἐζήτησα σοφίαν προφανῶς ἐν προσευχῇ μου,
ἔναντι ναοῦ ἠξίουν περὶ αὐτῆς,

suggests בקשתי׳ (פן 13 ובקשתיה) as containing the initial *beth*. Or with Bickell we may begin the line at ἐν προσευχῇ μου. Better than ἔναντι ναοῦ would be ἔναντι λαοῦ as a parallel to προφανῶς.

ג

Bickell's suggestion for the *gimel* is convincing. Starting from the Latin *Effloruit tanquam praecox uva, laetatum est cor meum in ea* as a rendering of the Greek, he gives for the latter "vielleicht ἐξήνθησεν ὡς περκάζουσα σταφυλή," and for this in Hebrew גמלה כו׳. A slighter emendation of ἐξ ἄνθους, with ἐν αὐτῇ run back from the next line, would give,

ΕΞΑΝΘΟΥϹΑ ΩϹ ΠΕΡΚΑΖΟΥϹΑ ϹΤΑΦΥΛΗ
ΕΥΦΡΑΝΘΗ Η ΚΑΡΔΙΑ ΜΟΥ ΕΝ ΑΥΤΗ.

The Authorised Version reads, "Even from the flower till the grape was ripe hath my heart delighted in her: my foot went the right way, from my youth up sought I after her." Less suitable is "From her flower &c." (R. V.), the context referring only to the writer's own immaturity when he began to seek wisdom. Fritzsche *male*, "post ἄνθους adde αὐτῆς, quod interpres addere neglexit."

"*till the ripening grape*]. The writer has in mind Isa. xviii. 5. If the reading adopted by the A. V. be right, the author is referring to his own lifetime....Most MSS. however have ὡς *as for* ἕως *till*, giving a difficult verse, which might be explained with Fritzsche, 'from her [Wisdom's] flower, as from the ripening grape,' &c." (E).

APPENDIX.

ἐξανθοῦσα] Bickell ἐξήνθησεν, גמלה. See in xiv. 18ᶜ ואחר גומל, 18ᵃ צומח over גומל erased. For ἐξανθοῦσα...ἡ καρδία μου 𝔐 may have had גומל...ולבי, or גמלתי... In Prov. xxxi. 12 גמלתהו gives the ג.

ὡς περκάζουσα σταφυλή] Bickell כענב בושל, which 𝔊 is assumed to have rendered idiomatically. But perhaps Ben Sira, having in mind Isa. xviii. 5 (E), wrote בְּבֹסֶר עָנָב, and 𝔊 mistook בסר for an adjective prefixed to עָנָב, cf. xlii. 9 ἀπόκρυφος ἀγρυπνία (xxxi. 1 n.). On this hypothesis it may be suggested that 𝔐 read,

נמלתי כבסר ענב   ולבי שמח בה :

Referring to Holmes and Parsons, I find MS. authority for the conjectural reading ἐξανθοῦσα κ.τ.λ., and for A. V. till, in the note, "'Εξ ἄνθους] ἐξανθούσης 23. ἐξανθούσῃ 253. ἐξανθούσα 254. ὡς περκαζούσης] ἑως περκαζούσης 111." The documentary evidence for a wrong reading is overwhelmingly preponderant, but the A. V. by an exercise of sound judgement has brought out a right result.

Lastly, it is suggested that the *t* of *Effloruit* is a doublet and should be omitted. With this emendation we have in the Latin, exactly agreeing with the proposed נמלתי כו in 𝔐,

Efflorui tanquam praecox uva,
laetatum est cor meum in ea.

ד

The initial *daleth* is preserved in דרכה, ܘܪܟܐ. 𝔊 15 *b* ἐπέβη, which Holmes and Parsons detach from ἐν αὐτῇ, reading in their text,

εὐφράνθη ἡ καρδία μου ἐν αὐτῇ, ἐπέβη ἡ πούς μου.

ה

Neglecting ὀλίγον in 𝔊 16 as perhaps out of place, read הטית אזני as the beginning of the *hé* line. The strange אדני in 𝔐 13⁽¹⁾ *b* (≡ 15 *a* מבו,) is like a transliteration of ܐܕܢܐ *my ear*, but see the note on 𝔐 li. 13⁽¹⁾. ≡ 16...וצלית may be a corruption from ואצלית אדני *I inclined my ear* (p. LXXXVI), of which 𝔐 14ᵃ would then likewise be a corruption.

ו

The *vau* of 𝔐 16ᵇ perhaps belongs to the "Alphabet" (Bickell).

ז

Bickell's seventh line is 𝔊 17 with זאת prefixed. It had occurred to me that the unmeaning 𝔐 14ᵃ ואתפלל כו *and I prayed a prayer in my youth* might be a corruption of something like זאת תפלתי *this* was my

l

prayer: he asked like Solomon not for anything else, but for wisdom. When ואת became את the reading ואתפלל כו׳ would easily have arisen. But perhaps this belongs to the ה line.

Bickell does not account for עלה which, as it stands, means *her yoke*; but, with מוסר masc. for 𝔊 παιδείαν just before, the reading may have been something like זה עלה לי לכבוד. Compare ABOTH IV. 18 (*Jewish Fathers*) ששגגת תלמוד עולה זדון for the use of עלה, VI. 2 הרי זה מתעלה for the idea of exaltation by Torah or Wisdom.

ח

The reading חשבתי (𝔥, Bickell) is attested by ܐܚܫܒܬܗ and gives the *cheth* of the acrostic. The same initial in the next line of 𝔥 is doubtless spurious.

ט

Under *teth* Bickell gives טבועה, but it is not easy to explain 𝔊 διαμεμάχηται and ܐܬܚܒܫܬ as renderings of it. Very suitable in itself would be the reading טרדה נפשי בה, and טרד is a word of Ben Sira (xxxii. 9). It is not at once obvious how the renderings of the Versions 𝔊 διαμεμάχηται, ܐܬܚܒܫܬ would be accounted for, but a not impossible explanation has occurred to me.

Under עשק we read in Gesen. *Thesaur.,* "in Kal inusit., chald. et talmud. עסק operam dedit rei, Ithpa. occupatus est in re, it. litigavit. Syr. ܐܬܚܒܫ pro περιεργάζεσθαι Sir. iii. 22...Hithpa. litigavit....Gen. xxvi. 20...עשק, (rixa) n. pr...."Ἔσκος...μάχην ἄν τις αὐτὸ φήσειε."

Again, under חשק we read, "pr. *coniunxit*...et intrans....*adhaesit*... Arab. عشق...et عشق...ח et ע permutatis," cf. in xxxix. 18 𝔊 (p. LVIII) ἐλάττωσις, for מחצור with *cheth* instead of מעצור with *ayin* (𝔥 ܐ).

The Cairo reading חשקה נפשי בה is attested by ܐ, and 𝔊 is explained by the phonetically slight change to עשקה. Conversely ܐ might be accounted for as reading *cheth* for *ayin*. But the acrostic as read thus far wants an initial *teth* here. The note on a saying of Hillel in ABOTH II. in the unpublished Appendix to *Sayings of the Jewish Fathers* quotes the comment טרוד אינך אם לשמוע איפשר שאי תאמר ואל ועסוק במלאכה. As טרד and עסק are thus synonyms, טרדה in the acrostic may have been first explained by עסקה (עשקה) in the margin, and then replaced by עשקה, afterwards read חשקה, in the text. The same note on ABOTH contains the words לשמוע אזנך הט לאחר אלא, cf. הטיתי אזני (?) in the acrostic.

APPENDIX.   LXXXIII

א

Passing over for the present נפשי נתתי אחריה כו׳, we come in the Cairo text to

20ᵃ⁽²⁾ ידי פתחה שעריה   ולה אחוז ואביט ב:
20ᵇᵒ¹ ובטהרה מצאתיה ולב קניתי לה מתחלתה בעבור כ...:

Here ידי (𝔖 ܐܝܕܝ) gives the initial *yod*, 𝔊 reading perhaps ידי פתחתי שמימה *I spread out my hands heavenward*. Another letter of the acrostic is wrapped up in the next line.

The punctuation of 𝔐 is faulty. According to 𝔖 the verse 20ᴬ⁽²⁾ from ולה continues thus:

ܘܐܫܬܘܕܥܬ ܨܦܪ ܠܗ ܘܐܫܟܚܬܗ ܟܕ ܕܟܝܐ ܘܐܬܒܩܝܬܗ.

אחוז] Having opened her gates, he would next see Wisdom, or look about for her. As possible readings, it may be suggested that 𝔐 had אחור from חור, Syr. ܚܪ, *vidit*, or אחזור or אחור (𝔖).

ואביט ב....] If there is vacant space here for four letters, 𝔐 may have read בטהרה ואביט *and I perceived her brightness*. The words ובטהרה מצאתיה *and in pureness I found her*, 𝔊 καὶ ἐν καθαρισμῷ εὗρον αὐτήν, might then be cancelled as a doublet. Or, reading ואביט בה ובטהרה מצאתיה (𝔖), we may suppose this to be an expansion of ואביט בה בטהרה, or of ואביט בטהרה.

After 𝔐 ידי כו׳ *my hand opened her gates*, there cannot have been anything like 𝔊 *and I bewailed her ignorances*, A.V. and R.V. *my ignorances of her*. As an emendation of 𝔊 19 *d* as it stands (p. LXXVII) read,

ⲀⲄⲚⲞⲦⲎⲦⲀ ⲀⲨⲦⲎⲤ ⲈⲠⲈⲚⲞⲎⲤⲀ

for

ⲀⲄⲚⲞⲎⲘⲀⲦⲀ ⲀⲨⲦⲎⲤ ⲈⲠⲈⲚⲞⲎⲤⲀ.

The reading ἐπενόησα, for which there is the authority of the MSS. 23. 55. 248. 253. 254. (Fritzsche), necessitates an alteration of ἀγνοήματα. With the proposed ἀγνότητα αὐτῆς giving the sense *and I perceived her pureness*, cf. St James iii. 17 *But the wisdom that is from above is first* ἁγνή. On 𝔊 in connexion with the Latin see p. LXXXV.

ב

Bickell's כוננתי נפשי אליה represents 𝔊 τὴν ψυχήν μου κατεύθυνα εἰς αὐτήν. Supposing ת misread *nun*, נתן as in עת for *cloud* (xxxv. 20 n.), and noting that אליה *minus* the top of ל is like אריה, which according to the HEXAPLA would be a phonetic equivalent of אחריה (xiv. 22), we easily get as a corruption נפשי נתתי אחריה, after which should perhaps come ופני כו׳ from 18ᵇ⁽¹⁾. Having opened her gates and looked round for her and perceived her within, he directs his soul toward Wisdom, and cannot turn away his face from her.

l 2

THE WISDOM OF BEN SIRA.

ל—ת

Two of these letters only need be noticed here. To get the *samech* I first thought of reading with a transposition סכלים פנו אלי, but perhaps סורו is right. Compare in Jud. iv. 18 Jael's סורה (ܣܘܪ), *Turn in, my lord, turn in to me.*

The *shin* is contained in רבים שמעו כו׳, where 𝔐 mispunctuates and reads, *See with your eyes that I was little; And I stood in her and found her. Ye* MANY (or *great ones*), *hear my teaching in my youth.* 𝔊 ܣ read MUCH at the end of verse 27 instead of MANY at the beginning of verse 28, 𝔊 27 ending πολλὴν ἀνάπαυσιν (vi. 28), and ܣ 27—28 running thus, *See with your eyes that I laboured a little in her; And I found her abundantly. Hear my teaching while little.* Reading עמלתי for 𝔐 עמדתי, compare ch. vi. 19ᵃ—19ᶜ *And wait for the abundance of her increase. For in the tillage of her thou shalt toil a little.* Comparing 𝔐 ܣ 27 we might think קטן a mistranslation of ܩܠܝܠ ὀλίγον, or ܣܓܝܐܐ ܗܘ a corruption of ܣܓܝܐܐ ܗܘܐ, 𝔐 הייתי ועמלתי.

THE GREEK AND THE LATIN.

Different parts of 𝔐, as we have seen, correspond to one another. In connexion with the acrostic should be read especially ch. vi. 19ᵃ—37ᶜ and ch. xiv. 20—xv. 8 on Wisdom.

The Latin of the acrostic, as given by Bickell (p. 324) with some alteration, begins thus,

> Cum adhuc junior essem, priusquam oberrarem,
> quaesivi sapientiam palam.
> In oratione mea ante templum postulabam pro illa,
> et usque in novissimis inquiram eam.

The next three verses begin with *Effloruit[t]* (גמלתי), *Ambulavit* (דרכה), *Inclinavi* (הטיתי), the third of them perhaps giving also the ו by its "*et multam.*"

Next come the most difficult lines,

> Multum profeci (προκοπὴ ἐγένετό μοι) in ea;
> danti mihi sapientiam dabo gloriam.
> Consiliatus sum enim, ut facerem illam;
> et zelatus sum bonum et non confundar.
> Colluctata est anima mea in illa,
> et in faciendo (ποιήσει) eam confirmatus sum (διηκριβωσάμην).
> Manus meas extendi in altum,
> et insipientiam (τὰ ἀγνοήματα) ejus intellexi.
> Animam meam direxi ad illam,
> et in purificatione inveni eam.
> Possedi cum ipsa cor (καρδίαν ἐκτησάμην μετ᾽ αὐτῆς) ab initio;
> propter hoc non derelinquar.

APPENDIX.   LXXXV

The ? line *Multum profeci in ea &c.* probably began with זה or זאת.
Its *danti mihi sapientiam* (τῷ διδόντι μοι σοφίαν) suggests למחכמי for
למלמדי, cf. מן vi. 37ᵉ יחכמך, Psalm cxix. 98—99 כי תחכמני מאיבי.
מכל מלמדי השכלתי. Next comes *Consiliatus sum* (חשבתי).

The original of *Colluctata est* may have been טרדה (p. LXXXII).
Fritzsche writes on this verse, "νόμου ex coniectura scripsi; III. 106. 155.
157. 254. praebent μου, Vet. Lat. in faciendo eam; vulgo legitur λιμοῦ,
etiam in X." Dr Swete gives for it, with variants,

διαμεμάχισται ἡ ψυχή μου ἐν αὐτῇ,
καὶ ἐν ποιήσει λιμοῦ διηκριβασάμην.

The Latin *et in faciendo eam* (𝔊 18 τοῦ ποιῆσαι αὐτήν) may be retranslated
ובעבדתה, cf. מן vi. 19ᶜ כי בעבדתה כו, and the variant μου (Swete,
Fritzsche) accounts for the impossible reading of "The best MSS." (p. IX).
For -ει write -αι and we get in uncials,

ΠΟΙΗϹΑΙΜΟΥ

ΠΟΙΗϹΛΙΜΟΥ

and then   ΠΟΙΗϹΕΙ ΛΙΜΟΥ

Cf. in Hexaplar renderings of בשוע (Ps. xxviii. 2, xxxi. 23) αναβοήσαι
(-ήσει).

The *yod* line begins *Manus meas* (ידי), and ends with *intellexi* (W *luxi*,
23. 55. 248. 253. 254. ἐπενόησα). Before *intellexi* comes *insipientiam
ejus*, the *unwisdom* of Wisdom. This suggests ΑΓΝΟΗΜΑ sing.
(for 𝔊 ἀγνοήματα), which is not unlike ΑΓΝΙϹΜΑ. According
to 𝔐 𝔖, *intellexi* should be followed immediately by *et in purificatione*
(W *agnitione*) *inveni eam*.

The next letters are given by *direxi* (כוננתי), *cor* (לב); and to the
remaining initial words correspond more or less aptly, *Venter meus, Dedit,
Appropiate* (𝔊 ἐγγίσατε) which does not suggest סורו (Bickell), *Quid
adhuc, Aperui os meum, Collum vestrum, In proximo, Videte, Assumite*
(𝔊 μετάσχετε) a substitute for "Hear," *Laetetur*. The shortening of the
ק line (𝔐 26ᶜ) to *In proximo est invenire eam*, 𝔊 ἐγγύς ἐστιν εὑρεῖν αὐτήν,
is explained by the homœoteleuton (αὐτήν...αὐτήν) of its hemistichs.

Bickell's Latin, which is interspersed with words from 𝔊, is "bereits
nach dem Resultate des Herstellungsversuches abgesetzt" (p. 323). The
letter W refers to Walton's Polyglot. On the Vet. Lat. see also E
p. 29 sq.

THE HEBREW AND THE SYRIAC.

𝕳 li. 13—30 (p. LXXIX) agrees closely with 𝔖 (p. LXXVIII) and differs from 𝔊 (p. LXXVII).

א—ד

The ב and ג lines having disappeared, and 𝕳 חכמה being rendered by 𝔖 "julpônô," there is no mention of Wisdom, the subject of the poem, in 𝔖 until verse 25; pronouns which should refer to Wisdom are masculine; and verse 13 seems to refer to the name of the Lord (Bickell).

ה—ו

On 𝔖 Bickell writes (p. 323), "In V. 16 a habe ich mir eine ganz evidente Emendation nach dem Griechischen erlaubt; die absurde jetzige Lesart *und ich betete sein Gebet als ich klein war* ist nämlich dadurch entstanden, dass man die Form 'vaç'lît' als 'v'çallît' aussprach, dann aber, um wieder Sinn in den Satz hineinzubringen, 'ç'lûtěh' hinzufügte und 'ednô' durch Weglassung eines Buchstabens in '-nô' verwandelte." With this explanation of 𝔖, the Hebrew here would seem to have been derived from the Syriac. But the conjecture is open to criticism, and does not end so well as it begins. To read ܐܢܓܒ τὸ οὖς, instead of ܐܢܓܒ τὸ οὖς μου (iv. 8, vi. 33 אונך), is an artificial way of accounting for ܐܢܕ ܘܗܒܐ ܒܓ, 𝔊 ὀλίγον *a little*. The same verse may give the ו (Bickell), but this is not certain.

ז—ט

If 𝕳 17 is the ז line, it may have begun with a זה or זאת now missing. The "yoke" of Wisdom (vi. 30) is seemingly out of place here: it comes in better below in the line וצואריכם בו, with which compare in Buber's *Midrasch Mishlé* 25 *b* אם נתת צוארך בעולה של תורה בו (S. S.). Under 𝕳 on p. LXXXII it is conjectured that the true initial word טרדה of the line was replaced by a synonym עסקה (עשקה). Compare 𝕳 xxxviii. 4 *a*,

ברא יהֹוה   אל מארץ מוציא תרופות

In the ח and ט lines 𝔖 follows 𝕳 which has אהפך in both, in the former case perhaps as a corruption of ארפה (vi. 27, li. 10ᵇ). For the original of 𝔊 18 διενοήθην we might have thought of זממתי (Prov. xxxi. 16) if 𝕳 had not preserved the ח word חשבתי.

י—ל

𝕳 נתתי for 'כוננתי (𝔊 κατεύθυνα) in the כ line, and so 𝔖, both placing it wrongly before the י line. Ending the י line with ואבים בְּטָהֳרָה, note that

APPENDIX.

𝕳 𝕲 xlii.—xliii. (C. & N. pp. 14, 16) quote Ex. xxiv. 10 וכעצם השמים
לטהר, and compare what is said of her brightness in the book of Wisdom.
𝕲 20 ἐν καθαρισμῷ, xliii. 1 καθαριότητος. 𝕲 20 rightly καρδίαν for
ולב in the ל line.

מ—ת

𝕳 פנו a synonym for סורו in the ס line, ܠ better סטו. 𝕳 wrongly
רבים at the beginning of the שׁ line. ܠ סני at the end of the ר line, 𝕲
πολλὴν ἀνάπαυσιν. 𝕲 at the end of the צ line παιδείαν, ܠ ܪ̈ܚܡܬܐ.
Comparing 𝕳 vi. 21—25 משא כו׳ ושאה, we may suppose that we have
the original form of the צ line with a *vau* prefixed in 𝕳 26ᵃ,

וצואריכם בעולה הביאו   ומשאה תשא נפשכם:

Some things in the Cairo Text require fuller consideration than was
practicable in this edition (p. X). In places it is "manifestly corrupt," as
in the passage described as "A chaos of variants" (p. XXXVII). On the
whole it is not unlike the part of it which contains the acrostic in ch. li.,
where much of Ben Sira's Alphabet is given by 𝕳 as it stands (p. LXXIX),
other letters can be recovered with the help of the Versions, and a few
remain doubtful. Possibly Bickell's initial words are right or nearly right
everywhere except in the ט line.

ECCLUS. LEWIS-GIBSON FOLIO. VERSO.

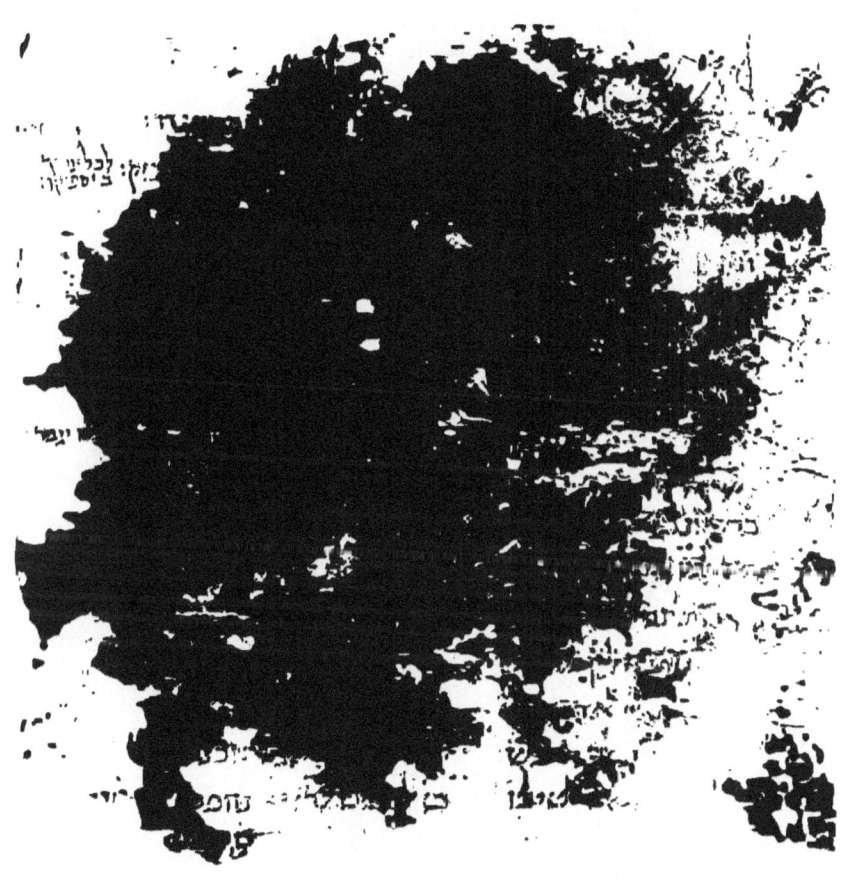

ECCLUS. LEWIS-GIBSON FOLIO. RECTO.

III.

PREFATORY NOTE
INTRODUCTION
NOTES ON THE TEXT
THE TEXT

PREFATORY NOTE.

IN presenting to the learned public the following pages it is my first duty to state that on me falls the sole responsibility for the Introduction, the transcription of the Text, and the Notes to it. The only exceptions are the transcription of the Persian Glosses in the text (pp. 13—15) and the commentary on them in the notes; these are the work of an Oxford scholar whose well-known modesty and dread of publicity forbid me to disclose here his name.

In the Introduction the reader will find a description of the MSS. used in this edition, as well as a discourse on the Relation of Ben Sira to the O. T. The former needs no apology, whilst the latter will probably call forth a good deal of opposition; but this is no reason for suppressing views which are the result of studies pursued for a long time with earnestness and devotion. In the printed text the lines and pages correspond exactly to those of the MSS., of which I have endeavoured to make the transcript as faithful a copy as possible. This was fortunately no difficult task, since the MSS. from which this copy is prepared are in fairly good preservation. But where the *slightest* reason for doubt existed, where a word or a letter was not quite legible at the first glance, the words or letters in question were provided with the sign ٠ in contradistinction to the sign – occurring as *raphe* over various letters in the MSS. In places where there is some real reason to doubt the reading in the text special warning is always given in the notes. In the numbering of the verses I have followed that of the *Authorised* Version; this version recommending itself to me both on account of its fulness (or, as it has been considered, richness in interpolations) and its arrangement of the chapters. Verses not to be found in it (which means in most cases not to be found in any Greek MS.) are indicated by repeating the number of the preceding verse enclosed in brackets. In the Notes I give a commentary on such passages as seemed to require an explanation. This I have chiefly endeavoured to accomplish by giving as many references to parallels or echoes in the Hebrew literature, Biblical and post-Biblical, as were in any way calculated to throw light on the words of our author. The hitherto published Hebrew portions of B. S. are of course of the greatest importance and in the chapters are referred to as O. H. (=Original Hebrew), whilst the references to the Hebrew chapters included in this volume use the terms *above* and *below*. Portions again of B. S. which at present exist only in the Versions are cited as *Ecclus*. Of the versions, Greek as well as Syriac, I have, while consulting them throughout, made little use in my notes; reproducing their variants only in cases when the reading suggested by them seemed to be an improvement upon that afforded by our MSS., or (as in some few instances) when the misreadings and the mistranslations of the versions were calculated to bring our text into more prominent relief. In consulting the Greek I have mostly used Fritzsche's edition of the Apocrypha; the Hebrew text, as already pointed out by many specialists, affording many readings and giving whole verses not to be found in the Codices used by Professor Swete in his edition of the Septuagint but included often in Fritzsche's text or noticed at least in the *Apparatus Criticus*. I need hardly say that I do not consider my commentary as definitive. The obscurities are too many to allow us to hope for finality in a preliminary edition; and I am as anxious for the instruction of fellow-students as they are for the publication of these texts. I am also convinced that finality will not be reached without a more thorough-going study of the post-Talmudic literature in its various branches—philosophic, gnomic and liturgical—than students are wont to accord to it. But if it is not my "duty to complete the work," neither did I feel at liberty to desist from it altogether. Thus the attempt is made, whilst time and further study, added to "ministering to the sages" and "discussion with the disciples," will do the rest.

In conclusion it is my pleasant duty to record my thanks to the Rev. Aaron Bensimon, Chief Rabbi of Cairo, and Mr Jussef M. Cattaui, Warden of the Jewish Community in Cairo, for their exceptional liberality in placing the treasures of their Genizah at my disposal, which alone made this publication possible. To my friend Mr L. D. Barnett of Trinity College I am indebted for assistance in reading the greater part of the proofs. I have also to express my thanks to my friend Mr Reginald Q. Henriques of Cairo (originally of Manchester), to whose kindness, beginning during my stay and still continuing, I am indebted for many a precious document and important MS.

S. SCHECHTER.

March 1899.

AUTHORITIES QUOTED.

Aruch Hashalem (ערוך השלם) ed. by A. KOHUT. Cited *Aruch Hashalem*.

BACHER. The Hebrew Text of Ecclus. Jewish Quarterly Review, 1897, IX. 543–573. Cited sometimes Bacher.

BENZEEB. חכמת יהושע ב״ס נעתק ללה״ע. Cited Benzeeb.

COWLEY-NEUBAUER. The Original Hebrew of a portion of Ecclus. Oxford, 1897. Cited O. H.

EDERSHEIM, A. In the Holy Bible...with an explanatory and critical commentary, &c. London, 1888. Cited Ed.

FRITZSCHE. Kurzgefasstes exegetisches Handbuch zu den Apokryphen d. A. T. Leipzig, 1859. Cited Fr. Com.

FRITZSCHE. Libri Apocryphi V. T. Lipsiae, 1871. Cited Fr.

HALÉVY, J. Étude sur la partie du texte Hébreu de l'Ecclésiastique récemment découverte. Paris, 1897. Cited Halévy.

JASTROW, M. A Dictionary of the Targumim, the Talmud Bably and Jerushalmi. Cited Jastrow.

KAHANA, David. ס׳ ב״ס במקורו העברי. (Periodical השלח for 1898.)

LAGARDE. Libri V. T. Apocryphi Syriace. Lipsiae, 1861. Cited Syr.

LÉVI, Israel. L'Ecclésiastique, texte original Hébreu. Paris, 1898. Cited Lévi.

LEVY, Jacob. Neuhebräisches und Chaldäisches Wörterbuch. Cited sometimes Levy.

PERLES, F. "Notes Critiques sur le Texte de L'Ecclésiastique." Revue des Études Juives, 1897. Cited Perles.

SAADYAH. ספר הגלוי in Studien u. Mittheilungen aus der Kaiserlichen Oeffentlichen Bibliothek zu St Petersburg von Dr A. HARKAVY. St Petersburg, 1891. Cited Saadyah.

SCHLATTER. Das neu gefundene Hebräische Stück des Sirach. Gütersloh, 1897.

SMEND. Das hebräische Fragment der Weisheit des Yesus Sirach. Berlin, 1897. Cited Smend.

STRACK, HERM. L. Lehrbuch der Neuhebräischen Sprache. Cited Strack.

(This list does not include authorities quoted by their full titles.)

INTRODUCTION.

THE Fragments of the "Wisdom of Ben Sira" published in this volume come from the Genizah at Cairo to which we owe the former discoveries of this Apocryphon[1]. These Fragments, twenty pages of which are now edited for the first time, represent *two* Manuscripts, the one occupying pp. 3—10, the other the rest of the text pp. 11—24[2]. For convenience' sake we shall designate them as MS. A and MS. B.

I.

MS. A.

MS. A consists of 4 leaves of paper. Size of the paper 18 x 11 cm., whilst the space given to the writing measures only 15 x 8·5 cm. The MS. is fairly well preserved except in four places where the paper is a little damaged[3]. But even there the injury done is not of a serious nature, affecting only two or three letters at a time, and these can easily be supplied.

There are no marks of guiding lines in the body of the MS., but the writing is bounded by vertical lines drawn through the length of the paper. In a few cases the letters overlap these lines[4]. In other places the scribe prolonged a letter in order to bring up the writing as close as possible to the marginal line[5]. Only in three places we have something like a waving[6] stroke (-) intended to fill up the line, the space left being too small for the word with which the next line begins.

---

[1] See *Times* of July 6, 1896, and Mrs Lewis' *In the Shadow of Sinai*, Ch. VII.
[2] pp. 21, 22 were given as a Genizah specimen in the *Jewish Quarterly Review* of January, 1898.
[3] Cf. 5 6ᵃ, 13 23ᵃ, 16 3ᵃ and 24.
[4] Such are the ך of ישינוך (3 8), of לח מאלף (6 6), the יא of יחליא (12 10), and the דנה of ילמדנה (15 10).
[5] For instance, the ל of מכל (3 18), the ר of צורו (4 6), the ח of בתחבולתיה (6 25), and the final ם of חייהם (16 26).
[6] These are to be found after תדע (7 20), רגלי (16 10), and שמעשיו (ibid. v. 15).

חכמת בן סירא

The number of writing lines on each page is 28 (pp. 3, 5, 6, 7, 10) and 29 (pp. 4, 8, 9) respectively. On pp. 3 and 5 the scribe made use of the 29th line to insert there one word (p. 3) or two (p. 5), which enabled him to commence the following page with a new verse.

With the exception of the prolonged letters, naturally distorted, the MS. is written in square characters, with a very slight tendency towards cursive, in a rather minute hand, as may easily be imagined from the small size of the paper and the large amount of writing it contains. The only real approach to cursive is visible in the ל, which sometimes (in the minority of cases) resembles the ל in various later MSS.[1] and in the א combination, the basis of which is rather rounded. This fact however need not be interpreted as pointing to a late age. We have now in the Genizah collection *dated* MSS. of a decidedly cursive character from the middle of the 11th century, and our Fragment may thus without serious objection be attributed to the same if not to an earlier period.

The country in which our MS. was written is unknown, the MS. in its defective state giving no clue. But considering the place of its discovery it may safely be attributed to the Orient or to North Africa. So far as my examination of the Genizah allows me to judge, the great majority of its documents come from these parts of the world.

The number of words in a line varies between seven and eleven. Some words are provided with vowels and *raphe*-signs[2]; this however is not peculiar to this MS. The tetragrammaton is represented by two *Yods* crowned by a third *Yod* (ייִ)[3]. The words are written in one continuous line across the page, not in the two columns which are such a conspicuous feature in MS. B. It should be noted that this hemistichal division is only an imitation of the mode in which the Book of Proverbs was intended

---

[1] See Steinschneider, *Vorlesungen über die Kunde Hebräischer Handschriften* p. 31 and the *Schreibtafel* at the end of the book.

[2] Cf. 3 18, 24—4 2, 21—6 5, 11, 22—12 6, 13—13 2', 6, 8, 9—14 9, 11, 16, 26—15 10—16 5, 6, 18.

[3] See Steinschneider *Abbreviatur des Tetragrammaton* in the *Monatsschrift für Geschichte und Wissenschaft des Judentums* vol. 40, pp. 130 seq. His conclusion that this way of representing the tetragrammaton originated with the Franco-German Jews cannot well be accepted; as may be seen from the Genizah specimens published by S. S. in the *Jewish Quarterly*, X. p. 654 seq. reproducing a ritual never known in Europe in which the tetragrammaton is given by three *Yods* ייִ. The ספר יוחסי (in the *Mediaeval Jewish Chronicles*, II. published by Dr Neubauer) has also the ייִ.

INTRODUCTION.

to be written, but which was only observed by the "eminent scribe" (סופר מובדק), not as it seems by the usual copyists[1]. Our scribe, as we shall see presently, has no claim to this honourable title, and the division of the verses is marked by two dots (:), sometimes by one dot (·)[2]. But even these are sometimes wrongly placed, which shows that our scribe is not always very reliable[3]. Altogether he must be described as a very careless copyist. For not only may he be fairly suspected of having corrupted many words and even omitted whole verses[4], but it can hardly be doubted that he was not always competent to read the MS. from which our copy was prepared[5]. Occasionally however he corrects his own mistakes. This he does either by drawing a line through the word or letter written wrongly[6], or (mostly in the case of single letters) by providing it with a dot[7], or by inserting the letter or the word omitted by mistake between the lines[8].

In this class of mere self-corrections must, I think, be included the few readings to be found in the margins or between the lines[9]. They are all supplied by the same hand, and probably taken from the same MS. Had our scribe been in the possession of a second codex, it is not only likely that the number of the glosses would have been much larger (as may be seen from MS. B), but it is certain that he would have corrected from it such passages as 4 14, it being highly improbable that one and the same verse should be illegible in two distinct MSS. Unfortunately even these self-corrections were, as it seems, sometimes neglected. This fact is suggested by the dot-signs (.·.) on certain passages, apparently indicating some wrong reading in the body of the MS. but unaccompanied by the right one in the margin[10].

As to orthographical peculiarities, they are mostly confined to the

---

[1] See *Masechet Soferim*, ed. Müller, text c. XIII. § 1 and notes pp. 172, 173.
[2] E.g. 3 17—4 10ᶜ—6 16—13 2ᵉ⁽¹⁾.
[3] See 4 14, 17ᵃ—6 3—16 15.
[4] See notes 4 19—5 4—6, 6 16—7 15, 12 13, etc.
[5] See note on 4 14.
[6] See 3 19ᵇ—12 13—14 18ᵃ, 18ᶜ, 23—15 3—16 15, 22.
[7] See 4 21—15 14, 19—16 8.
[8] See 5 10—6 11—12 13—13 2ᵃ, 2ᶜ—22ᵃ—14 9, 18ᵃ—15 14—16 22, 23.
[9] See 3 14—12 14—14 16⁽¹⁾, 18ᶜ—15 3, 9.
[10] See pp. 4, 5, 6, 8, and 9. I suspect strongly that the .·. of רוּגַח (4 2) ought to have been placed above the word, marking it as a mistake, the correct reading being רוּחַ (see note). The same was probably the case with צָרִיךְ (13 6) and וּתָיִן (14 16).

חכמת בן סירא

frequent use of the Yod[1]. Other strange phenomena in the MS. cannot well be reduced to a system and are discussed in the notes[2].

Lastly I must remark that our MS. shows no indication of division into chapters; unless we take as such the two blanks, the one on p. 4 (before 4 11) and the other on p. 7 (before 13 2ª). The first, closed at both ends by writing, may perhaps have been meant as a סתומה, whilst the second, in which the blank continues to the end of the line, was intended for a פתוחה. The objection to this explanation is that the context in these places would rather lead us to expect a פתוחה before 4 11, the matter following being of a decidedly fresh nature, whilst 13 2ª is so closely connected with the preceding verses as to leave scarcely room there for a סתומה.

II.

MS. B.

This MS., consisting of seven leaves of paper (pp. 11—24), comes from the same codex of which the Lewis-Gibson Fragment, as well as the Fragments in the Bodleian, once formed a part. It is now well known[4] and thus requires no detailed description. The only new feature is the letter פׄ to be found in various places, viz.: on the top of p. 16 and ibid. on the margin against line 17 (*v.* 18); on the top of p. 18; on the margin of p. 22 against the 12th line (*v.* 12ᶜ⁽¹⁾). I have no satisfactory explanation for it. One naturally thinks of the abbreviation פ in the Bible standing for פתוחה. But none of the different functions which the *pethuchah* is supposed to perform[3] could satisfactorily account for the omission of the פ in p. 17 (before 38 1), p. 18 (before 38 25), and p. 23 (before 51 13),—which are certainly quite separated

---

[1] E.g. יחן (4 15), היבנע (4 25ª), תשיים (6 32, see however 16 20 י׳ם), איותה (6 37ʳ), יסיר (7 23), צריך (13 6, but צורך in 12 5ᵈ). Cf. on this point Rapoport in the Hebrew periodical *Bikkure Haittim*, x. p. 104. See also O. H. p. xxxvi.

[2] An exception may be made in the case of the peculiar confusion between על and אל (see notes on 4 22, 28⁽¹⁾, 5 5, 6ʳ), which may perhaps be accounted for by the אל combination (ﭏ) resembling somewhat a reversed ע.

[3] See on this point Müller (as above), notes p. 30, No. 74.

[4] For the best description see I. Lévi's Introduction to his *L'Ecclésiastique*, p. ix. seq.

[5] See Müller (as above) p. 24.

INTRODUCTION.

from the previous verses[1],—nor for its appearance on the top of p. 18, where the verse with which the page begins[2] is closely connected with those that precede it.

Another feature of our Fragment is the greater number of pointed words than were to be found in the hitherto discovered pages of the same MS.[3] Particularly worth noting is the pointing of וְהֹם (38 17ᵃ gl.). Two more instances appear in וָאָרח and in חֹקְךָ (O. H. 42 3, 18). It is difficult to account for these dots except by describing them as representing the ō vowel of the well-known Babylonian system of pointing[4]. But in this case we shall have to assume that there is some mistake in the former place (38 17ᵃ) on the one hand—since וְהֹם would give no sense—whilst on the other hand we shall have to explain all the other pointings as added by another hand, for there is some difficulty in accepting that one and the same scribe would use both the Oriental and the Babylonian system, though such dual punctuation is not unknown. Lastly I shall call attention to the two Persian glosses found in this Fragment, which teach the same lesson as those known from the O. H., namely that copies of the Hebrew Ecclesiasticus were not so scarce, as its later disappearance would lead us to believe[5].

Of vital differences between the two MSS. there are only to be noticed: the ניסיון in MS. A and ניסוי in MS. B[6], the יחשׂוּף in MS. A and מחסוף in MS. B[7], and the representation of the Tetragrammaton, which MS. A, as already mentioned, gives by ֔֔ and MS. B by ״׳.

It is also to be noticed that MS. A shows a closer agreement with the Syr. than MS. B. Whilst the latter in many cases corresponds with the Gr. as against the Syr. we have very few instances of this kind in MS. A, which fact points to various classes of MSS. existing in the Hebrew itself.

---

[1] Cf. also O. H. 42 9, 15 and 44 1. I must however call attention to Dr Ginsburg's statement in his *Introduction to the Massoretico-Critical Edition of the Hebrew Bible* (pp. 18, 19) that in a certain Paris MS. there occur in the Book of Proverbs seven sectional divisions "simply preceded by a vacant line without the letter פ."

[2] כי יש עת, etc. It is not impossible that it indicates that there is a *pethuchah* on the page, but in that case we should also expect one on the top of pp. 17 and 23.

[3] See 30 17⁽¹⁾ (gl.), 20ᵇ⁽²⁾—36 8 gl. and 33 26. About O. H. cf. Smend, p. 5.

[4] See Smend, ibid.

[5] See notes on 32 1ᵇᶜ, 35 20⁽¹⁾ and O. H. 40 18 gl. and 45 9 gl.

[6] See note on 4 17ᵈ and text 33 1. Cf. also O. H. 44 20ᵈ.

[7] See 6 9 and O. H. 42 1.

חכמת בן סירא

III.

Relation of Ben Sira to the Old Testament.

The Fragments published in this volume have revealed so many important linguistic features that an examination of the style and language of the Wisdom of B. S., particularly in its relation to the canonical Writings, is most desirable. Such an examination of course suggested itself to every Biblical student as soon as the first discovery of the original was made, and I hinted at it in my essay "*A Fragment of the Original Text of B. S.*"[1]; but as the whole of the first find consisted of one leaf—amounting to about a fiftieth part of the whole book—I did not consider it sufficiently representative to justify serious conclusions. It is true, as was pointed out at the time, that among the two hundred words which the first Fragment restored to us of the original Hebrew of B. S. only three occurred that could not be found in the O. T. But the statistical test, laying so much stress on the proportion which the New-Hebrew words bear to others, did not recommend itself to me as satisfactory in the case of B. S.[2] For B. S., though not entirely devoid of original ideas, was, as is well known, a conscious imitator[3] both as to form and as to matter, his chief model being the Book of Proverbs[4]. Now Jewish writers have at almost all periods fairly succeeded in writing a pure Biblical Hebrew. To give an instance lying near at hand I shall refer here to Benzeeb, who flourished about twenty-one centuries after B. S. and in whose Hebrew re-translation of the latter's '*Wisdom*' hardly more than a dozen Rabbinisms could be

[1] See *Expositor*, July 1896, p. 1.
[2] See Professor Driver's notice in the *Guardian*, July 1896, p. 1029, as well as his *Introduction to the Literature of the O. T.* (ed. 1891), p. 483.
[3] The statement by some writers that the Jews were imitators is as far as the canonical writers are concerned still to be proved. It is based on the assumption that certain Biblical books could not have been composed at the date which tradition has assigned to them. The books admittedly written "after the turning-point in the Hebrew style in the age of Nehemiah," such for instance as the books of Daniel, Ezra, Nehemiah, Ecclesiastes, Esther, and Chronicles, do not show any real effort to imitate the older literary productions. They write the style of their own age.
[4] Among others see Schürer, *Geschichte des Jüdischen Volkes im Zeitalter Jesu Christi*, II. p. 593, Bickell, *Zeitschrift für Kat. Theologie*, 1882, and Seligmann, *Das Buch der Weisheit*, etc. p. 20. R. Saadyah (*Sepher Haggalui*, ed. Harkavy), p. 150, considers it also as a ספר מוסר הדומה לספר משלי.

discovered¹. His success is of course due to his skill in imitating the Biblical style. The test therefore for divining the real state of the language in an age of such productions is not to be sought in what the writers have succeeded, but in what they have failed, in accomplishing. B. S.'s production is undoubtedly a successful imitation on the whole, but it is not less certain that he failed in parts. Judged by this test, which I think is the only right one, we shall arrive at the conclusion that at the period in which B. S. composed his 'Wisdom,' classical Hebrew was already a thing of the past, the real language of the period being that Hebrew idiom which we know from the Mishnah and the cognate Rabbinic literature.

Before examining the evidence of B. S.'s failure it is necessary to point out that even his success need not deceive us, for, as in the case of other imitators, it is simply due to the fact that he had already made ample use of the Bible.

The following list, containing the phrases, idioms, typical expressions, and even whole verses about which there can be no reasonable doubt that they were either suggested to him by or directly copied from the Scriptures, will best show how well he was acquainted with the Bible and how much he made use of it :—

[Uncertainty of reading or interpretation is denoted by asterisks; in each case notes and text should be consulted. In O. H., Lévi's excellent commentary should be specially consulted.]

Ecclus.	3	8	ישיגוך וג'	Deut.	28	2
,,		13	עזוב לו	Exod.	23	5
,,		18, 21	גדולת עולם...פלאות ממך	Ps.	131	1
,,		23	אל תמר	Exod.	23	21
,,		26	לב כבד	,,	8	28
,,		29	ואזן מקשבת לחכמה	Prov.	2	2
,,		30	צדקה תכפר חטאת	Dan.	4	24

¹ Benzeeb died 1811. See Steinschneider's *Catalogue (of the Bodleian Library)*, col. 795. A similar production of proverbs in elegant Biblical Hebrew, betraying only a very few Rabbinisms and later philosophical phrases, are the משלי אסף by Isaac Satanow, who died about 1803. As an example of a failure I will notice here, Joshua Duklo's Hebrew Version of B. S. in which the Rab. dialect is predominant. See Zeitlin's *Kiryath Sepher*, p. 71.

חכמת בן סירא

Ecclus.	4	1	ומר נפש	1 Sam..	22	2	(etc.)
"		3ᵃ	תחמיר מעי	Lam.	1	20	
"		10ᵃ	כאב ליתומים	Ps.	68	6	
"		12	אהבו חיים..יפיקו וג'	Prov.	8	35	
"		13	ותמכיה וג'	"	3	16, 18	
"		"	בברכת יי'	Gen.	39	5	(etc.)
"		14ᵃ	ואל אהב מאהביה	Prov.	8	17	
"		17ᵈ	ימלא לבו בי	Exod.	35	35	
"		20ᵃ	עת וג'	Eccles.	3	1	
"		21	משאת עון	Lev.	22	16	(Zeph. 3 18)
"		"	כבוד וחן	Ps.	84	12	
"		24	במענה לשון	Prov.	16	1	
"		28	ויי' נלחם לך	Exod.	14	14	
"		28⁽¹⁾ᵃ	ו' לשונך אל תרגל	Ps.	15	3	
"		29	ורפי..במלאכתך	Prov.	18	9	
5		1	יש לאל ידי	Micah	2	1	(etc.)
"		1⁽²⁾	תאות נפשך	Ps.	10	3	
"		2	אל ת' אחרי לבך וג'	Num.	15	39	
"		3	מבקש נרדפים	Eccles.	3	15	
"		4	אל ארך אפים	Exod.	34	6	(etc.)
"		7ᶜ	וביום נקם	Is.	34	8	(etc.)
"		8	לא יועילו וג'	Prov.	11	4	
"		11	ובארך רוח	Eccles.	7	8	
"		12	ידך על פיך	Prov.	30	32	
6		1ᵇ	וקלון ת' חרפה	"	18	3	
"		3	כעץ יבש	Is.	56	3	(etc.)
"		4	נפש עזה	"	"	11	
"		5	חיך ערב	Cant.	5	16	
"		"	ושפתי חן	Ps.	45	3	(Prov. 22 11)
"		8	ביום צרה	2 Kings	19	3	(etc.)

INTRODUCTION. 15

Ecclus.	6	9	ריב חרפתך	1 Sam.	25	39	
,,		16*	צרור חיים	,,	,,	29	
,,		22*	ולא לרבים וג׳	Job	32	9	
,,		27	דרש וחקר	Deut.	13	15	
,,		,,	וההזקתה וג׳	Prov.	4	13	(Job 27 2)
,,		30	פתיל תכלת	Num.	15	38	
,,		31	ועטרת תפארת	Prov.	4	9	(etc.)
,,		33	והט אזנך	,,	,,	20	
	7	15	מלאכת עבדה	Lev.	23	7	(etc.)
,,		11	מרים ומשפיל	1 Sam.	2	7	(Ps. 75 8)
,,		12	אל תחרוש	Prov.	3	29	
,,		17	ת׳ אנוש רמה	Job	25	6	
,,		17(1)	גל אל אל	Prov.	16	3	(etc.)
,,		18	בזהב אופיר	1 Chr.	29	4	(etc.)
,,		19	וטובת חן	Nahum	3	4	
	12	3*	וגם צדקה וג׳	Is.	58	2	
,,		6	ישיב נקם	Deut.	32	41	
,,		10	אל תאמין בשונא	Prov.	26	24, 25	
	13	12	קושר קשר	2 Kings	12	21	(etc.)
,,		19	פראי מדבר	Jer.	2	24	(Job 24 5)
,,		21	נרדה מרע וג׳	,,	9	2	(Prov. 14 32)
,,		23ª	עב יגיעו	Job	20	6	
,,		25	ישנא פניו	Eccles.	8	1	
,,		26	ושיג ושיח	1 Kings	18	27	
	14	3	רע עין	Prov.	23	6	(etc.)
,,		15	הלא לאחר וג׳	Ps.	49	11	
,,		,,	ליודי גורל	Joel	4	3	(etc.)
,,		17	כבגד יבלה	Is.	51	6	(Ps. 102 27)
,,		19	ימשך אחריו	Job	21	33	
,,		20	אשרי אנוש...	,,	5	17	

חכמת בן סירא

Ecclus.	14	20	בחכמה יהגה	Ps.	**1**	1, 2 & **37** 30
,,		23*	ומשקיף וג'	Jud.	**5**	28 (etc.)
,,		26	וישם קנו	Num.	**24**	21 (etc.)
,,		27	וחוסה בצלה	Jud.	**9**	15 (Eccles. **7** 12)
	15	1	ותופש תורה	Jer.	**2**	8
,,		4	יבטח ולא יבוש	Ps.	**22**	6
,,		5	ובתוך קהל תפתח פיו	Prov.	**24**	7
,,		6	ששון וג'	Is.	**51**	3
,,	,,		ושם עולם	,,	**56**	5
,,		7	ידריכוה מתי שוא	Job	**22**	15
,,		9*	לא נ' תהלה	Ps.	**33**	1
,,		13	ולא יאננה ל'	Prov.	**12**	21
,,		14	אלהים מבראשת ברא	Gen.	**1**	1
,,		17	לפני...חיים ומוות וג'	Deut.	**30**	15 (Jer. **21** 8)
,,		19	עיני אל וג'	Ps.	**33**	15, 18
	16	1	בבני עולה	2 Sam.	**3**	34 (etc.)
,,		3ª	אל תאמין בחייהם	Job	**24**	22
,,		5	רבות כאלה	,,	**16**	2
,,		6	יוקדת אש ובגוי חנף	Is.	**65**	5 & **10** 6
,,		10	שש מאות אלף רגלי	Num.	**11**	21 (etc.)
,,		13	תאות צדיק	Prov.	**10**	24
,,		15	הקשה את לב פרעה	Exod.	**7**	3
,,		17ᶜ	בעם כבד	Num.	**20**	20
,,		18	הן השמים ושמי השמים	1 Kings	**8**	27
,,		19	קצבי הרים	Jonah	**2**	7
,,		23	חסרי לב	Prov.	**6**	32 (etc.)
,,		25	במשקל רוחי	Job	**28**	25
,,	,,		אחוה דעי	,,	**32**	10
	30	11⁽¹⁾, 12ª*	כפתן וג'	Ez.	**29**	7
,,		12ᶜ	מפח נפש	Job	**11**	20

INTRODUCTION.

Ecclus.	30	13	והכבד עלו	1 Kings	12 10
,,		19 (gl.)*	לאללי הגוים וג׳	Ps.	115 6
,,		20⁽ᵃ⁾	וייי מבקש מידו	1 Sam.	20 16 (etc.)
,,		21*	אל תתן לד׳...בעונך	Ps.	31 11
	31	5	ר׳ ח׳ לא ינקה	Prov.	28 20
,,		6⁽¹⁾	להושע ביום עברה	,,	11 4
,,	32	3 (gl.)*	והצנע לכת	Micah	6 8
,,		4	תשפך שיח	Ps.	102 1
,,		16, 16⁽¹⁾	יבין משפט	Prov.	28 5
,,		17⁽¹⁾	ישמור לשנו	,,	21 23, 24
,,		22⁽ᴸ⁾	בדרך רשעים	,,	4 19
,,		22⁽ᵐ⁾	שמור וג׳	,,	19 16
,,		24	נוצר תורה	,,	28 7
,,	35	9 gl.	מלוה ייי וג׳	,,	19 17
,,		11	כי אל׳ וג׳	Jer.	51 56
,,		,,	ושבעתים ישיב	Ps.	79 12
,,		12ᵃ	אל תשחד וג׳	Deut.	10 17
,,		12ᶜ	עמו משוא פנים	2 Chr.	19 7
,,		15	דמעה על לחי	Lam.	1 2
,,		17ᶜ	ושופט...יעשה משפט	Gen.	18 25
,,		18ᶜ	עד ימחץ מתני וג׳	Deut.	33 11
,,		18ᶠ	ומטה רשע	Ez.	7 11
,,		19ᵃ	עד ישיב וג׳	Jer.	25 14 (Prov. 24 29 & 12 14)
,,	36	2	פחדך על כל הגוים	1 Chr.	14 17
,,		3 gl.	הניף יד על	Zech.	2 13 (etc.)
,,		5	כי אין וג׳	1 Chr.	17 20
,,		6	ח׳ אות...האדר יד וג׳	Ps.	74 11 & 44 4 (Exod. 15 6)
,,		7	ושפוך חמה	Jer.	10 25
,,		7*	צר...איב	Ps.	74 10
,,		8ᵃ	קץ...מועד	Dan.	11 35

Ecclus. 36	8⁽¹⁾	כי מי וג׳	Job	9	12	(Eccles. 8 4)
,,	10*	השבת ראש	Ps.	74	13	(& 8 3)
,,	10*	פאתי מואב	Num.	24	17	
,,	11	שבטי יעקב וג׳	Is.	49	6	(Ps. 74 2)
,,	13	מכון שבתיך	Exod.	15	17	(2 Chr. 6 30)
,,	14	ומכבודך וג׳	1 Kings	8	11	(etc.)
,,	17ᵃ	תפלת עבדיך	Dan.	9	17	(1 Kings 8 30)
,,	17ᵃ*	ברצונך על עמך	Ps.	106	4	
,,	17ᵃ gl.	ויראו כל אפסי ארץ וג׳	Is.	52	10	
37	31	בלא מוסר וג׳	Prov.	5	23	
38	2	ישא משאות	Gen.	43	34	(2 Sam. 11 8)
,,	3	ולפני וג׳	Prov.	22	29	
,,	10	ומהכר פנים	,,	24	23	(etc.)
39	15ᶜ	נבל...בתרועה	Ps.	33	2, 3	
,,	17ᶜ*	ומוצא פיו אוצרו	,,	,,	7	
,,	18	ואין מעצור לתשועתו	1 Sam.	14	6	
,,	19	ואין נסתר מנגד עיניו	Amos	9	3	
,,	20*	מספר ל	Ps.	147	5	
,,	23	גוים יוריש	Exod.	34	24	(Ps. 44 3)
,,	,,	ויהפך למלח משקה	Gen.	13	10	(Ps. 107 34)
,,	26ᶜ	דם ענב	Deut.	32	14	
,,	28	הרים יעתיקו	Job	9	5	
,,	29	אש וברד	Ps.	148	8	
,,	30*	וחרב נוקמת	Lev.	26	25	
,,	30ᶜ	והמה באוצר ולעת	Job	38	22, 23	
,,	31	ישישו	Ps.	19	6	
,,	,,	ימרו פיו	Num.	20	24	(etc.)
,,	35*	וברכו את שם קדשו	Ps.	145	21	
40	1ᶜ	צאתו מרחם אמו	Num.	12	12	
,,	,,	אם כל חי	Gen.	3	20	

INTRODUCTION.

Ecclus.	40	3	יושב כסא	Prov.	20	8	
,,	,,	,,	עפר ואפר	Gen.	18	27	
,,	,,	4	אימת מות	Ps.	55	5	
,,	,,	5ᶜ	נוחו על משכבו	Is.	57	2	
,,	,,	9	חרחר וחרב	Deut.	28	22	
,,	,,	,,	שד ושבר	Is.	60	18	
,,	,,	11	כל מארץ וג׳	Eccles.	12	7	
,,	,,	13	כנחל איתן	Amos	5	24	(Deut. 21 4)
,,	,,	,,	בחזיז קולות	Job	38	25	
,,	,,	14	כי פ׳ לנצח יתם	,,	4	20	
,,	,,	15	שן סלע	,,	39	28	
,,	,,	17	וחסד...ימוט	Prov.	10	30	
,,	,,	18	יין ושכר	Lev.	10	9	(etc.)
,,	,,	19	יעמידו שם	Deut.	25	7	
,,	,,	22	צמחי שדה	Ez.	16	7	
,,	,,	23	אשה משכלת	Prov.	19	14	
,,	,,	24*	אח...צרה	,,	17	17	
,,	,,	,,	צדק מצלת	,,	10	2	
,,	,,	26ᶜ	ביראת יײ מחסור	Ps.	34	10	
,,	,,	27	כבוד הפתה	Is.	4	5	
,,	,,	30	תבער כמו אש	Jer.	20	9	
,,	41	2ᶜ	ואבד תקוה	Ez.	37	11	(etc.)
,,	,,	4	זה חלק וג׳	Job	20	29	(27 13)
,,	,,	,,	תמאס בתודת	Is.	5	24	
,,	,,	9	תולידו לאנחה	Prov.	17	21	
,,	,,	9ᶜ	לשמחת עולם	Is.	35	10	
,,	,,	11	אך שם...לא יכרת	,,	56	5	
,,	,,	14ᵃ	שמעו בנים	Prov.	1	8	(etc.)
,,	42	1ᶜ	ומצא חן בעיני	Gen.	6	8	(etc.)
,,	,,	1ᶠ	תשא פנים	Deut.	10	17	(etc.)

3—2

חכמת בן סירא

Ecclus.	42	4ᵃ	שחק מאזנים	Is.	40	15	
״		4ᵇ	בין רב למעט	Num.	26	56	
״		6	ידים רפות	Is.	35	3	(Job 4 3)
״		13	כי מבגד יצא עש	״	50	9	
״		15	אזכר נא מעשה אל	Ps.	77	12	
״		״	וזה חזיתי ואספרה	Job	15	17	
״		16	וכבוד ייי וג׳	Ps.	104	31	
״		17	לא...לספר וג׳	״.	40	6	
״		18	תהום ולב חקר	Job	38	16	
״		20ᵃ	לא נעדר	Is.	40	26	(etc.)
״		21ᶜ	ו׳ צ׳ לכל מבין	״	״	14	
43		1ᵇ	ועצם שמים	Exod.	24	10	
״		2	מה נורא מעשי ייי	״	34	10	(Ps. 66 3)
״		5	כי גדול ייי עושהו	Ps.	95	3, 5	
״		6	ואות עולם	Gen.	1	14	(Is. 55 13)
״		8ᶜ	גבלי מ׳	Job	38	37	
״		10	בדבר אל וג׳	Ps.	33	6	
״		11ᵃ	ראה קשת...בכבוד	Ez.	1	28	
״		14 gl.	למענו ברא	Prov.	16	4	
״		17	קול רעמו וג׳	Job	37	5	(Ps. 29 3, 9)
״		״	סופה וסערה	Is.	29	6	
״		19	כפור כ׳ י׳	Ps.	147	16	
״		״	ויציץ...ציצים	Num.	17	23	
״		20ᶜ	וכשרין ילבש	Is.	59	17	
״		21 gl.	יבול הרים	Job	40	20	
״		24	יורדי הים וג׳	Ps.	107	21, 23, 31	
״		״	לשמע אחננו	״	18	45	(Job 42 5)
״		25	שם פלאות וג׳	״	107	24 & 104 25
״		״	מין כל חי	Gen.	7	14	
״		27	וזקן דבר וג׳	Eccles.	12	13	

INTRODUCTION.

Ecclus.	43	28	נגדלה עוד וג'	Ps.	145	3	(Job 5 9)
,,		30ᶜ	תחליפו כח	Is.	40	31	
,,	44	1	אנשי חסד	,,	57	1	
,,		3	ואנשי שם בגבורתם	Gen.	6	4	
,,		5	ח' מזמור על. חוק	Ps.	119	54	
,,		6	אנשי חיל	Gen.	47	6	(etc.)
,,		9ᶜ	כאשר לא היו היו ·	Job	10	19	(Obad. 16)
,,		11	עם זרעם וג'...ונחלתם	Prov.	13	22	
,,		13	עד עולם וג'	Ps.	112	6, 9	
,,		16ᵃ	והתהלך לפני יי' וילקח	Gen.	5	24	
,,		17	נמצא תמים	,,	6	9	
,,		18	באות עולם...כל בשר	,,	9	12, 16	
,,		19	אברהם אב המון גוים	,,	17	4	
,,		20ᵇ, 20ᶜ	ובא בברית וג'	Nch.	9	8	
,,		21	לברך בזרעו גוים	Gen.	22	18	
,,		21ᶠ	מים ועד ים ומנהר ועד אפסי ארץ	Zech.	9	10	(Ps. 72 8)
,,		22ᵃ	הקים כן	Gen.	26	3	
,,		22ᶜ	ברית כל וג'	Lev.	26	42, 45	(Is. 42 6)
,,	45	3ᵉᵃ	ויצוהו אל	Exod.	6	13	
,,		5ᶠ	ביעקב חקיו וג'	Ps.	147	19	
,,		6	וירם קדוש וג'	Num.	18	19	
,,		7ᵇ	ויתן עליו הוד	,,	27	20	
,,		7ᵈ	בתועפות ראם	,,	23	22	
,,		8	בכבוד ועז	1 Chr.	16	28	(etc.)
,,		10	בגדי קדש זהב וג'	Exod.	28	4, 15, 32	
,,		11ᵇ	אבני חפץ	Is.	54	12	
,,		,,	פתוחי חותם	Exod.	28	21	
,,		11ᵈ	כל אבן יקרה	Ez.	28	13	
,,		,,ᵉ	למספר...ישראל	Josh.	4	5	
,,		12	עטרת פז	Ps.	21	4	

חכמת בן סירא

Ecclus.	45	14	כליל תקטר	Lev.	6	15	
,,		15ᶜ	ולזרעו וג'	Ps.	89	30	
,,		16, 16ᵈ	עלה והלבים...ולכפר..	2 Chr.	35	14	(Lev. 16 34)
,,		17ᶜ	וילמד...חק ומשפט את בני ישראל	Ps.	147	19	(Deut. 4 14)
,,		18	ויקנאו וג'	Ps.	106	15, 16	
,,		19ᶜ	בשביב אשו	Job	18	5	
,,		21ᶜ, 22ᶜ	אשי יי יאכלון וג'	Deut.	18	1, 2	(Num. 18 3)
,,		23ᶜ	ויעמד בפרץ	Ps.	106	23	
,,		23ᶜ	ויכפר על בני ישראל	Num.	25	13	
,,		24	ברית שלום	,,	,,	12	
,,		25ᶜ	ייי הטוב	2 Chr.	30	18	
,,		,,	המעטר...כבוד	Ps.	8	6	
,,	46	1	משרת משה	Num.	11	28	(etc.)
,,		1ᶜ	להנקם וג' ולדגחיל	Josh. 10 13 & 1 6			
,,		3	מ' ה' לפניו יתיצב	Josh.	1	5	
,,		,,	מלחמות ייי נלחם	1 Sam.	25	28	
,,		6ᶜ	למען דעת וג' גוי חרם	Josh.	4	24	(Is. 34 5)
,,		6ᶜ	כי מלא	Num.	14	24	
,,		7ᵈ	להשיב חרון	,,	25	4	(etc.)
,,		8	משש מאות אלף רגלי	,,	11	21	(etc.)
,,		8ᶜ	ארץ זבת וג'	Exod.	3	8	(etc.)
,,		9ᶜ	להדריכם וג' נחלה	Josh.	14	9	(Amos 4 13)
,,		11ᶜ	ולא נסוג וג'	Ps.	44	19	
,,		13ᶜ	נזיר ייי	Jud.	13	5	
,,		13ᶜ	וימשח נגידים וג'	1 Sam.	9	16	
,,		16ᶜ, 17*	בעלתו...וירעם...	1 Sam.	7	9, 10	
,,		19	נוחו וג'	Is.	57	2	
,,		,,	העיד ייי ומשיחו	1 Sam.	12	5	
,,		19ᶜ*	כופר וג'	,,	,,	3	
,,		20	ויגד וג' דרכיו	Job	21	31	
,,		20ᶜ	וישא מארץ קולו	Is.	29	4	

INTRODUCTION. 23

Ecclus.	47	2	כי כחלב טורם וג׳	Ps.	89	20
,,		5	ויתן בימינו עז	1 Sam.	2	10
,,		9 (gl.)	מזמור הנעים	2 Sam.	23	1
,,		10ᶜ*	לפני וג׳ משפט	Ps.	119	62
,,		11	יי׳ העביר	2 Sam.	12	13
,,		,,	וירם...קרנו	1 Sam.	2	10 (etc.)
,,		11ᶜ	וכסאו הכין	1 Chr.	17	12
,,		12	בן משכיל	Prov.	10	5
,,		13	הניח לו מסביב	2 Chr.	20	30 (Josh. 21 42)
,,		18	בשם הנכבד	Deut.	28	58
,,		19	ותתן לנשים	Prov.	31	3
,,		,,	ותמשילם וג׳	Is.	3	12
,,		20	ותחלל את יצועך	Gen.	49	4
,,		22	ולא יפיל וג׳	2 Kings	10	10
,,		22ᶜ	נין ונכד	Is.	14	22
,,		,,*	ואוהביו וג׳	Ps.	145	20
,,		23ᶜ	ירבעם וג׳	2 Kings	3	3
,,		25	ולכל רעה התמכר	1 Kings	21	20 (etc.)
	48	1	כתנור בוער	Mal.	3	19
,,		2	וישבר וג׳	Lev.	26	26
,,		3*	עצר שמים	Deut.	11	17
,,		10ᵇ,ᶜ*	לפני וג׳ להשיב וג׳	Mal.	3	23, 24
,,		12ᶜ	פי שנים	2 Kings	2	9
,,		12ᵈ	מוצא פידו	Deut.	8	3
,,		12ᵉ	לא זע	Est.	5	9
,,		,,	משל ברוחו	Prov.	16	32
,,		13	לא נפלא וג׳	Gen.	18	14 (etc.)
,,		15	בכל זאת לא שב	Is.	5	25
,,		,,	ע׳ א׳ נסחו מארצם	Deut.	28	63 (Prov. 2 22)
,,		,,	ויפצו וג׳	,,	,,	64

חכמת בן סירא

Ecclus. 48	18ᶜ	ויגדף וג׳	2 Kings	19	22	(etc.)
״	19	ויחילו כיולדה	Is.	13	8	
״	21	ויהמם במגפה	1 Sam.	7	10	
״	24	ברוח גבורה	Is.	11	2	
״	״	אבלי ציון	״	61	3	
49	1	כקטרת סמים וג׳	Exod.	31	11	
״	5	לגוי נבל	Deut.	32	21	
״	6ᶜ	מרחם...נביא	Jer.	1	5	
״	7ᵃ	לנתוש וג׳	״	״	10	
״	13ᶜ	וירפא וג׳	1 Kings	18	30	
״	״	דלתים ובריח	Deut.	3	5	(Josh. 6 26)
״	16	תפארת אדם	Is.	44	13	
50	5	מבית הפרכת	Exod.	26	33	(etc.)
״	6	ככוכב אור	Ps.	148	3	
״	7	וכקשת נראתה בענן	Gen.	9	14	
״	8ᵃ	יבלי מים	Is.	30	25	(etc.)
״	8ᶜ	כפרח לבנון	Nahum	1	4	
״	9ᵃ	לבונה על המנחה	Lev.	6	8	
״	9ᵇ	אבני חפץ	Is.	54	12	
״	10	כזית רענן	Jer.	11	16	
״	12ᶜ	וי׳ כערבי נחל	Job	40	22	
״	13ᵇ,ᶜ	נגד כל קהל ישראל	1 Kings	8	22	
״	16ᵃ	בחצצרות מקשה	Num.	10	2	
״	17ᵃ	כל בשר וג׳	״	16	22	
״	17ᶜ	קדוש ישראל	Is.	1	4	(etc.)
״	19ᵃ	וירנו כל עם	Lev.	9	24	
״	25	קצה נפשי	Num.	21	5	
״	״	איננו עם	Deut.	32	21	
״	26	גוי נבל	״	״	״	
״	28	אשרי איש...יהגה	Ps.	1	1, 2	(Prov. 3 13)
״	29ᵇ	יראת ייי חיים	Prov.	19	23	

INTRODUCTION.

Ecclus.	51	1ᶜ	אספרה וג׳	Ps.	22	23	
,,		2ᵃ	פרית...נפשי	,,	34	23	(etc.)
,,		2ᵇ	חשכת...משחת	Job	33	18	
,,		2ᶜ	מרבת עם	Ez.	36	3	
,,		,,	משוט לשון	Job	5	21	
,,		,,	שטי כזב	Ps.	40	5	
,,		3ᵃ	כרוב חסדך	Neh.	13	22	(Is. 63 7)
,,		3ᵈ	מרבות צרות	Ps.	71	20	(Deut. 31 17)
,,		5ᵈ	ומפלי שקר	Job	13	4	
,,		5ᵇ	וחצי לשון מרמה	Ps.	120	4, 3	
,,		6	ותגע וג׳ וחיתי וג׳	,,	88	4, 7 & 86 13	
,,		8ᵃ	וחסדיו וג׳	,,	25	6	
,,		10ᵇ	אל תרפני ביום צרה	Prov.	24	10	
,,		,,	ביום שואה ומשואה	Zeph.	1	15	(etc.)
,,		11ᵃ,ᶜ	אהללה שמך...אז שמע וג׳	Ps.	145	2 & 143 1	
,,		12ᶜ	ואברכה את שם ייי	,,	,,	1	
,,		12ᵈ⁽¹⁾	הודו וג׳	,,	136	1	(etc.)
,,		12ᵈ⁽²⁾	לשמר ישראל	,,	121	4	
,,		⁽⁴⁾	ליוצר הכל	Jer.	10	16	
,,		⁽⁵⁾	לגואל ישראל	Is.	49	7	
,,		⁽⁷⁾	למקבץ נדחי ישראל	,,	56	8	(Ps. 147 2)
,,		⁽⁸⁾	למצמיח קרן לבית דוד	Ps.	132	17	
,,		⁽¹⁰⁾	לאביר יעקב	,,	,,	2	(Gen. 49 24)
,,		⁽¹¹⁾	לבוחר בציון	,,	,,	13	
,,		⁽¹⁴⁾	וירם קרן וג׳	,,	148	14	
,,		13	אני נער	,,	71	17 & 119 9	
,,		13⁽¹⁾	א׳ מנעורי וג׳	,,	,,	17	
,,		18ᵃ	חשבתי וג׳	,,	119	59	
,,		20ᵃ	ולנצח נצחים	Is.	34	10	
,,		28, 29	בנעורתי...בשיבתי*	Ps.	71	17, 18	

This list speaks for itself; it extends almost over the whole Canon of the O.T., and, what is of special importance, it covers all the books

4

חכמת בן סירא

or groups of the Psalms[1]. In fact the impression produced by the perusal of B. S.'s original on the student who is at all familiar with the Hebrew Scriptures is that of reading the work of a post-canonical author, who already knew his Bible and was constantly quoting it. A few words of comment however as to the nature of these quotations are necessary.

The greatest number of these are what we may perhaps term adaptive[2]. By this I understand such Scriptural passages, phrases, and groups of words as could not have been embodied by B. S. in his 'Wisdom' without subjecting them first to the process of adaptation. This he managed mostly by slightly altering the Biblical text, by transposing words or giving them a different pointing, or by omitting or adding some words, or by combining various phrases, sometimes also by giving to the Biblical expression a meaning foreign to its original purport. The following few specimens will illustrate these various alterations:

B. S.	3	8	ישינוך כל ברכות	Deut.	28	2	ובאו עליך כל הברכות האלה והשינוך
"	13	23ᵃ	שכלו עד עב יגיעו	Job	20	6	וראשו לעב יגיע
"	15	6	ששן ושמחה ימצא	Is.	51	3	ששון ושמחה ימצא

[1] Cf. especially the references in the list to Pss. 1—8—15—19—21—22—25—28—31—33—34—37—40—44—49—55—71—74—77—84—88—89—95—102—104—106—107—112—115—119—120—121—131—132—136—145—147—148. A study of the list will show that some of these Pss. furnished B. S. with more than one quotation. Again, as regards Ps. 19, though only one verbal quotation from it is given, there can be little doubt that B. S.'s description of the planets (O. H. 42) was partly at least suggested by this Ps. Very instructive in this respect is B. S.'s epilogue (51 13—30). In form, as is well known, it is an imitation of the last 23 vv. of Proverbs (31 10—31), whilst the matter was undoubtedly largely suggested to B. S. by Pss. 71 and 119. But both in language and in style it is as far removed from the Psalms as is any Rabbinic composition from the book of Deuteronomy.

[2] For merely reminiscent passages, see the various commentaries on Ben Sira. Cf. also Ehrt, *Abfassungszeit und Abschluss des Psalters*, p. 126 and Dr C. H. H. Wright, *The Book of Koheleth*, p. 41 seq. (B. S. an imitator of Koheleth). With regard to this latter I will only draw particular attention to O. H. 43 27 וסוף דבר הוא הכל נשמע and Eccles. 12 13 את האלהים which B. S. had undoubtedly borrowed from Eccles, where it is only at the *end* of the book that the סוף דבר can give a real sense. Lévi, who also drew attention to this parallel, does not think it convincing, but he gives no reasons. With regard to Job see Halévy, p. 67 seq. (cf. also Baethgen, *Die Psalmen übersetzt*, etc. 2nd ed. p. xxvi. seq.). In fact the whole of B. S.'s cosmography is a mere echo of the last chapters of Job, whilst his teleology (e.g. 39 21—34, and 43 14) is based on Job 37 12, 13, and 38 22, 23. The אוצרות of the Bible (cf. besides Job, Deut. 28 12, 32 34, Jer. 50 25, and Ps. 33 7) seem to have much occupied the thoughts of post-canonical writers, cf. the book of Enoch, cc. 41, 60, and 68, and B. T. *Chaggigah* 12ᵇ. [I am informed now that Mr Thomas Tyler has also pointed out the reference of Ben Sira 43 27 to the epilogue of Eccles. 12 13, in the *Guardian*, Feb. 17, 1897. Dr Taylor has also noticed this reference, *Jewish Fathers*, second edition, p. 172.]

INTRODUCTION.

B. S.	15	7	לא ידריכוה מתי שוא	Job	22 15	¹אשר דרכו מתי און
"	"	14	אלהים מבראשית ברא	Gen.	1 1	²בראשית ברא אלהים
"	16	25	במשקל רוחי	Job	28 25	לעשות לרוח משקל
"	30	12*	ובקע מתניו	Ez.	29 7	³ובקעת...כתף...והעמדת מתנים
"	44	20*, 20*, 21	ובא בברית עמו... ובניסוי נמצא נאמן על כן בשבועה הקים לו לברך בזרעו	Neh.	9 8	ומצאת את לבבו נאמן לפניך וכרות עמו הברית ...לתת לזרעו ותקם את דבריך
"	45	6	וירם קדוש את אהרן... וישימהו לחק עולם	Num.	18 19	⁴כל תרומת הקדשים אשר ירימו...אתך לחק עולם
"	"	17*	וילמד את עמו חק ומשפט את בני ישראל	Ps.	147 19	מגיד דבריו ליעקב חקיו ומשפטיו לישראל
"	50	17*	כל בשר יחדיו נמהרו ויפלו על פניהם	Num.	16 22	⁵ויפלו על פניהם ויאמרו אל א' ח' לכל בשר
"	"	19*	וירנו כל עם הארץ	Lev.	9 24	⁶וירא כל העם וירנו

Others again are simple verbal quotations⁷. But both in this and in the former class the most noteworthy feature is the artificial or Paitanic⁸

---

¹ Cf. also Job 11 11 (מתי שוא). See also O. H. 46 9° להדריבם על במתי ארן, which is taken from Amos 4 13, but the application of it to Caleb was undoubtedly suggested by Jos. 14 9 דרכה. (Cf. Messrs Cowley and Neubauer, O. H. p. 30, n. 4.) This strongly recalls the Rabbinic גזירה שוה.

² It is difficult to account for this deviation from the verbal order of the Scriptures. It is the more significant in view of the tradition that אלהים ברא בראשית was the order adopted by the Septuagint translators. Cf. Müller as above text 1. and notes p. 14. See also Geiger, *Urschrift*, p. 345, and Frankel, *Vorstudien zur Septuaginta*, p. 32.

³ See also note on 11⁽¹⁾.

⁴ See Prof. D. H. Müller, Vienna *Oriental Journal*, XI. p. 105. Cf. also Ps. 106 16 לאהרן קדוש ח'.

⁵ Cf. also Zech. 2 17.

⁶ The addition of the הארץ is probably taken from Ez. 46 3 and 9.

⁷ E.g. 3 23—4 1, 24—5 1, 4—6 30—7 17—12 6—15 6—16 10, 18—36 2, etc.

⁸ See Zunz, *Gottesdienstliche Vorträge*, p. 393 (2nd ed.) about the use of the terms פייטן, פייטם, פייטנא (ποιητής), by which are generally understood the poets or the hymnologists of the Synagogue. They created many new grammatical forms and words. Their writing is mostly a mosaic and their style is allusive. This style was fashionable among Jewish authors for many centuries. Moses Ibn Ezra, Sepher ha-Tarshish, where the references to Scripture are given in lines corresponding to the text, will give an idea of this form of composition to one unacquainted with it.

tendency betrayed by them. It consists (to use the words of Prof. Bacher, who first pointed it out) in borrowing a number "of ready-made expressions and phrases from the Scriptures, hereby already exhibiting that mosaic style which is characteristic of the later post-Talmudical authors¹." Referring the reader to the Professor's list as far as the O. H. is concerned, I will confine myself here to a few instances from the pages included in this volume:

B. S.	4	28	ויי׳ נלחם לך	B. S.	36	10	פאתי מואב'
"	6	30	פתיל תכלת	"	38	2	ישא משאות
"	13	23ᵃ	עב יגיעו	"	49	13ᶜ	וירפא את הריסתינו
"	14	23	המשקיף בעד חלונה	"	"	"	דלתים ובריח
"	16	19	קצבי הרים	"	"	16	תפארת אדם
"	"	25	אחוה דעי	"	50	8ᶜ	כפרה לבנון
"	35	15	דמעה על לחי	"	"	12ᶜ	ויקיפוהו כערבי נחל
"	"	18ᶜ	עד ימחין מתני	"	51	9	וארים מארץ קולי

These specimens are taken at random from all over our texts, and their number might easily be doubled and trebled. I have only to add that this Paitanic fashion can also be detected in various allusive adjectives and terms which form such a prominent feature in the later liturgy of the Synagogue. As such we may consider the expression נושבת (43 4ᶜ), an epithet for the earth³, the word רבה (ibid. vv. 23 and 25), a poetic name for the sea⁴, the term חכמי שיח (44 4ᶜ) applied to men occupying themselves with the study of the Torah⁵, the term כלה (ibid. v. 17), by which the deluge is understood⁶, the epithet ראשון (ibid. v. 22ᶜ), for the patriarch⁷ and the מלא תשלומות

¹ See *Jewish Quarterly Review*, July 1897, pp. 555 and 556. I will here only call attention to one more interesting specimen in O. H. not mentioned by Professor Bacher. I refer to 48 12ᶜ ומשל ברוחו וג׳ ולא מסל ברוחו בכל בשר. The phrase מ׳ ב׳ is evidently taken from Prov. 16 32, but with B. S. it means the same as the Rab. expression לא שלט בהן רמה ותולעה (B. T. *Baba Bathra* 17ᵃ.)

² See however gloss. For the Biblical references to all these quotations, see notes and the list.

³ In allusion to Exod. 16 35 ארץ נושבת, cf. also Is. 45 18 לשבת יצרה.

⁴ In allusion to רבה תהום Gen. 7 11, Is. 51 10 and elsewhere. This latter verse (25 in B. S.) as well as that which precedes it were undoubtedly suggested by Ps. 104 25 and 107 24.

⁵ It alludes to Ps. 119 vv. 15 (בפקודיך אשיחה), 23, 48, 78. The דרשונים במחקרותם of the preceding verse in B. S. (O. H. 44 4) was perhaps suggested by Prov. 25 2.

⁶ Alluding to Nahum 1 8 ובשטף עבר כלה יעשה.

⁷ In allusion to Lev. 26 42 and 45.

(48 8) by which Jehu is meant¹. The eulogistic term זכרו לטובה
(45 1), given to great men removed by death or otherwise translated
into the superlunar spheres, reminds us also, as I may here remark,
more of the Rabbinic usages of this expression² than of the similar
Biblical phrase³. The fact again, that there occur in B. S.'s 'Wisdom'
a number, however small, of forms and expressions to be found only
in the Paitanic literature, can hardly be considered as a mere accident.
At least it points to a certain similarity in its object and its treatment
of Biblical themes, as well as in its language⁴.

Another noteworthy feature is that B. S.'s production is not quite
free from Agadic elements or Midrash. These are traceable in certain
passages which already show a tendency towards expanding or developing
the word of the Scripture into some instructive lesson or edifying story⁵.
Such passages are:

B. S. 3 18—24, which is undoubtedly based on Ps. 131 1. But
whilst the Scriptural words were probably meant as a confession of
humility in a political respect, B. S. interpreted them as a warning against
spiritual pride and heresy⁶.

¹ See however Prof. Kaufmann in the *Monatsschrift*, vol. 41, p. 338, who takes the תשל in a different sense.
² B. T. *Berachoth* 3ª אליהו זכור לטוב. Cf. Zunz, *Zur Literatur u. Geschichte*, p. 321 seq.
³ Neh. 5 19, cf. also Prov. 10 7.
⁴ See notes on 3 14—6 36—7 16—13 10—50 5—to which may be added נעימות צדרה (*Kobez*, ed. Rosenberg, p. 113), partly suggested by לחת נעימה כצעדיו O. H. 45 9ᵇ; שביב אשו (*Kobez*, p. 112) O. H. 45 19ᶜ; וריח מפעליו כרקח כדרתיו (*Kobez*, p. 3) O. H. 49 1. The description of the beauty of בניהו בן יהוידע in the *Targum Sheni* to Esther 1 3 נגהא לכוכב, דמי etc. is probably also taken from B. S. 50 6, 7, 8. R. Simon b. Isaac in the Ophan to פסח חוה״ש שבת has the form לְיָשִׁש, cf. O. H. 47 23 (?מיושש). Of other possible quotations from B. S. are to be added R. Hai Gaon in his didactic poem קחה שירה (ed. Filib, Lemberg, 1889), lines 56 and 57 (כמת); reading כמה וולמר את ידריך מלאכה...וליטים ולשנים נשיבה בצפעונים תהי לחם הפיכה l. 89 (according to one MS.) ואל תדרוש לך מה בנכוחים l. 116 (4 4°); ותשכח שאלת רל על דלתך (3 21). R. Samuel Hannagid in his *Ben Mishle* (ed. Harkavy), p. 122 סור יהי חושף (O. H. 42 1); p. 133 אל תעש חברים עם רשעים (12 2, 3). Again, R. Abraham Ibn Ezra in his *Divan* (ed. Egers, Berlin, 1886), p. 77 עין אל על מפעלו גמול ירו ישיב לו p. 82 או מארץ מצרים ככורי כניתיך (36 12); אלו פינו מלא שירה...אין אנו מספיקים להודות prayer נשמת (15 19 and 35 19ᵃ). The passage in the was probably also suggested by B. S. (O. H. 42 17). It is rather questionable whether the author of the שיר היחוד (incorporated in the German Ritual for the Day of Atonement) who has such passages as לא החסרת ולא (O. H. 42 15ᵈ reading לָקְחוֹ) or כי בדרכך כל יצורך ומעשה חפצך במאמרך הערפת (O. H. 42 21ᶠ) was acquainted with our work or not. Thus far at least there is no sign indicating that the German Jews have ever made use of it.
⁵ See Zunz, *Gottesdienstliche Vorträge*, cc. 3 and 4, and Steinschneider, *Jewish Literature*, § 5, about *Midrash* and *Agadah*.
⁶ See Baethgen (as above) on this Ps. Interesting is the use of אל תמד (3 23), copied from Exod. 23 21, which verse is also made a subject of interpretation by a Rabbi in connexion with a heretical controversy (B. T. *Sanhedrin* 38ᵇ).

In B. S. **6** 17^(א) and 22¹ we have interpretations of words in a punning way, the Midrashic character of which will be best illustrated by the following passage from the Midrash, שמות נקרא לעני...אביון שהוא ז' מתאוה ממכן שהוא מסוכן'. Very interesting is the Rabbinic parallel to B. S.'s interpretation of the word מוסר. It runs thus: לדעת חכמה ומוסר אם חכמה למה מוסר אם יש באדם חכמה ר"ת נמסרין בידו', the only difference between the two Agadists being that, whilst B. S. plays upon the root יסר, the Rabbi makes the same pun upon the root מסר. As regards B. S.'s interpretation of names, his pun on Joshua נוצר להיות תשועה (46 1ᶜ) recalls the Rab. interpretation יושיעך יה יהושע"יהושע', whilst his pun ירבעם רחבעם...רחב אולת (47 23ᶜ) has a parallel in the Rab. passage ירבעם שעשה מריבה בעם', though it is possible that this method was suggested to him by Biblical etymologies of a similar nature⁴.

B. S. **15** 9 לא נאוה תהלה בפי רשע (suggested by Ps. 33 1 לישרים נאוה תהלה) and O. H. **47** 22ᶜ ואוהביו לא ישמיד (suggested by Ps. 145 20 ואת כל הרשעים ישמיד) are rather commonplace. But they are nothing but a דרשה on the Biblical verses just given, in accordance with the rule מכלל לאו אתה שומע הן ומכלל הן לאו'.

B. S. **16** 7 speaks of the נסיכי קדם המורים עולם'. The commentaries justly see in it an allusion to Gen. 6 1—4. But that the בני האלהים were princes, that they were thought entitled to be called 'the dominators of the world,' belongs of course to the region of legend or to the אגדה'. Perhaps we have here an allusion to נמרד, who according

---

¹ Cf. also O. H. **43** 8, gl. חדש כשמו וכ' and the blessing on the appearance of the new moon (B. T. *Sanhedrin* 42ᵃ) וללבנה אמר שתתחדש...שהן עתידין להתחדש כמותה. The preceding verse in B. S. (O. H. **43** 7) ומני חוק corresponds with the words חוק וזמן נתן להם in the same blessing. Probably **48** 20ᶜ ויושיעם ביד ישעיהו also belongs to this class.
² See *Midrash Mishleh*, ed. Buber, XXII. § 22, text and notes.
³ Ibid. I. § 2 and XXII. § 15.
⁴ B. T. *Sotah* 34ᵇ, cf. also N. T. Matt. 1 21.
⁵ B. T. *Sanhedrin* 101ᵇ. For other similar interpretations (רתן, קרה, etc.) see ibid. 109ᵇ.
⁶ Gen. 5 9—10 25, etc. It is to be noticed however that the Rabbis also claimed to have for this mode of interpretation a precedent in the Scriptures. See T. Jer. *Rosh Hashanah* 59ᵃ מכאן היה ר' מאיר דורש שמות, referring to Num. 21 9 (נחש נחשת). Cf. Bacher, *Agada der Tannaiten*, II. 38.
⁷ See notes to the vv. quoted from B. S. and cf. Siphré (ed. Friedmann), p. 83ᵃ (§ 46). See also L. Dobschütz, *Die Einfache Bibelexegese der Tannaim*, p. 40. Cf. also notes on 3 10 and 32 14. See also **15** 5 and Prov. 24 7.
⁸ See notes on the verse. I am now inclined to think that המורדים עליו is the most probable reading.
⁹ See Fr. and Ed. for references to the Agadic literature.

INTRODUCTION. 31

to the Rabbis was a king and also made the world rebel against God. נמרד הרשע שֶׁהִמְרִיד אֶת כל העולם כולו בְּמַלְכוּתוֹ[1].

B. S. **38** 5 חלא בעץ וגו׳ *Midrash* Tanchuma on Exod. **15** 24 derives a similar lesson from that verse ויורהו ה׳ עץ...הורהו בדרכיו...כמה מופלאין דרכיו של הקב״ה[2].

B. S. **44** 16 חנוך...וילקח אות דעת לדור ודור (cf. Jud. **3** 1 למען דעת דרת) is undoubtedly connected with some legend about Enoch's translation[3].

B. S. **45** 15ᶜ ולזרעו בימי שמים (cf. **50** 24⁽¹⁾) is, as Prof. Lévi points out, borrowed from Ps. **89** 30. He adds it is surprising that the authority for his description of the prerogatives of the priests should have recourse to a chapter of the Psalms which treats of the privileges of the dynasty of David. But this is a regular Rabbinic method. כיוצא בו גם זרע יעקב ודוד עבדי אם אינו ענין ליעקב...תנהו ענין לאהרן[4].

B. S. **46** 13ᶜ Samuel is called נזיר יי. There is no mention in the Scriptures that Samuel was a Nazir, but the Rabbis deduce it from certain verses in 1 Sam. and Jud. by means of גזירה שוה[5].

B. S. **47** 2 כי בחלב מורם מקדש כן דויד מישראל is suggested by Ps. **89** 20 הרימותי בחור מעם and Lev. **4** 8 ואת כל חלב...ירים, but the application, it is hardly necessary to say, strongly recalls the גזירה שוה[6].

B. S. **47** 10ᶜ לפני בקר ידרנן משפט is based on Ps. **119** 62 חצות לילה אקום להודות לך על משפטי צדקך (cf. also Ps. **57** 9), from which verses the Rabbis also inferred that David awoke in the middle of the night when he applied himself to the study of the Torah[8].

---

[1] B. T. *Pesachim* 94ᵇ.
[2] This would suggest כחו as the original reading. With regard to the reading in the Tanchuma see also Nachmanides, Com. to the Pentateuch Exod. **15** 25, who quotes דרכו ה׳.
[3] Cf. especially *Beth* Hammidrash, ed. Jellineth, v. p. 171 ממני שאני חנוך בן ירד בשחטא דור המבול ואמר לאל סור ממני...הצילני הקב״ה מפניהם (נו״א העלני הקב״ה מביניהם) להיות עד עליהם בשמי מרום לכל באי העולם. This would suggest the reading ל ולעדת (cf. Is. **19** 20 לאות ולעד) instead of דעת ל. It is however impossible to say how far back such legends may go.
[4] Cf. לב מדות of R. Eleazar, § 20. The same thing may also be observed of O. H. **44** 21ᶜ, directly copied from Ps. **72** 8 and applied by B. S. to Jacob.
[5] Mishnah, *Nazir*, IX. 5; C. Bacher, *Revue des Études Juives*, Vol. XXXVII. p. 315.
[6] Cf. also Num. **18** 29 and 30.
[7] See above, p. 27, note 1.
[8] B. T. *Berachoth* 3ᵇ. Of course it is possible that the correct reading in B. S. is ידין (instead of ירנן, cf. Smend, who reads ירין, and Lévi to this verse) and thus based on Jer. **21** 12 בית דוד דינו לבקר משפט. But the converting of a wish as to what the descendants of David should do into a fact that David has really done is also Agadic.

32   חכמת בן סירא

B. S. **49** 1 שם יאשיה כקטרת סמים is based on Cant. 1 3 לריח...שמן
תורק שמך, but the application of it to the righteous man is already
Agadic. Thus Gen. *Rabbah* xxxix. § 2 applies this verse to Abraham
דומה לצלוחית של אופפלסמין (ὀποβάλσαμον)¹.

Advances towards הלכה we have in such passages as ועל כל אלה
ברך וג' (**32** 13) which implies the institution of ברכת המזון, and ראה
קשת וברך עושיה (O. H. **43** 11) which formed the subject of a benediction
with the later Rabbis².

The foregoing remarks tend to show that B. S. was not free
from the interpreting tendencies which are the main characteristics of
a Rabbi. In fact he thought like a Rabbi and so did his contem-
poraries whom he invites to the בית המדרש (**51** 23) the *House of
Research*, the regular meeting place of the ordinary Rabbi⁴. The
subject of the research was naturally the Scriptures. The משל, either
in the sense of metaphor, or of parable, or of pregnant sayings was
the favoured way of illustrating the Scriptures⁵. But if he thought like
a Rabbi he wrote like a Paitan. His success in producing a work, "the
predominant character" of which "is classical," is, as already hinted at,
to be ascribed to the author's knowledge of the Bible, the language
and style of which he was imitating and from which he was constantly
copying, whilst his most admired "boldness and freedom" in employing
Biblical phrases is in most cases nothing more than a mere Paitanic
artificiality so common in post-Biblical Hebrew poetry⁶. In fact B. S.
should be rather described as the first of the Paitanim than as one

¹ Cf. also Cant. *Rabbah* to this verse and *Agadath Shir Hashirim*, pp. 12, 54 and 55.

² See B. T. *Berachoth* 48ᵇ where this institution is attributed to various Biblical personages, which is mere legend; but still points to a high antiquity. Of course the origin is to be sought in Deut. 8·10.

³ See B. T. *Berachoth* 59ᵃ. From **38** 17ᵈ (see notes) and **22** 7 it is also clear that certain customs about "the days of mourning" codified in the later *Halachah* were already known to B. S. On this Halachic activity of B. S. see also Stade, *Geschichte des Volkes Israel*, II. 302 (Berlin, 1888).

⁴ Cf. *Mishnah, Berachoth*, IV. 2.

⁵ See Rab. Dict. under משל. Cf. also *Siphre* (ed. Friedmann, 117ᵇ) דורש מן התורה במשל.

⁶ It will be noticed that when Canonical writers reproduce Biblical history (cf. for instance Pss. 78, 104, 105, and Neh. 9), though naturally they sometimes use phrases from the Pentateuch, their style is homogeneous throughout; they tell their tale in their own way without the least conscious imitation or artificiality. On the other hand the language of B. S.'s Hymnus Patrum impresses one at the first glance as more ancient than that of Nehemiah, but the impression passes away when we find that it is a mere patchwork. Cf. for instance the praise of Abraham extending only over five verses (O. H. **44** 19–21ᵃ), which is made up of quotations borrowed from three Canonical books, Genesis, Psalms, and Nehemiah (see list).

INTRODUCTION.

of the last of the canonical writers. But great as his acquaintance with the Scriptures was, and strained as his efforts were in imitating them, he failed in the end. For, as is the case with all imitators, in unguarded moments such phrases, idioms, particles and peculiar constructions escaped him as to furnish us with a sufficiently strong number of criteria, betraying—as already indicated—the real character of the language of his time.

It must first be pointed out that the statement made, by some students, that the relative שׁ never occurs[1] in B. S.'s 'Wisdom,' is not borne out by the new discoveries. It does occur not less than nine times[2]. This however would prove very little, as we meet the שׁ even in the early books of the O. T. As the real criteria of his failure we may consider such words and phrases as the following:

B. S.	3	10	אל תתכבד בקלון אביך	B. S.	31	3	לקבל תענוג
"	"	16	מזיד	"	"	8	ואחר ממון
"	"	24	ידעות מתעות	"	32	5(1)	נאים דברים יפים
"	4	8	והשיבהו שלום	"	38	17ª	כיוצא בו
"	5	10	סמוך עלדעתך	"	40	29	אין חייו למנות חיים
"	7	18	ואח תלוי	"	42	8*	ונוטל עצה
"	13	13	יוהיה זהיר	"	45	1	זכרו לטובה
"	"	22ª	ודבריו מבוערין	"	"	24	כהונה גדולה
"	14	18ᵉ	בשר ודם	"	49	8	מרכבה
"	16	14	כל העושה צדקה וג'	"	51	12ᵈ(14)	למלך מלכי מלכים
"	30	12ª	כשהוא קטן	"	"	17	אתן דודאה
"	"	17(1)	וליורד שאול	"	"	23	בבית מדרשי
"	"	18	לפני גלול	"	"	24	אילו

[1] See Messrs Cowley and Neubauer, *O. H.* p. xiii. note. Cf. also Prof. Driver's notice in the *Guardian*, July, 1896, p. 1029.
[2] Viz.:—3 22—13 5 (?)—14 16(1) and 18ª—16 3ᵉ and 15—30 11(1), 12—31 10ᵃ.
[3] Post-Talmudical philosophic writers have רעות המשבשות.
[4] Cf. also O. H. 42 8ᵉ והיית זהיר באמת. Even Eccles. 12 12 has הזהר. *Pirke Aboth*, II. 1 הוי זהיר.
[5] See notes, but the use of יפה in connexion with דבר as well as the whole phrase gives it a decided Rab. complexion.
[6] See above p. 29, note 2.
[7] A regular Rab. term. Cf. *Siphra*, ed. Weiss 80ᵈ בגדי כהונה גדולה. See also Lévi's Com. on this passage in B. S.
[8] As a term of the vision of Ezekiel occurs only in the Rab. literature. Cf. Rab. Dict. *s. v.* מרכבה.

חכמת בן סירא

It should be observed that the above specimens are strictly confined to Rabbinic instances, omitting all those New-Hebraisms occurring frequently enough in B. S., but for which some authority can be found in the later canonical writings[1]. Nor are there included in it a whole number of Aramaisms, as נתקל (13 23ᶜ), יתבעבע (14 4) etc., or such strange forms as ותמור (3 14), נבהן (4 29), עברון (7 16), קצפון (30 23ᵃ).

These specimens are however enough to show that in the times of B. S. the New-Hebrew dialect had long advanced beyond the transitory stage known to us from the later Biblical books, and had already reached, both in respect of grammar and of phraseology, that degree of development to which the Mishnah bears testimony. Had B. S.'s ambition not been to produce a second Proverbs he would have written his 'Wisdom' in the style of the *Pirke Aboth*. But being an imitator by choice he did not escape the fate of his class. He would of course be niggardly with the use of the perfect with the simple *Waw*, but he would not fail to blunder into such a decidedly Rab. construction as 16 14 exhibits. He would use the Biblical חרוץ and פנינים for money and boundless treasures (31 5, 6) but would betray himself three lines further by ממון (31 8). He would even be most careful to avoid the New-Hebrew conjunction שמא (substituting for it the Bib. פן 7 3, 13 10, 42 9ᶜ etc.), but would employ such infinitive forms as לירד and such particles as כיוצא בו.

The results at which we thus arrive with regard to B. S. are the following: (1) that he was a conscious imitator; (2) that the classical portions in his work are due to his skilful manipulating of Biblical passages and patching them together; (3) that his composition shows already such traces of an artificial way of interpreting and using the contents of the Scriptures as are only to be found in post-Biblical writers; (4) that with all his skill and caution his language is full of later Hebrew expressions, even furnishing us with criteria pointing to the highest development of the Rabbinic dialect.

Now none of the canonical writings ever shows the least sign of conscious imitation; no trace of Paitanic artificiality is to be detected in any of them, even when they reproduce words and sentiments of their

---

[1] A complete list of New-Hebraisms of this kind would fill many pages. In fact the book is full of them. Many are indicated in the notes. See also Lévi's Com. on the portion of B. S. included in O. H.

INTRODUCTION.

predecessors; and lastly they are free from late developments of the language such as are displayed by B. S.

From these results two conclusions appear to follow:

(1) that when the same phrases occur in one of the canonical writers and in B. S., the balance of probability is strongly in favour of the supposition that B. S. was the imitator of the canonical writer and not *vice versa*.

(2) that as clear examples of such imitation by B. S. can be found (see list, pp. 13—25) in the case of *all* the canonical books, with the doubtful exception of the Book of Daniel, these books must as a whole have been familiar to B. S., and must therefore be much anterior to him in date.

This view, especially as regards the Psalms, is further confirmed by the hymn of B. S. which the new discoveries have brought to light. I am referring to *vv.* $12^{c(1)}$—$12^{c(15)}$ in the fifty-first chapter, omitted by the Versions but nevertheless restoring to us an authentic piece of Ben Sira's 'Wisdom.' The reason for its omission by the Greek translator, who in this respect, as in so many others, was followed by his Syrian successor, is not hard to conjecture. Living at a time when the house of Zadok was already superseded by the Maccabean line, the grandson of B. S. recoiled from giving publicity to a hymn which claimed that the בני צדוק were specially selected for the priesthood[1]. But it is just the prominence given to the house of Zadok in the hymn which establishes its authenticity. For after the unworthy part played by the high priests of the house of Zadok during the Hellenistic troubles, it is highly improbable that any pious Jew—such as the author of this hymn evidently was—would feel so enthusiastic about this family, that their continuance in the sacred office would form the special theme of his thanksgiving to God[2]. Such an enthusiasm could only have been displayed by one

---

[1] See **51** $12^{c(9)}$. Cf. Geiger, *Zeit. d. Morgenländischen Ges.* XII. 536, who attributed the exclusion of Ecclesiasticus from the Canon to the Sadducean tendencies of its author. This hypothesis however assumes the close of the Canon at a much later period than 200 B.C., which is very doubtful.

[2] See *Mishnah*, Middoth v. 5 וכך היו אומרים...וברוך הוא שבחר באהרן ובבניו לעמור ולשרת לפני ה' בבית וכו'. The formula seems to be very old, though it is omitted in the Cambridge MS. (ed. Lowe, p. 188ᵃ). Cf. J. T. *Yoma*, 44ᵇ where it is stated that one of the eight benedictions of the High Priest on the day of Atonement was concluded with the words הבוחר בכהנים, thus omitting all reference to any special priestly family.

חכמת בן סירא

who knew the best of the Zadokides, namely Simon the Just, and who prayed so fervently for the perpetuation of God's grace upon the high priest and his children (**50** 24, 24$^{(1)}$), that is by Ben Sira himself. Now the model for this hymn is, it is hardly necessary to say, Ps. **136**. I think it also probable that our hymn is in a defective state, having had originally the same number (26) of verses as Ps. **136**. But enough remains of it to give us some insight, however slight, into the state of religious thought in the times of B. S. We learn first from it that the theocratic tendency of those ages has been unduly emphasized by some writers. At least it never went so far as to suppress the devotion to the house of David. Even with such a strong partisan of the High Priest Simon as B. S. was, loyalty to the descendants of Zadok (**51** 12$^{(9)}$) went hand in hand with prayer for the restoration of the Davidic family (**51** 12$^{(9)}$), in which the Messianic hope was embodied. If the first was commanded by the Torah, the second was guaranteed by the Prophets, the fulfilment of whose words is a subject of prayer with B. S. (**36** 16). To the harmony of these two loyalties, antagonistic as they may appear to some modern eyes, all subsequent Jewish literature bears witness, in which the restoration of the priestly order to the service in the temple and the advent of the Messiah ben David form such a prominent part and are equally prayed for.

We learn further from this hymn that what occupied the minds of such latter-day psalmists was the history of their own times, not the events of the remote past. Thus living, as it would seem, in comparatively peaceful times, which however were preceded by a great crisis in the history of the nation, B. S. gives thanks for the rebuilding of the city and the temple and for the gathering of the outcast of Israel (**51** 12$^{(d(6)}$ $^{(7)})^1$. What he further praises God for are the two great religious institutions of his age; the priesthood as represented by the house of Zadok, and "the house of David," which, embodying the hope of Israel in the future, passed with B. S. for a living reality. The praise of the God

---

[1] These two verses may perhaps refer to the troubles in Palestine about 312 B.C. (see Grätz, *Geschichte*, 1J. p. 229 seq.). The peaceful times which followed would then fall in the reign of Simon I. The date of B. S. would accordingly have to be placed about 280 B.C. But the history of those times is still so obscure that it is hardly possible to arrive at any certain conclusion.

of the Fathers (51 12ᵈ⁽¹⁰⁾ ⁽¹¹⁾ ⁽¹²⁾), though Biblical in its origin, is at the same time a characteristic feature of the Jewish liturgy. In fact the first Benediction of the Eighteen Benedictions is called אבות "Fathers¹." The expression "King of Kings of Kings" (51 12ᶜ⁽¹⁴⁾) shows also the marked Persian influence to which B. S. was as much subject as any later Rabbi who uses the same appellation for God². We see thus clearly that what inspired our psalmist was the present and the future of his people. To these he refers in plain language, and in the language of his time. Is it now possible that Psalms written about the same age or even later should not have a single distinct and unmistakeable reference to the events of their own time? Is it conceivable that B. S., writing in comparatively uneventful times, should be entirely given to the present, whilst the author of the 136th Psalm for instance, writing 50 (if not 130) years later, should not have a single reference to the great events of his generation or a generation before him³, and instead of making the Maccabean victories the subject of his thanksgivings should praise God for the Exodus from Egypt? Is it possible that B. S. should make the selection of the house of Zadok the theme of his thanks to God, whilst no Maccabean writer should thank God in plain language for replacing it by the new dynasty? Is there any adequate reason why B. S. in celebrating his hero should give us his name, "Simon b. Johanan" (50 1), whilst the Maccabean heroes should be typified by Joshua, David, Solomon, Saul, and alluded to in all possible obscure ways, but never called by their right names⁴? Is it again possible that B. S., with all his care as an imitator and writing only two or three hymns, should so forget himself as to use an appellation of God מ׳ מ׳ מ׳ on which the Persian influence is so manifest, whilst all the hosts of Psalmists of the Persian and the Greek period which the Psalter is supposed to represent should so far succeed in escaping this influence that it left no decisive mark on their language? All these considerations make it a certainty that the Psalms cannot possibly be a production of

---

¹ B. T. *Megillah* 11ᵃ. For the expression אבות עולם (O. H. p. 20 at the top) cf. *Mishnah Edoyoth*, l. 4.
² See Landau, as referred to in the notes.
³ See Prof. Cheyne's *Origin of the Psalter*, p. 50.
⁴ See Prof. Cheyne's index to the above cited book under Maccabees. See also ibid. p. 26 about Simon the high priest, the supposed subject of Ps. 110.

the age in which B. S. composed his 'Wisdom.' The literary ambition of that age did not, as the Wisdom of B. S. clearly shows, presume either to write Scripture or even to add to it; it was content with studying the inspired documents of the past, interpreting them, and imitating them.

S. SCHECHTER.

NOTES.

III.

8. [במאמר] See Esther i. 15. Usually אָמַר. Cf. below, iv. 24, O. H. xlii.
15. [יְשִׁינוֹךְ כל ברכות] Cf. Deut. xxviii. 2. [עֲבוּר] Usually with the prefix בְּ. Cf. below, xxxviii. 5, 17ᶜ, li. 20ᵇ and 21. But some Jewish authorities wrote עֲבוּר; see *Ha-Tishbi*, *s. v.*
9. [חיסר שרש] Gr. and Syr. ת' בית. [תנתש נטע] Is. li. 16 לנטע ש' וליסר א'.
10. [אל תתכבד בקלון] A Rab. term, see Gen. *Rabbah* i. 5, T. Jer. *Chagigah* 77 c, *Derech Erez Zutta* vii. For the second clause, cf. Prov. xvii. 6.
11. [ומרבה חטא מקלל אמו] Agrees more with the Syr. Cf. Lev. xxvi. 16.
12. [תעצבהו] Gr. תעצבנו, see Ed.
13. [עזוב לו] מעזוב לו Exod. xxiii. 5, which according to some commentaries means to support, to help. [חיין] Gr. חילך.
14. [ותמור] Cf. below, iv. 10. The form תמור instead of תמורת occurs often in the *Paitanic* literature. See קובץ מעשי ידי גאונים קדמונים ed. Rosenberg pp. 12, 112 and 113. Cf. also Zunz *Syn. Poesie* p. 409. For this and the next verse, see the Syr.
16. [ומזיר] Part. *hif.* of זור never occurring however in the O. T. See Rab. Dict. [בוראו] Eccles. xii. 1.
18. [מעט] imper. *piel* of מעט, see B. T. *Chulin* 60 b לכי ומעטי את ולא הלכתי בגדלות ובנפלאות ממני. Cf. [גדולת] Ps. cxxxi. 1 עצמך. also Jer. xlv. 5 and Job xlii. 3. The Gr. and the Syr. took it a different way. [עולם] in the later sense of *world*. Cf. Eccles. iii. 11 and Comm. as well as below, xvi. 7.
19ᵇ. Only to be found in the Syr. and in some Gr. MSS., see Fr. *v.* 18 n. The first ינלה is cancelled in the MS.
21. פלאות etc.] This is undoubtedly the correct reading (not במופלא), the saying being suggested by the Ps. quoted *v.* 18, see also Original Hebrew xliii. 25. The versions agree more or less with Rabbinical quotations. Cf. The Quotations from Ecclus. in Rab. Literature by S. Schechter in the *Jewish Quarterly Review*, III. pp. 690 and 689, and Messrs Cowley and Neubauer, Original Hebrew, etc. p. xix. [אל תחקור] Cf. O. H. xliii. 30ᶜ.
22. [שהורשית] *hof.* of רָשָׁה to have power, or authority. Cf. Levy and

40   חכמת בן סירא   [CH. 3

Kohut s. v. In the O. T. only the noun רשיון occurs (Ezra iii. 7). Note the use of שֶׁ for אשר occurring for the first time in the Cairo text. [עסק See below xxxviii. 24, O. H. xl. 1, Glossary, *ibid.* p. xxxiv.

23. [תמר Exod. ויותר מרמה בני הזהר. Eccles. xii. 12 [וביותר ממך xxiii. 21.

24. ורמיתות] Cf. Ps. xvii. 12 (דמינו). In the sense of illusions it occurs frequently in the post-Talmudic literature, see Ibn Tabbon's פירוש מלות זרות at the end of the מורה נבוכים. [רעות מתעות for which the versions read רעות. For a similar confusion see LXX. Dan. xii. 4 (reading הרעות for הדעת—see *Die Heilige Schrift* ed. Kautzsch, *Beilagen* p. 88). See also Ed. Ecclus. xxv. 9.

26. [לב כבד Cf. Exod. viii. 28. [ואורב טובות ינרע בהם Agrees with the Syr., cf. Eccles. ii. 3 נהג בחכמה. The Gr. (reading with Fr. after several MSS. ἀπολεῖται) seems to have read וא' חובות ירבץ בהם; see LXX. to Dan. i. 10 (וחיבתם) and to Gen. xx. 4 (תהרג).

27. [ומתחולל Cf. Jer. xxiii. 19 and Job xv. 20 and commentaries and Heb. and Rab. Dict. s. חול and חיל. In our case the parallel passage below, v. 5, is decisive for the meaning "waiting" (cf. Ps. xxxvii. 7 והתחולל) i.e. "he who abides in his sin."

25. The order agrees with the Syr., but neither the Gr. (which is only to be found in some MSS., see Fr. v. 23 n. and Ed.) nor the Syr. agrees with our text in the second clause. The simile was probably suggested by Prov. vii. 2.

28. [אל תרוץ לרפאות... כי These words are omitted both in the Gr. and the Syr. For the sentiment cf. Prov. ix. 8, 9.

29. [אזן מקשבת לחכמה תשמח Cf. Prov. ii. 2.

30. [וצדקה תכפר חטאת Cf. Dan. iv. 24. See also O. H. xl. 24. *Aboth* and *R. Nathan* iv. כפרה אחת...ואיזו זו גמילות חסדים.

31. [פועל טוב יקראנו ברכיו Is. xli. 2 צדק יקראהו לרגלו. The Gr. probably read יזכרנו for יקראנו.

IV.

1. [ואל תדאיב נפש א' תעשק Cf. Prov. xvii. 5. Gr. perhaps [אל תלעג Cf. Deut. xxviii. 65 and Jer. xxxi. 12. [ומר נפש 1 Sam. xxii. 2.

2. [רווח Probably corruption of רוח. Syr. לא תכאיב רוחה. [אל תפוח Cf. Ps x. 5. Cf. also Num. *Rabba* xx. לפוח את נפשו "to annoy his soul." [ואל תתעלם ממדכדי נפש ממדכדך Read, part. pass. *pilp.* of דוך. Cf. *Lev. Rabbah* xxxiv. 6 דך מרובדך, "The poor man is called דך because he is crushed" (see Jastrow, p. 306).

3. חמרמרו מעי דך. [אל תחמיר מעי דך *hif.* of חמר. Cf. Lam. i. 20 ונחמרו. בני מעיה 3. Mishnah *Chullin* III. The Gr. possibly understood it in the sense of to "pile up," to "load." Cf. Rab. Dict. s. חמר. See however LXX. Lam. i. 20, ii. 11 Heb. 15. The second clause is omitted in the Gr. and only a trace of it is to be found in the Syr. (לא תכאב).

4ᵃ. תָבוֹה וּ] etc. Cf. Ps. xxii. 25. שְׁאִלוֹת [Read שְׁאֵילוֹת.

5ᵇ. וְלֹא תִתֵּן לוֹ מָקוֹם לְקַלְּלְךָ] · Cf. Job xvi. 18, see also *Mishnah, Parah* III. אַל תִּתְּנוּ מָקוֹם (var. יד) לִצְדוּקִים לִרְדוֹת בָּנוּ.

6. בְּכַאֵב] Syr. בְּבַל. צוֹרוּ] Gr. and Syr. יוֹצְרוּ.

7. הָאֹהֵב] imper. *hif.* of אָהַב. See Rab. Dict. s. אָרַב. הַכְאֵף] imper. *hif.* of כָּאַף or כּוּף—Cf. below, xxx. 20ᵃ. See also Levy, *s. v.* כָּאַף and כּוּף. מכס

8. וְהֵשִׁיבוּהוּ שָׁלוֹם] *Mishnah, Berachoth* II. I וּמֵשִׁיב שָׁלוֹם. Cf. O. H. xli. 21ᵇ.

9. תִּקְצַר] Gr. תִּקְרִין.

10ᵃ. אָב לִיתוֹמִים] Cf. Ps. lxviii. 6. See also Job xxix. 13, 26. וַתָּמוּר] See above, iii. 14.

10ᶜ. וְאַל יִקְרָאֲךָ בֵּן] Cf. 2 Sam. vii. 14 and Hosea ii. 1. וְיַצִּילְךָ מִשַּׁחַת] Omitted in the Syr., with which the verse agrees mostly.

11. חָכְמוֹת] in the *singular*, as in Prov. i. 20 and ix. 1. See Olshausen's *Lehrbuch d. Hebräischen Sprache*, p. 418. לְמֹרָה] Syr. אַלְפַת. The Gr. probably read רוֹמְמָה. Cf. *Perek R. Meir*, where it is said of the Torah (the *Chochmah* of the Rab. literature) וּמְרוֹמַמְתּוֹ עַל כָּל הַמַּעֲשִׂים. וְתָעִיר] for which the Syr. read וְתָאִיר, whilst the Gr. perhaps read, as was suggested to me, תְּעוֹדֵד. See however LXX. to Jer. xxvi. (Gr. xxxviii.) 4, where some MSS. have for תְּעוֹדֵד, ἐπιλήψῃ. This points to the reading וַתַּעַד (Hos. ii. 15) "adorned," cf. Prov. i. 9 and below, vi. 30 (note).

12. Cf. Prov. viii. 35.

13. וְתֹמְכֶיהָ] etc. Cf. Prov. iii. 16, 35. וַיְחֹנֵּנּוּ] for which the Gr. and Syr. probably read וַיְחֻנֵּנּוּ.

14. The textual corruptions of the second clause of this verse can only be accounted for by assuming that the scribe was not always able to read the MS. he had before him, and thus copied as many letters as he could discern. The Gr. suggests the emendations וְאֵל אוֹהֵב מֵאֲהָבֶיהָ, cf. Prov. viii. 17. For the expression מְשָׁרְתֵי קֹדֶשׁ see J. T. *Berachoth* 14ᵇ.

15. אֶמֶת] Cf. Prov. viii. 7. בַּחֲרִי] The Gr. בְּטַם, cf. Prov. i. 33. Verse 16 is omitted.

17ᵃ. כִּי בְהִתְנַכֵּר] Cf. Gen. xlii. 7. 17ᶜ. יִבְחָרֻנוּ] The versions suggest אֲבַחֲנֵנּוּ. בְּנִסְיוֹנוֹת] Cf. below, vi. 7 and xiii. 11ᶜ. 17ᵈ. וְעַד עֵת יִמָּלֵא מָלֵא אוֹתָם חָכְמַת לֵב] Cf. Exod. xxxv. 35. לִבּוֹ בִי] Cf. also Ecclus. ii. 17.

18. וְגָלִיתִי] Cf. *Perek R. Meir* וּמְגַלִּין לוֹ רָזֵי תוֹרָה.

19. וְיֹסַרְתִּיהוּ] "I will bind him." Cf. Hosea vii. 15, A. V. וְנָטָה מֵאִתִּי probably corruption of וּנְטֹתִיהוּ.

19⁽¹⁾. לַשְּׁדָרִים] Cf. below, xv. 14. The verse agrees more with the Syr., whilst the Gr. shows traces both of 19 and 19⁽¹⁾.

20. עֵת הַמֹּן] Read זְמַן. Cf. Eccles. iii. 1 עֵת וּזְמַן.

21. בְּשֵׂאת] The dot indicates that the letter has to be cancelled. מַשְׂאֵת עָוֹן] Cf. Lev. xxii. 16, see also Zeph. iii. 18. כָּבוֹד וְחֵן] Cf. Ps. lxxxiv. 12.

חכמת בן סירא

22. 'נ על] Read אל. Cf. Lévi on O. H. xlii. 1ᶜ. תכשל] Read with the Gr. and Syr. תכלם.

23. בעולם] Syr. בעתו (cf. Prov. xv. 23), Gr. בשלום (or perhaps בעת שלום), which latter seems to be the correct reading. אל תצפין] Cf. O. H. xli. 15.

24. במענה לשון] Cf. Prov. xvi. 1.

25⁽¹⁾. אל תסרב] *piel* from סרב, see Driver, O. H. p. xxxiv., meaning to contradict, to refuse. It occurs frequently in the Rab. literature. Cf. the phrase in B. T. *Pesachim* 86 b ואין מסרבין לגדול. Syr. אל תסרוב, Gr. μὴ ἀντίλεγε. האל] Gr. and Syr. האמת. The second clause is in both versions quite different.

הי ב ל ר

26. לשוב] Gr. and Syr. מלהורות. שבולת] Is. xxvii. 12. The Syr. שבלות. The dots on the margin point to some corrections which the scribe intended but failed to supply.

27. תצע] Apocop. *imperf.* of the root צעה. תמאן] Gr. תשא.

27⁽¹⁾. כאשר כרצונו] Read רצונו. This verse corresponds with Gr. and Syr. viii. 14. Our text agrees more with the latter.

28. היעצה על] Probably the *imper. nif.* (with *scriptio plena*) of עצה. See Heb. and Rab. Dict., *s. v.* עצה (or עצי). In our case it would mean to be pressed or fixed. The *nif.* does not occur anywhere else, unless the איעצה עליך עיני in Ps. xxxii. 8 is interpreted to mean "I will fix my eyes upon thee," which is not impossible (notwithstanding the traditional punctuation). See commentaries to this verse, especially Delitzsch (English ed. 1897, p. 497) and Baethgen about the rendering of the Septuagint. Gr. and Syr. "strive" understood התעצם to which it is related, see Rab. Dict. *s. v.* עצם.

28⁽¹⁾. בעל שתים] B. T. *Baba Mezia* 48 a שלא ידבר אחד בפה ואחד בלב. ואל לש'] Read ועל as in Ps. xv. 3. Cf. below v. 14ᵃ.

29. נבהן] See Levy, *s. v.* גבהות and נאות (from גאות). ורפי etc. Cf. Prov. xviii. 9. ורשיש] part. *Qal* of רשש, see Heb. Dict. As this scarcely goes well with רפה, the Syr. נשיש is probably to be restored.

30. בכלב] so Syr. Cf. Septuagint, 1 Sam. xxv. 3 (*Keri* כלבי). Gr. בלביא, see Ed. במלאכתך] which probably came in from the preceding verse. Gr. and Syr. בעבדיך.

31. מתן] Cf. O. H. xl. 28.

V.

1. יש לאל] See Gen. xxx. 29, Micah ii. 1 and below xiv. 11.

1⁽¹⁾. This verse agrees with the Syr.

2. Omitted in the Syr., but the Gr. ἐξακολουθεῖ represents תלך אחרי though it shows also traces of 1⁽¹⁾. בחמודות] Cf. below xiv. 14.

3. בחו] Read as suggested by the Syr. בחי. The second clause agrees with the Syr. Cf. Eccles. iii. 15.

4. ומה] Read ומי. Cf. below, vi. 36.

4⁽¹⁾. The first clause of this verse is to be found in the Syr.

NOTES ON THE TEXT.

5. אל] R. Saadyah (*Sepher Haggalui*, ed. Harkavy, p. 176) ואל. R. Nissim's quotation in the *Sepher Maasiyoth* (ed. pr. Constantinople, 1519) ועל הסליחה. Later editions have ובסליחה. Cf. *Jewish Quarterly Review*, III. pp. 695 and 704.

6ª. Cf. Gr. below, vii. 9. R. Nissim, *ibid.* ותאמר רחמיו רבים לרוב עונותינו.

6ᶜ. ואל רשעים] Read (with R. Saadyah, and R. Nissim, *ibid.* and the parallel below, xvi. 11ᶜ) ועל. רנזו] R. Saadyah, *ibid.* and R. Nissim, *ibid.* עז, cf. Ezra viii. 22. Below xvi. 11ᶜ יגיה רנזו.

7. ואל תתעבר] Cf. Prov. xiv. 16, of which the verse would seem to be a mere paraphrase. But the parallel passages below, vii. 16, suggest that we have to correct the ב in those places into כ derived from a root עבר meaning, as in Syriac, to continue, to tarry.

8. Cf. Prov. xi. 4.

9. שבולת] Gr. and Syr. שביל.

10. סמוך על דעתך] B. T. *Baba Mezia* 84b סמך ר"א בר"ש אדעתיה. See also *Aruch Hashalem s. v.* סמך.

11. ובארך רוח] Cf. Eccles. vii. 8.

12. אם יש אתך] to which the Syr. added (probably after Job xxxiii. 32) ידך על פיך] Cf. Prov. xxx. 32. חכמה the Gr. דבר.

13. ביוד] Read ביד. Cf. Prov. xviii. 21.

14ª. בעל שתים] See above, iv. 28⁽¹⁾. See also Ecclus. xxviii. 13.

14ᶜ. רעהו] Gr. and Syr. רעה.

15. תשגה] Gr. תשחת. Cf. Fr. and Ed.

VI.

1ᵇ. וקלון ת׳ חרפה] Cf. Prov. xviii. 3 ועם קלון חרפה.

2. אל תתנני] Cf. above, iv. 22. See also Ps. xxvii. 12 אל תפול ביד נפשך. ותעבה חילך עליך] *piel* of עבה to make thick, fatten, see Deut. xxxii. 15 אלוה...ויטש עבית. שמנת Perhaps we should read חלבך על שארך for חילך עליך, cf. Ps. xvii. 10, lxxiii. 7 and Job xv. 25—27, which would account both for the mistake of the versions reading שרך for שארך, or לשרך (cf. Prov. iii. 8) and for the corruption of the Hebrew text caused by the על with which the next verse begins. Micah vii. 3 suggests the emendation ותעבת, but the meaning there is obscure. The Syr. תבעא איך תורא חילך (See Dr Taylor's note on the English Translation).

4. נפש עיה] Cf. Is. lvi. 1. See also O. H. xl. 20. תשינם] Gr. and Syr. תשימם.

5. חיך ערב] Cf. Cant. v. 16. See also O. H. xlix. 1ᶜ. שואלו] Read שואלות. Syr. שאלות. Gr. perhaps מלאות.

44   חכמת בן סירא   [CH. 6

6. אנשי ש׳] Syr. שאלי ש׳. Cf. the quotation in B. T. *Sanhedrin* 100 b. R. Saadyah *Sepher Haggalui*, p. 178: רבים יהיו אנשי שלומיך גלה סודך לאחד מני אלף agreeing in the second clause more with the Talmud.

7. בניסון] Read בניסיון as above, iv. 17ᵃ and below, xiii. 11ᶜ. R. Saadyah (as above) במסה. See Ecclus. xxvii. 17 (Syr.).

8. ואל י׳] R. Saadyah (as above) ולא.

9. ריב חרפתך] Cf. 1 Sam. xxvii. 39. יחשוף] Cf. O. H. xlii. 1 and Driver's Glossary, p. xxxii.

10. Cf. Ecclus. xxxvii. 5. חבר שלחן] Cf. the Rab. expression נירי שולחן מלכים (T. Jer. *Kiddushin* 65ᵇ).

11. The second clause agrees with the Syr.

12. יהפך בך] Cf. Amos iv. 11 in a different sense.

13. השמר] R. Saadyah (as above) הזהר.

14. תקוף. See Dan. iv. 27. Cf. Siegfried-Stade's *Heb. Wörterbuch*, p. 894. Cf. the forms גלול xxx. 18 and צדוך O. H. xxix. 33 and xlii. 23ᵇ, Gl.

16. צרור חיים] 1 Sam. xxv. 29. Gr. and Syr. צרי ח׳. ישיגם] Read with the Gr. ישיגנו or refer the affix to חיים.

17ᵇ. The omission of the first clause of this verse is due probably to the fact that it began with about the same words ירא י׳ יישר with which the last verse finished. 17⁽¹⁾. וכשמו כן מ׳] Cf. Ecclus. xxxvii. 1. Perhaps it is a play upon the word רע, cf. Prov. xviii. 24 ואיש רעים להתרועע. B. S. had decidedly a tendency towards playing on words. Cf. below, v. 17ᵇ and O. H. xliii. 8 (Gloss), xlvi. 1ᶜ (reading with Gl.—see Lévi, Smend and Schlatter—כשמו for בימיו) and xlvii. 23ᶜ.

19ᵃ. The context proves that v. 18 was omitted by mistake and has to be supplied from the versions.

19ᶜ. ולמתר] Cf. B. T. *Erubin* 22ᵃ למחר לקבל שכרם. Gr. and Syr. ולמדר.

20. חסר לב] Prov. vi. 32, vii. 7 and elsewhere. See also below, xvi. 23.

21. משא] Cf. Zech. xii. 3 מעמסה. Gr. מסה.

22. כשמה] Read בשמו. Perhaps a play upon the verb יסר, that is to say, that מוסר means more than mere instruction, but also implies discipline and chastisement. Cf. above, v. 17⁽¹⁾. ולא לרבים היא נכוחה] See Dict. s. נכחה. For the sentiment see Job xxxii. 9. See Dr Taylor's note on the English Translation.

21⁽¹⁾. This verse and the next are to be found in the versions in chapter xxvii. 5 and 6. The verse agrees more with the Gr.

22⁽ᵃ⁾. עבדת עין] which is confirmed by the versions. Still I am inclined to consider it an Aram. and read עברת, meaning branch or bough (see Levy, *Ch. Wb.* II. p. 200, s. v. עוברא i.). For a somewhat similar confusion (of עֲבָרָה and עֲבָדָה) see Nestle, *Marginalien*, p. 52. Cf. also R. Joseph Kimchi (in the *Sepher Ha-shorashim* of R. David Kimchi, ed. Lebrecht, col. 498) who takes

NOTES ON THE TEXT.

the עֶבְרָתוֹ in Prov. xxii. 8 to be related to the Aram. עִיבּוּרָא and thus meaning as much as תְּבוּאָה, whilst the Septuagint reads there עֶבְרָתוֹ, ἔργων (see Wildboer's Commentary to Prov. p. 64, German edition). חֶשְׁבּוֹן עַל יֵצֶר] The Gr. ἐνθύμημα occurs also for יֵצֶר מַחֲשֶׁבֶת (1 Chr. xxviii. 9). אֶחָד] Perhaps a corruption of אָח. Gr. and Syr. אָדָם.

Vv. 23 and 24 omitted by mistake, as the context proves, and must be supplied from the versions.

25. הָט שִׁכְמְךָ] Cf. Gen. xlix. 15. תַּחְבּוּלוֹתֶיהָ] read חֲבָלֶתָה as below, v. 29.

27. דְּרֹשׁ וְחַקֵּר] Cf. xiii. 15. וְהַחֲזִקְתָּה וְאַל תֶּרֶף] Cf. Prov. iv. 13.

28. וְנֶהְפַּךְ] Perhaps we should emend וְנֶהְפְּכָה.

30. עֲלִי זָהָב] Gr. עֶדְיִי.

31. בִּגְדֵי כָבוֹד] Cf. below l. 11 and Ecclus. xxvii. 8. תִּלְבְּשֶׁנָּה—תְּעַטְּרֶנָּה] Syr. תַּלְבִּישֵׁךְ—תְּעַטְּרֵךְ. עֲטֶרֶת תִּפְאֶרֶת Prov. iv. 9, xvi. 31. See also *ibid*. i. 9.

32. תְּעָרֵם] Prov. xv. 5, xix. 25.

33. תּוֹבָא] See Prov. i. 10 (תֹּבֵא). תִּתְחַכָּם] Eccles. vii. 16. After לִשְׁמֹעַ some verb has to be supplied, as תָּבִין or תִּלְמַד (see versions). וְהַט אָזְנֶךָ] Prov. iv. 20.

35. וּמָשָׁל ... שִׂיחָה] Job xv. 4 and Ps. cxix. 97 and 99, and O. H. xliv. 4. Cf. *Aboth d' R. Nathan* 15[b] שִׂיחִין וּמְשָׁלִים; *Var.* שִׂיחוֹת. יְצָאֲךָ] Cf. Jer. x. 20 בְּנֵי יְצָאֻנִי.

36. מָה] Read מִי. Cf. above, v. 4. וְשֻׁתְרִיהוּ] Cf. the Rab. phrase מַשְׁכִּים לְפִתְחוֹ, B. T. *Berachoth* 14 a and 28 a. בַּסִּפִּי] Read בַּסִּפִּין. The Targum to Prov. viii. 34 וְנִשְׁקוֹד עַל אִסְקוּפָתִי (Benzeeb). The Paitan Solomon Habbabli has also שְׁקַדְנוּ סִפּוֹת (Baer's *Abodath Israel*, p. 603).

37ᵃ. וְהִגָּה] Read תֶּהְגֶּה.

37ᶜ. יָבִין] Gr. and Syr. יָכִין. אֱיֻתָהּ] Read אִיּוּתָהּ. Cf. Ecclus. i. 26.

VII.

3. אַל תֵּרַע חֲדוּשִׁי] Read (as required by the context and the parallelism) אַל תּוֹרַע חֲרִישִׁי and supply (after the versions) the word עֹל or אָוֶן. Cf. Hos. x. 13, Prov. xxii. 8 and Job iv. 8.

5. מֶלֶךְ] Cf. Prov. xxv. 6. Gr. and Syr. אֵל, as in the preceding verse.

6ᶜ. וּנְתוּנָה בֶצַע] Read וְנִתְּנָה Syr. מוּמָא וְתֵעָבַד. Cf. O. H. xliv. 19 and xlvii. 20.

7. בְּעֶדְרַת שַׁעַר] Read בְּעֶדְרַת שַׁעַר as O. H. xlii. 11ᶜ. The אַל is probably a mere dittography. See however Ecclus. xxiv. 2. וְאַל תַּפִּילֵךְ] See versions. Perhaps the author thought of Deut. xxv. 1, 2 ... וְהִרְשִׁיעוּ אֶת הָרָשָׁע וְהִפִּילוֹ הַשּׁוֹפֵט. Cf. however above, i. 30. See also Prov. v. 14.

46   חכמת בן סירא   [CH. 7

8. תקשור] "conspire," see 1 Sam. xxii. 8 and elsewhere.

15. בצבא] Probably in the same sense as in Is. xl. 2, Job vii. 1 and xiv. 14. See R. V. Siegfried-Stade, *s. v.* "*poet. Kriegsdienst von der Mühsal des Lebens.*"

מלאכת עבודה] Lev. xxiii. 7, 8 and elsewhere. הי כאל] Read כי מאל. Cf. below, xv. 9.

10. See *Jewish Quarterly Review*, III. 690 and 698 for the Talm. quotation in *Erubin* 65ᵃ. Perhaps we should read there קצר for בצר. תתעבר] Cf. below, xxxviii. 9.

11. Cf. above, iv. 1.

12. Cf. Prov. iii. 29.

13. על] Gr. and Syr. בל. תקותו] Read תקותך.

14. תמור] imperf. of סור. Cf. O. H. xlii. 12 and Lévi's Com. on it. Gr. תשוח (Perles). תישן] Read תשנה, but it is possible that we have here an apocop. form. Cf. Eccles. v. 1 and O. H. xlii. 1 (ומשנות דבר). The Syr. תשנה.

16. עברון] Read עברון = עברה. Syr. עמך. Gr. ב' עון. במתי עם]. See however R. Jehudah Hakkohen b. Misatyah's *Selichah* in the Roman Ritual to the 17th of Tammus where the words וְנֶעְבַּר עָבְרוֹן occur. Cf. Zunz *Syn. Poesie* 401 and *Literaturgeschichte ed. Syn. Poesie* p. 100. יתעבר] see above, v. 7ᵃ.

17. Cf. Job xxv. 6. See also *Sayings of the Jewish Fathers*, 2nd ed. p. 165 (no. 40).

17⁽¹⁾. לאמר לפריץ] Perhaps corruption of לעמד בפרץ. Cf. Ps. cvi. 23 and O. H. xlv. 23. גל אל אל ורצה] Cf. Ps. xxii. 9.

18. תלי] Cf. the Rab. term אשם תלוי (*Mishnah, Zebachim* v. 5), which means the trespass offering of one who is in *doubt* whether he has committed an act that has to be atoned for by a sin offering. אח תלי would then mean a doubtful, question-able, indifferent friend. See also the expression טהור ותלוי (B. T. *Niddah* 60 a), which latter word means one who is in a doubtful state as to his ritual purity. The Gr. ἀδιαφόρου is probably the equivalent for תלוי (though it occurs in the first clause), contrasting with γνήσιον (ודאי). The original order of the Hebrew was probably אוהב תלוי במחיר ואח ודאי which suggests for the original of the Greek text μὴ ἀλλάξῃς φίλον ἀδιάφορον (תלוי) ἕνεκεν διαφόρου (מחיר), and tends to confirm Casaubon's emendation διαφόρου, which is further supported by the fact that in xxvii. 1 and xlii. 5 there is some MS. authority for the same change. The ἀδιάφορον here has probably been lost through its resemblance to διαφόρου, but the latter for the same reason has been corrupted to ἀδιαφόρου. See Jastrow, *s. v.* אשם.

19. תמאס] Syr. תמיר. For the second clause cf. Prov. xxxi. 10. Perhaps we should supply after חן the word רחוקה or יקרה. Syr. בפנינים for מפני.

20. תרע] Read תרע. באמת] Perhaps corruption of באמר "offend not by word." שובר נותן נפשו] Read שביר. The parallel in Deut. xxiv. 14, 15 would suggest the reading נשא instead of נותן; see however below, li. 20ᵃ.

NOTES ON THE TEXT.

21. Agrees more with the Syr. Cf. Ecclus. xxxiii. 30, 31.

22. עֵינֶיךָ] Perhaps corruption of בְּעֵינֶיךָ, or perhaps עֶדְרְךָ. Cf. Prov. xxvii. 23. אֲמָנָה] Perhaps related to אָמְנוֹת 2 Kings xviii. 6; the original meaning according to Ges. ed. Buhl *s. v.* אָמְנָה is *festtragend*. Cf. also Levy *s. v.* אוֹמֵן (I. p. 97). The meaning of this term seems however to be very doubtful; cf. *Aruch Hashalem s. v.* אָמָן (I. p. 121) and *Landwirtschaft in Palästina* by Dr Vogelstein, p. 59, note 21. Possibly the root אמן which means among other things, "to nourish," "to nurse," etc. was also used in the sense of breeding (cf. the Rab. use of גדל) which would give excellent sense here; but so far we have no authority for it. Gr. perhaps as was suggested to me סֹכְנָת. Cf. Job xv. 3 Benzeeb's translation : וְאִם יִסְכֹּן לָךְ.

23. יָסִיר] Cf. Prov. xxiii. 13 and below, xxx. 12, 13.   וְשָׁא etc.] Cf. 2 Chr. xi. 21 and elsewhere.

25. עֶסֶק] in the sense of strife (Heb. Dict. *s.* עֵשֶׂק and Rab. Dict. *s. v.*). Cf. Prov. xxii. 10 גָּרֵשׁ לֵץ וְיֵצֵא מָדוֹן. נָבוֹן גֶּבֶר] For the position of the adjective see Gesenius § 112 note.

26. תִתְעָבָה] Gr. and Syr. תְּעוּבָה. For the second clause, see xii. 10. This clause agrees with the Syr.

XI.

34[b]. וַיִּנָּכֵר] *Piel* of נכר. Cf. the Rab. expression ר"א אוֹמֵר לֹא תְנַכְּרֵהוּ (B. T. *Sanhedrin* 7[b]) "to alienate," "to treat as a stranger." See Rab. Dict.

XII.

2. תשלומת] See below, xiv. 6, xxxv. 11 and O. H. xlviii. 8.

3. לָמְנוֹחַ] *inf.* of a lost verb מָנַח (cf. the Heb. noun מִנְחָה and the Arab. verb مَنَحَ) meaning to bestow gifts. The Gr. seems to have taken it from נוח to rest, to abide.   וְגַם צְדָקָה לֹא עָשָׂה] Read וְגוּ'. Cf. Is. lviii. 2.

5[b]. מֵאֲנִי זִינָךְ Syr. (cf. בְּלִי לֶחֶם Judg. v. 8 and 2 Sam. i. 27), which the Gr. mistook for לֶחֶם (bread).

6. יָשִׁיב נָקָם] Cf. below xxxv. 17[c].

8. יוֹדֵעַ] See Ed.

9. Cf. Prov. xix. 4.

10. אַל תַּאֲמִין] Cf. Prov. xxvi. 25. רֵעוּ] Syr. רֵעוּ.   יַחֲלִיא] denom. *hif.* from חַלָּאָה.

11[a]. וְיֵהָלֵךְ בְּנַחַת] Cf. for this expression, Maimonides *Mishnah Torah, Hilchoth Beth Habbechirah* VII. § 2, which he probably took from some older source.

11[c]. כִּמְגֻלֶּה רז] Syr. גְּלָא רָזָא, Gr. perhaps כְּרֹאִי.

הכמת בן סירא

12ᵉ. ולאמרתי] Gr. and Syr. ולאמרתי.

13. מי יוחן] Read יחון, unless we emend ממי for מי. חית שן] O. H. xxxix. 30.

14. אשת זדון] Gr. and Syr. איש. The עז on the margin is doubtful. The signs can also be read נון or עז. Perhaps they represent עון and thus are meant as a variant to זדון.

14⁽¹,⁹⁾. Omitted in the Gr. יפול] Read יוכל, Syr. תוכל.

15. יופיע] = יתגלה of the preceding verse of which this (omitted in the Syr. but represented by the Gr.) seems to be only a doublet. נמוט] Gr. תמוט. יתכלכל] Cf. O. H. xliii. 3.

16ᵃ. יתמרמה] Gr. יתמתק, cf. Job xx. 12 and Ecclus. xxvii. 23. מהמרות] Ps. cxl. 11.

17. יחפש עקב] "seek reward." The Gr. and Syr. suggest something like ישוף עקב

18. ולרובה—ישנא] Read as partly suggested by Gr. and Syr. וירבה—וישנא. Cf. below xiii. 25.

XIII.

2ᶜ⁽¹⁾. Found only in the Syr.

3. יענה] The context as well as the versions suggest the emendation יעוה. The mistake is probably due to the scribe's thinking of Prov. xviii. 23 ועשיר יענה (עזות) of which our verse is in fact only a sort of paraphrase. יתנוה] Read יתנוה, he will "praise himself," "boast." Cf. Exod. xv. 2. See Heb. and Rab. Dict. s. v. נוה נוי. ועל] Perhaps corruption of ועלב, cf. Rab. Dict. s. v.

4. תברע יחמל] The Gr. suggests תברע. Perhaps we should supply לא before יד, but there is no absolute necessity to emend the text. Gr. and Syr. יחמול עליך יזוב אותך (instead of יזוב אותך).

5. שלך] Read יש לך.

6. והשיע] Hif. of שוע, see Bib. and Rab. Dict. s. שוע. Possibly also hif. of שעע (reading והשע), cf. O. H. xli. 19ᵈ Gl. מיהשע) and Glossary, p. xxxv. Gr. perhaps והתיע. Syr. והתרע. Cf. Prov. xxii. 24.

7. ועריץ] Gr. ישדך from ערה "to empty." Cf. Symmachus to תער in Ps. cxli. 8 (Field, II. p. 298).

8. תרהב] Probably alluding to Prov. vi. 2 (ורדב רעיך) but not to exaggerate it. בחסירי מרע] See Ed. and Bissel on this verse.

10. תשנא] Agrees with the Syr. Gr. תנשה (Perles). Cf. Smend, Bacher and Lévi, O. H. xlii. 9 and 10 (Text and Gloss). Is. xliv. 21 תנשני. The word תנשה also occurs in the Paitan Kalir (Zunz, Jubelschrift, p. 202).

11ᵃ. לחפש] Cf. above, vii. 21.

11ᶜ. נסיון] See Rab. Dict. Cf. also above, iv. 17ᵉ and vi. 7. R. Saadyah as above כי ברב שיח מנסה אותך ושחק etc.

CH. **13**]   NOTES ON THE TEXT.   49

12. מוֹשֵׁל The פֶּן תִּתֵּן לַ ה' וּשְׁנָתְךָ לַאֲכָזָרִי [אכזרי יתן מושל Prov. v. 9 is thus the subject. Gr. מָשָׁל, or מָלָה. If this reading is correct it must be taken in the same sense as Ps. xliv. 15 תְּשִׂימֵנוּ מָשָׁל בַּגּוֹיִם. It is also possible that the יתן must, as was suggested to me, be taken as an apocop. form of תנה, thus meaning "to repeat," cf. ed. on Ecclus. xix. 6 and O. H. xlii. 1. Cf. also O. H. xlii. 11 Gl. and Lévi's note to it (p. 53). Syr. שָׁלוֹם. קוֹשֶׁר [קשר Misunderstood by the Gr. Cf. above, vii. 8.

13. [והיה זהיר O. H. xlii. 8ᶜ. Cf. Mishnah, *Aboth* ii. 1. For the second clause, see Prov. i. 15.

15. See *Jewish Quarterly Review*, III. p. 690 for Rab. quotation.

17⁽¹⁾. [נאצל Cf. O. H. xlii. 21ᶜ and Glossary s. אצל.

18. [מאיש Read מאין "whence." [צבוע Jer. xii. 9.

19. [פראי מדבר Cf. Jer. ii. 24 and Job xxiv. 5.

20. Omitted in the Syr. Cf. Prov. xxix. 27.

21. [מוט בסמך Read נמוט יסמך. [מרע So Gr. Syr. רַע, in the whole verse רַע or רֵעָה. Cf. Jer. ix. 2 and Prov. xiv. 32.

22ᵃ. [מדבר So in the Syr. Gr. נמוט. [מכוערין from the Rab. כער ugly, hateful. דברים מכוערין is a constant expression in the *Tanna debbe Eliyahu*, cf. i. *cc.* 18, 19, 20. See also B. T. *Yoma* 86ᵃ. [מופין Read מחופין from חוף or חפה. *Sifra* 91c (ed. Weiss) מפני שמחפין עליו, "because they palliate his crime." The Syr. suggests מִפִּין, cf. Jer. x. 4.

22ᶜ. [דל נמוט Syr. מדבר. [נע נע See Rab. Dict. (especially *Aruch Hashalem*) s. v. געגעא, כעכע and קוקן, קעקע נע גע is thus onomatopoetic, imitating the sound of the frogs (which confirms Rapoport's explanation of געגעא). It is however possible that we have to emend here קעקע = "to cackle." Syr. גוע. [ושא Read ישא. [ואין לו מקום Mishnah, *Berachoth* iv. 2 מה מקום לתפלה זו. Cf. Eccles. ix. 16.

23ᵃ. [נסכתו *Nif.* of סכת. Cf. Deut. xxvii. 9 (הסכת) and see Job xxix. 9. [ואת The MS. is here much faded, and it may also be ואמת or ואהת. [ושכלו etc. Cf. Prov. xii. 8. [עב יניעו Cf. Job xx. 6.

23ᶜ. [נתקל Aram. Cf. below xv. 12, xxxi. 7 and xxxii. 20.

25. [ישנא Cf. Eccles. viii. 1. Cf. above xii. 18 and see also *Jewish Quarterly Review*, III. p. 693, for Rab. quotation.

26. [עקבת *plur.* of עָקָב. [וישיג ושיח 1 Kings xviii. 27. The Gr. took שיח in the same sense as above, vi. 35.

XIV.

1. [אבה עליו Read אבל (cf. Job xiv. 22), or perhaps אנה, cf. Is. iii. 26 and xix. 8.

2. [הסרתו Read חסדתו.

50   חכמת בן סירא   [CH. 14

3. [חרוץ] Prov. iii. 14 and elsewhere. Cf. also below, xxxi. 5.

4. [מונע נפשו] We should expect here מטובה or some such word (cf. Eccles. iv. 8 and vi. 2 and below verse 14). Perhaps originally מַעֲנָה. Cf. Ps. xxxv. 13. יִתְבַּעְבַּע "rejoice," from the root בע or בוע. See Levy, Ch. Wb. I. 85 and *Aruch Hashalem*, II. 136, 137; see also below, xvi. 2.

5. [יקרה] Perhaps related to the Rab. קורת רוח "refreshment of the spirit" (*Aboth* IV. 24). Cf. also the *Kethib* in Prov. xvii. 27 וקר רוח. The Syr. however suggests an Aramaism קרה which may be taken to mean to rejoice.

6. [תשלומת] Cf. above, xii. 2.

9. [כושל] Perhaps a corruption of מושל (cf. Prov. xxiii. 1 and O. H. p. 9, n. 7) or perhaps of אוכל or זולל. Syr. בסיל. [וְרָעֵהוּ] Cf. below, v. 14. [מאבד חלקו] The Syr. with which this clause agrees on the whole reads מ' נפשו. The Gr. מיבש נפשו cf. Num. xi. 6.

10. [עין] The leg of the *Waw* is very short, and the word may thus be read עין. [תעט] I Sam. xiv. 32. (*Keri* וַיַּעַט.) [ומהומה] Cf. *Aboth* v. 11 ומהומה של רעב.

10(1). Only to be found in the Syr. which however seems to be corrupt. Cf. Ecclus. xxxi. 13.

11. [שדות] Read שמח. Syr. suggests שרת. The Gr. omits this clause. [ולאל ידך הדשן] Cf. above, v. 1. [הדשן] Prov. xi. 25 and elsewhere. "As long as it is in the power of thy hand, become fatted" (or be happy). The Gr. translated לאל "unto God," whilst thinking of Ps. xx. 4 in connection with הדשן. Cf. also below, xxxviii. 11. For the Rab. quotation of this and the succeeding verse see *Jewish Quarterly Review*, III. p. 690. Cf. also for this and the next eight verses Eccles. i. 4, iii. 12, iv. 8, 16, v. 17, 18, 19, vi. 2, viii. 15, ix. 7, 10, xi. 9.

12. [לא בשאול תענוג] These words are only to be found in the Rab. quotation. [וחוק] in the sense of a fixed limit, definite period. Cf. O. H. xli. 23 and Bacher's comment on it. [לשאול] Gr. and Syr. שאול. Tal. quotation בשאול. See below, xxxviii. 22.

13. [והשיגנת ידך] Perhaps we should read 'ו וכהשגת, cf. below, xxxv. 10. See also Prov. iii. 27.

14. [מטובת יום] etc.] Cf. Eccles. vii. 14. [ובהלקת] Gr. (μέρις) suggests ובחלק (cf. above, v. 9), whilst in the second clause we must point וחמוד חמר for חמר. רע (not רע as in the Syr.). Cf. Sept. reading in Num. xvi. 15 חמר for חמר. See also with regard to the Rab. tradition Müller's ed. of *Masecheth Soferim*, Text p. ii. and notes p. 16.

15. יָדוּ גוֹרָל Joel iv. 3 [לוידי גורל] [זה' ל' תעוב חילך] Cf. Ps. xlix. 11.

16. [ותין] Gr. and Syr. וקח. [ופנק] Cf. Prov. xxix. 21.

16(1). Omitted in the Gr. [דבר שיפה] alluding to Eccles. v. 17.

CH. 14]   NOTES ON THE TEXT.   51

18ᶜ. בשר ודם] See Rab. Dict.

19. ופעל ידיו] Gr. (ופעל. Cf. Deut. xxxiii. 11. ימשך אחריו] Cf. Job xxi. 33.

20. אשרי etc.] Cf. below, l. 28. ישעה] Cf. O. H. xliv. 8 (gloss.) above, xiii. 6, see also Ps. cxix. 117.

21. ובנתיבותיה] Read (with the Syr.) ובנתיבותיה.

22. בחקר] The versions suggest בחקך. יִרְצַד] Ps. lxviii. 17.

23. יצותת] Aramaism. The Paitan R. Meshulam b. Kalonymos has in the *Abodah* to the Day of Atonement German Ritual the form צוּתָתִין. Cf. Levy, *Ch. Wb. s. v.* צית, צות. Cf. also Jud. v. 26 and Prov. viii. 34.

24. יתירו] Gr. and Syr. יתרתיו. Cf. Bissel, *a. l.*

26. ישים קנו] Cf. Num. xxiv. 21. Gr. בנין. בעופיה] Cf. Ps. civ. 12 (עפאים). יתלונן] Ps. xci. 1 and Job xxxix. 28.

27. בצלה] Cf. Eccles. vii. 12.

XV.

1. ותופש תורה] Cf. Jer. ii. 8.

2. אשת נעורים] Cf. Prov. ii. 17.

3. לחם שכל] Cf. Prov. ix. 5.

4. ובה יבטח וג'] Cf. Ps. xxii. 6, xxv. 2 and elsewhere.

5. ורוממתהו] etc. Cf. above iv. 11 (note). ובתוך קהל וג'] Cf. Prov. xxiv. 7.

9. נאמר] Gr. and Syr. נאוה. Cf. Ps. xxxiii. 1 and Prov. xvii. 7. נחלקה] Cf. above, vii. 15, below, xvi. 16 and O. H. xxxix. 25, xl. 1 and xliv. 2ᵃ For the latter cf. also B. T. *Berachoth* 58ᵃ ברוך שחלק מכבודו ליריאיו. See also Job xxxix. 17.

10. ומשל etc.] agrees with the Syr. Cf. O. H. xlv. 17 וימשילהו בחוק ומשפט.

12. התקילני] Cf. above, xiii. 23ᶜ. Perhaps a protest against Jer. vi. 21 הנני נתן מכשולים ... In the Gr. the verse commences אל ת' (instead of פן). In the preceding verse the Gr. read תעשה (instead of עשה).

13. יאנגה] Exod. xxi. 13 לידו אנה והאלהים. Cf. also Prov. xxii. 21. Gr. יר', Syr. יאהבוה, יתננה.

14. אלהים מבראשית] see Gen. i. 1. Syr. מן בראשית, cf. below xvi. 26. The כי between the lines (the reading of which word however is not quite certain) probably belongs to the beginning of the verse thus commencing כי אלהים etc. ואמנידנו לשדדים. בידי חותפו] Cf. above, iv. 19⁽¹⁾ In the Rabbinic literature the evil *yetzer* is called among other names also צר (*Gen. Rabbah* xxii. 6) and שונא (B. T. *Sukkah* 52 a) as well as מלאך המות (B. T. *Baba Bathra* 16 a). In Sirach (below, l. 4) we find the חתף as apposition to צר. יצרו] This clause (probably a doublet) is represented by the Syr. See Dr Taylor, *Sayings of the Jewish Fathers*, 2nd ed. p. 152. Cf. also *Gen. Rabbah* xciv. 8 מושלמים ליצרם.

15. ‎[ותבונה]‏ Perhaps corruption of ‎ותתבונן‏. Gr. ‎ואמונה‏, cf. Prov. xii. 22.

15⁽¹⁾. Only to be found in the Syr. Cf. Habakkuk ii. 4; the second clause of the preceding verse is probably a doublet of this.

17. Cf. Deut. xxx. 15 and Jer. xxi. 8.

18. ‎[ספקה]‏ "abundant." Cf. Job xx. 22. ‎[וחוזה כל]‏ Cf. O. H. xliv. 3ᶜ.

19. ‎[עיני]‏ Cf. Ps. xxxiii. 18 and xxxiv. 16. ‎[על]‏ cancelled by the dots.

20. ‎[החלים אנש]‏ See Is. xxxviii. 16, and cf. below, xli. 9. Ps. xxxvi. 3 however would suggest the reading ‎החליק לא‏.

20⁽¹⁾. Omitted in the Gr. and only partly to be found in the Syr.

XVI.

1. ‎[תואר נערי]‏ Cf. Jud. viii. 18 and see also Perles, *Analecten z. Textkritik d. A. T.* p. 68. Gr. and Syr. perhaps ‎תרבות‏.

2. ‎[תבע]‏ See above, xiv. 4.

3ᵃ⁽¹⁾. Cf. Prov. xxiv. 19.

3ᶜ. ‎[לה]‏ The reading is uncertain, the letters being much faded in this place. Probably ‎מעולה‏ as in the Syr. Or perhaps ‎לבהלה‏, cf. Is. lxv. 23. ‎ומאחרית [זדון]‏ in the sense of posterity.

4. ‎[מאחר ערירי]‏ The word ‎ערירי‏ probably came by mistake from the preceding line. R. Nissim in the *Sepher* Maasiyoth (ed. Warsaw 1886, p. 12) ‎וכן אמר בראש אחד תחישב עיר‏. Jellinek however in his *Beth Hammidrash* (v. 133 and 206) gives after the *Meil Zedakah* the same passage ‎וכן אמר בן סירא באחד מגין ת' ע'‏. Cf. Gr. which suggests ‎מבין‏. See also Kahana in the periodical ‎השלח‏ iii. p. 42.

5. ‎[רבות כאלה]‏ Cf. Job xvi. 2. ‎[כאלה שמעה]‏ Gr. and Syr. ‎מאלה‏.

6. ‎[יוקדת]‏ Is. lxv. 6. ‎[ובגוי חנף]‏ Is. x. 6.

7. ‎[המורים עולם]‏ O. H. xliv. 2 (Gloss) suggests the reading ‎הרודים ע'‏ for ‎המורים‏. Gr. derived it from ‎מרה‏ (or perhaps read ‎המורדים עליו‏, possibly also ‎המעלים מעל‏, see Perles) Syr. ‎הממלאים‏. Cf. Is. xiv. 21. ‎עולם‏ here in the sense of the *world*. Cf. above, iii. 18.

9. ‎[גוי הרם]‏ O. H. xlvi. 6ᶜ. Cf. also Is. xxxiv. 5. ‎[הנודשים]‏ Cf. 2 Kings xiii. 7 and Hab. iii. 12. Gr. ‎הנאספים‏; cf. Ed., or ‎הנשאים‏.

11ᶜ. See above, v. 6.

13. ‎[תאות צדיק]‏ Cf. Prov. x. 24 and xi. 23.

14. ‎[כל]‏ etc. Cf. Prov. xi. 18. Our text represents a regular Rab. construction. This may perhaps account for the awkwardness of the Gr., which perhaps read ‎אתר‏ for ‎שכר‏. See *Jewish Quarterly Review*, III. 697 for the Ecclus. quotation given there from the *Baraitha Kallah*, which is probably a paraphrase of this verse. ‎[יצא לפניו]‏ Cf. Ps. lxxxv. 14. Gr. and Syr. ‎ימצא ל'‏.

15. This verse as well as the next are omitted in some Gr. MSS. See Fr.

16. ‎[וישבחו]‏ Read with Gr. and Syr. ‎וחשכו‏.

CH. 16]　　　　NOTES ON THE TEXT.　　　　53

17*c*. בעם כבד] Num. xx. 20. ומי] R. Saadyah (as above), who quotes this and the preceding verse, reads מי אן. For this and the following verses cf. Ecclus. xxiii. 18—21.

18. הן השמים וג׳] Cf. Ps. cxlviii. 4, 7 and 1 Kings viii. 27. עמודים] Syr. קימין suggesting עומדים. Cf. Ps. xxx. 8 ברצונך העמדת להררי עז, according to which we should emend here ברצונו ע׳ עומדים, whilst the following בפקרו may be taken as a corruption of בקפדו, meaning to grow impetuous or wax wroth, see Rab. Dict. This would give an excellent parallelism. Perles suggests here a confusion between עמד and מעד referring to the well-known emendation in Ez. xxix. 7. (Cf. Psalm lxix. 4.) This would account for the Greek σαλευθήσονται. See also Graetz, *Geschichte der Juden* II. b where he corrects the passage quoted from the Ps. into להררי עז המעדת בחרונך. On the other hand, the Gr. may have had רועדים; cf. Psalm civ. 32. Cf. also Ecclus. xliii. 16. וכרגשו] Read ירגשו.

19. קצבי הרים] Jonah ii. 7. בהביטו] etc. Cf. Ps. civ. 32.

20[n]. To be found only in the Syr. Cf. Ecclus. xxiii. 18.

22. אצוק חוק] Read with the Gr. ירחק. The verse is omitted in the Syr. Cf. Micah vii. 11. It is also possible, as was suggested to me, that we have here a corruption of אצעק חמם. Cf. Job xix. 7.

23. וחסרי לב] Cf. above, vi. 20. עת ה] The ע is somewhat faded. The versions suggest the reading מעת or נעוה. The *Waw* over the *Beth* of ונבר should probably have been placed over the *Ain* of עתה, thus reading עותה. Cf. Lam. iii. 59.

25. ובהצנע] See O. H. xlii. 8, and below, xxxii. 3. Cf. also Prov. xi. 2 ואת צנועים חכמה.

XXX.

11. תמשילהו] Ps. viii. 7. Cf. also O. H. xlv. 17 and xlvii. 19. לשחיתותיו] Aram. pl. of שחיתה. Cf. Dan. ii. 9. For the Gr. see Fr. 11, 12.

11[b]. כתפן עוד חי תבקע [כפתן על חי תפגע] Perhaps we should emend Cf. Ez. xxix. 7 כתף ... ובקעת. The sentiment would be the same as is expressed in the next verse. Probably one of them is a mere doublet. רציין] Read רצוץ.

12*a*. כיף] See above, iv. 7, and vii. 23 (Gr.). כשרוא] See Geiger, *Lehrbuch zur Sprache der Mischnah*, pp. 84 and 114.

12*c*. ישקה] Gl. יקשיח (Job xxxix. 16). מפח נפש] Job xi. 20. The Gl. ולך is preserved in the Gr.

13. יסר בנך] See above, vii. 23. יתלע] "breed worms," for which the Bibl. term is ירם תולעים (Exod. xvi. 20), whilst the Rabbis use for it the *hif.* התליע (Rabb. Dict. *s. v.* תלע). The metaphor in this place has the same meaning as נבאש ב׳ or הבאיש ב׳ in 1 Sam. xiii. 4 and xxvii. 12. Gl. יתעל, cf. Jer. li. 3. Gr. and Syr. יתקל.

14. וחי] In the sense of "healthy," "strong." Cf. Is. xxxviii. 22, but more frequently in Rab. literature, cf. Levy, II. 41. עצם] "body." Cf. Lam. iv. 7.

15. שר] Perhaps connected with שרך (Heb. and Rab. Dict., s. v.) meaning strong, healthy. Gl. שאר, עשר which latter word is probably a corruption of בשר. Cf. Prov. xiv. 30 חיי בשרים. See also Prov. iii. 8 (לשרך) where the same confusion with שאר or בשר is suggested by some commentaries (Gesenius, ed. Buhl, p. 823).

16. שר עצם] The use of עצם in verse 14 suggests that שר has to be taken here as an *adjective*; though שאר עצם is not impossible.

17. תנוחת] St. cst. of a noun נוחה occurring in the O. T. only as *nom. prop.* See Heb. Dict. נאמן] Cf. Deut. xxviii. 59. This verse agrees with the Gr. (cf. Fr. Text and Commentary), whilst the next is preserved in the Syr.

17⁽¹⁾. ולירד] Rab. *inf.* Qal of ירד (Bib. Heb. לרדת). See Strack, *Lehrbuch der Neuhebräischen Sprache*, § 100 a.

18. פום] Gl. Aram. for פה. נלול] Cf. the Rabb. גולל (*Aruch Hashalem*, II. 282; Levy, I. 335), signifying the stone covering the grave.

19. The next three verses agree more with the Syr., by which the gaps may be supplied as [נהגה מהוגן מה ייטב לאלילי הגוים...כן מי שיש לו וג׳ *nif.* of הגי (הני). See Rab. Dict. After 'מה which might also be read ממנו the signs of a word or two are visible but are illegible.

20ᵃ. בעינו] There are signs of words visible after בעינו, but they are much faded. The signs at the end of this line look somewhat like חרק, cf. Ps. cxii. 10.

20ᵇ. סירים] Read סרים. באונם] Esther i. 8. In the second clause as well as in the next verse (which agrees with the Syr.) we have the same confusion with xx. 4 which Fr. noticed in several Gr. MSS.

20ᵇ⁽¹⁾. כן] Read with the Syr. כמו. נאמן] Syr. מהימנא. Perhaps we should read אמן (the נאמן having slipped in from v. 17), he who brings up, in the sense of guardian; cf. Esther ii. 7.

21. לדין] "strife" (Prov. xxii. 10). Gr. and Syr. דוון "grief." Cf. *Pirke Aboth* ii. 8 in Baer's *Abodath Israel* p. 275 where some authorities have דוון for דאגה. בעונך] Gl. בעצתך, which latter reading agrees with the Gr. and Syr. The parallel in Ps. xxxi. 11 בינון...כשל בעוני is decisive for the readings בעונך and דוון.

22. אפו] Gr. and Syr. חיין, which gives indeed better sense. The mistake of the copyist may be due to his thinking of Prov. xix. 11 שכל אדם האריך אפו.

23ᵃ. פוג...ופייג] This verb is sometimes used in Rab. literature in the sense of calming and rejoicing. See Levy, IV. 12 and *Aruch Hashalem*, VI. 288. וקצפון] which form is sometimes used in Rab. and Paitanic literature for קצף. Cf. Levy, s. v. and Zunz *Syn. Poesie*, p. 400.

23ᵇ. תעלה] O. H. xli. 14 c (text תועלה, Gl. תעלה). It does not occur in the early Rab. literature, except in the *Midrash Haggadol* MS. to Gen. xlii. 37 וכי מה תעלה יש בידי. The word תועלת is only to be found in post-Talmudic authors, though both Levy and Kohut notice it under יעל and refer us to letter ת, where as a fact they omit it.

CH. 30]   NOTES ON THE TEXT.   55

24. The place on which we expect the marginal reading to which the mark on ודין points is torn off. Probably it was וחרון, as suggested by the Gr. See Fr. Com. p. 118 for the Rab. quotations of these verses.

25. שנות] Prov. vi. 10 and xxiv. 33 (שְׁנוֹת). [וּמַאֲכָלוֹ יַעֲלֶה עָלָיו Aboth d' R. Nathan, c. xxvi. אוכלים שאינם עולים על גופו meaning "food which does not agree with one's body." Cf. Ed.

XXXI.

1. שֹׁקֵד] Gl., which is the correct reading, the "watching," the "sleeplessness," cf. Eccles. v. 11. [דראגתו Gl., omitting מחיה, which agrees with Gr. and Syr. (תפרינ] Gl. Occurring also in Rab. literature (Rab. Dict. s. פָּרַג) meaning "to destroy," "to cause to disappear." נומה] Prov. xxiii. 21.

2. ומחלי] Cf. below, xxxvii. 30 and xxxviii. 9 Text and Gl.   'חן] Gl. Probably חזקה.

2(1). רע וג' חרפה]. This verse seems to express the same sentiment as O. H. xli. 22ᶜ (cf. also Ecclus. xxii. 22 and xxvii. 17). [תניר hif. of נוד "to remove" (2 Kings xxi. 8), "to keep off." אוהב כנפש] Perhaps we should read אהב כנפש, cf. above, vii. 21.

3. לקבל תענוג] O. H. lxi. 1. לקבץ. Gr. and Syr. לקבל ח']

4. ינע] Read יניע.

4(1). כחו]. Probably in the sense of substance or wealth. Cf. Prov. v. 10, Job vi. 22. נחה] Perhaps נחת or נוחה, see above, xxx. 17. Or perhaps we should read לאנחה (instead of לא נחה), cf. O. H. xlvii. 20ᶜ ואנחה על משכבך, see also B. T. Moed Katon 25ᵇ שהיא למנוחה ואנו לאנחה. See also למעצבה תשכבון Is. l. 11.

5. ור' חרוץ לא ינקה] Cf. Prov. xxviii. 20.

6. חבולי זהב] Perhaps in the sense of חבלים in Amos ii. 8, "pledged," which would form a better parallelism to והבוטח (read והבוטחים) than the Gl. חללי. (Cf. Prov. vii. 26.) על פנים] Gr. על פניהם.

6(1). ביום עברה] Prov. xi. 4. Cf. above, v. 8. This verse is only to be found in the Syr.

7. תקלה] Cf. above, xiii. 23ᶜ. לאויל] Gr. לאל or לאליל. Cf. Mishle Shualim, § 59 חשוב אויל כצל אליל. פותה] Job v. 2. Gl פתה probably corruption of פתי. Cf. the Gr. יוקש] Cf. Eccles. ix. 12.

8. איש] Gr. and Syr. עשיר. נמצא תמים] Cf. O. H. xliv. 16 and 17. ממון] See Rab. Dict. s. v. Note the use of this word for the Bibl. כסף or מטמן. Probably we have also to read in O. H. xl. 26ᶜ ממון instead of מטמן as suggested by the editors. I have examined the MS. and found that there is no room for two such big letters as Teth and Mim. Cf. the reading given by Rabbinowicz in the Variae Lectiones to B. T. Taanith 31 b עשירות שבהן אומרות תנו עיניכם בבעלי ממון. Smend's suggestion to read מעין gives no sense, unless one thinks of Is. xii. 3 ממעיני הישועה, see versions. נלוו] Is. xxx. 12, Prov. iii. 32.

56   חכמת בן סירא   [CH. 31

9. [הפליא לעשות] Cf. Jud. xiii. 19 and Joel ii. 26. Cf. also below, l. 22².

10ᵃ. [שנדבק] Gr. שנבדק. The next two verses are omitted in all versions.

10ᵃ⁽¹⁾. This verse must be emended by the contents of the following. Probably it formed originally only a gloss.

10⁽ᵇ⁾. [מי ברכו] Ps. x. 3 וּבֹצֵעַ בֵּרֵךְ, A. V. "and blesseth the covetous." Here the object is מָמוֹן (= בֶּצַע). [וישלם] Job ix. 4. [היא] Read הוא. Verse 10⁽¹⁾ is undoubtedly only a corrupt doublet of this verse.

10ᶜ. [לסור] Cf. Deut. vii. 4, 1 Sam. xii. 20 and elsewhere. It is also possible that this word is in some way connected with the Aram. סָרִי used also of moral corruption. See Rab. Dict.

11. [ותהלתו יספר קהל] Cf. Ps. ix. 13 and cxlix. 1. See also O. H. xliv. 15 Gl.

XXXII.

1. "The Persian note is partly obliterated .. این نو... ابا آن فاسوق ایست. The word نسخها دیگر .. نوסכהא is not certain; the last three letters might be ברא. The meaning is probably "this *clause* is not found with that verse in the other copies." נוסכהא is somewhat irregular for נוסכתרא, but allowable (Vullers, *Instit. linguae Persicae*, § 194). The י of the construct state may have preceded דינר in the next line, a mode of writing found in Judaeo-Persian. The use of ני would not be impossible in this dialect; but since some letters seem certainly lost after it, the original import of the note must be doubtful." (D. S. M.)

1ᵇᶜ, 2¹. [חסוב... תרבין] *Mishnah, Berachoth* vi. 6 (לאכול) הסבו. Cf. Friedmann's סדר והגדה של לילי פסח pp. 16—25 for other passages bearing on the הסיבה question. The term is never employed in this sense in the O. T., though it is not impossible that the custom of reclining at meals was already known in very early times (Amos vi. 4, Ez. xxiii. 41). Gl. [ובכין], cf. Eccles. viii. 10, etc. and above, xiii. 7.

2ᵇᶜ. [בכבודם] Syr. בשמחתם. [ועל מוסר] Perhaps corruption of מסבה (Syr. פתורא). [שכל] Gr. כליל. Syr. כבוד. Perhaps we should read שכר —cf. for a somewhat similar confusion O. H. xl. 18 Text and Gloss, but it is possible that it is used in the sense of ומצא חן ושכל טוב (Prov. iii. 4).

3. [שב] O. H. xlii. 8. [והצנע] The sign on this word shows that there was another reading, which the copyist however failed to give. Perhaps we should read בהצנע. Cf. above, xvi. 25. [לכת] Gl. Cf. Micah vi. 8. This verse is omitted in the Syr.

4. [בם' האזין]. So the Syr. Gr. [במקום היין אל תשפך שיח ולבלא. מזמר] V. L. *ubi auditus non est*, which suggests the emendation ובלא משמע or מאזין. [ובל עת] In the O. T. only used with verbs. [תתחכם] Eccles. vii. 16.

4⁽¹⁾. [שיר... על משתה היין] Cf. O. H. xlix. 1ᶜ. This verse is preserved only in the Syr.

5. [כומז] Exod. xxxv. 22. More likely it is a corruption of כמו

CH. **32**]   NOTES ON THE TEXT.   57

נִיב [גוּב. Gl. Is. lvii. 19, where the *Keri* is נִיב and the *Kethib* is גוּב. For the meaning cf. Prov. xxv. 11.

5[1]. Only to be found in the Syr. [נָאִים] Cf. O. H. li. 16. בדרים [יָפִים] Cf. Eccles. iii. 11.

6. מְלוּאוֹת] See Exod. xxviii. 17 and 20.

7. בְּחֹזֶק] "by an effort." See Levy, *s. v.* חֹזֶק.

8. כָּל לֶאֱמֹר] Read כּוֹל (cf. Is. xl. 20) "measure" or "compress the speech." See Heb. Dict. *s. v.* כּוֹל. It is also possible that we have here the shortened *imper.* of כָּלָה in which case we read בַּל. וּמְעַט הַרְבֵּה Possibly however it is a corruption of בִּמְעַט. Cf. the Rab. phrase מֻעָט מַחֲזִיק הַמְּרוּבֶּה (Exod. *Rabbah* XI. 5).

9. תְּקוֹמֵם] Is. lviii. 12, Micah ii. 8. [תֵּרֵב] Ps. lxxi. 21. Syr. תַּאֲבָה. לִטְרֹד [Prov. xix. 13. For the second clause see Fr. n.

9[1], 10. יָנֻצָּח] Perhaps we should read with the Gr. יָחִישׁ "hasten" (1 Kings xx. 19). Cf. Prof. Fränkel's emendation in O. H. xliii. 5, quoted by Prof. Lévi, O. H. p. 67. See also *ibid. v.* 13. One of these two verses must originally have formed only a Gloss.

11. בְּעֵת מִפְקָד] Cf. Ez. xliii. 21. We might thus render it "in the appointed time." Cf. also O. H. xlii. 7 Gl. but in a different sense. וּשְׁלַם רָצוֹן] probably came in by mistake from *v.* 12. Originally we must have had here some such words as וְיֵלֶךְ בְּחִפָּזוֹן.

11[1]. Only partly to be found in the Syr.

12. כלבבך...] Perhaps we should supply after the Gr. שָׂמֵחַ or עֹשֶׂה after the Syr. בְּחֶסֶר] So Syr. Gr. בְּחֶסֶד ("reproach," cf. Ed.). Cf. Ecclus. xl. 6 Gr. and Syr. for a similar confusion. It is however probable that the whole clause בִּירְאַת אֵל וְלֹא בְחֶסֶר כָּל was suggested by Ps. xxxiv. 10 and Deut. xxviii. 47. Cf. also O. H. xli. 26°. There is thus no necessity to emend our text.

13[1]. The supplied letters are suggested by the Gl. and the next verse. וּמִתְהַלְּלָה] Prov. xxvi. 18. Cf. also below, *v.* 15.

14. וּמְשַׁחֲרֻהוּ] Cf. above, vi. 36.

14[1]. חֶפְצֵי אֵל] Cf. Is. liii. 10. See also B. T. *Shabbath* 150 a חֶפְצֵי שָׁמַיִם. This verse is only to be found in the Syr., whilst *v.* 14 is omitted. Of course this as well as the preceding verse express only (in a positive way) the same sentiment as Prov. xxviii. 9 מֵסִיר אָזְנוֹ מִשְּׁמֹעַ תּוֹרָה גַּם תְּפִלָּתוֹ תּוֹעֵבָה.

15. יְפִיקֶנָּה] Cf. Prov. iii. 13, see also above, iv. 12.

16, 16[1]. The latter verse is preserved in the Syr., whilst the Gr. seems to be based on the former, reading יָצִית for יוֹצִיא (cf. Ed.).

17. חָמָם] Gl. This is the correct reading, and is also supported by the Gr. תּוֹרָה Read [תּוֹכָחָה or תּוֹכָחָה Syr. אוֹרְחוֹ. The יִמְשׁוֹךְ (Syr. יַעֲשֶׂה?) may have been suggested by Job xxi. 33 and xxviii. 18.

17[(1)]. This verse is preserved in the Syr. (reading with the Gl. חכמה), though the preceding is retained.

18. The שכל of the Gl. is preserved in the Gr. (διανόημα—reading also יקח for ישכח), whilst in the second clause it agrees more with the text, reading of course זר (ἀλλότριος) for זד (cf. Ed.), and מורא for תורה.

20. [תתקל בננף] Cf. Is. viii. 14.

21. [מחתף] Cf. Prov. xxiii. 28, as well as above, xv. 14 and below, l. 4. The ink is much faded in the margins, which makes the reading of the Gl. (particularly רשעים) extremely doubtful. Perhaps it is משדדים which the Gr. again, as it would seem, read מישורים.

22[(1)]. Only preserved in the Syr., which however omits the preceding verse.

22[(2)], 23. In the Rab. literature (B. T. *Berachoth* 32 b) the exposing of oneself to danger is regarded as a transgression of the Scriptural words רק השמר לך ושמר נפשך (Deut. iv. 9).

24. [נוצר תורה שומר נפשו] Cf. Prov. xvi. 17, xix. 16 and Ps. xxii. 6.

XXXIII.

1. [יפנע רע] Cf. 1 Kings v. 18. The supplying of the missing letters is suggested by the Gl. and the versions. Cf. Ed.

2. [במס....] The rest is torn off. The *Beth* is doubtful, and may be taken as *Kaph*. Perhaps we had here במסה ומ', whilst the Gr. represents the Gl.

3. [כא..ן] Perhaps we have here the remains of כאורים (see Gr.) וכהן, but the letters are very doubtful. The one given as א may also be taken for ם, whilst of the ן only the leg is left, and may as well represent a trace of any final letter or of a *Koph*.

XXXV.

9. [מעשיך] Gr. (Swete xxxii. (xxxv.) 11, Fr. xxxii. 9) and Syr. probably משאותיך. Cf. Gen. xliii. 34 and below, xxxviii. 2.

10. [כמתתו] Gl. O. H. xli. 22 and xlii. 7. Cf. Deut. xvi. 15. [לאל] Gl. Preserved in the Syr. Gr. לאל עליון. Cf. Ps. l. 14. ובהשגת יד Read וכהשגת. Ez. xlvi. 7 כאשר תשיג ידו. The noun השגה does not occur in the O. T. In Rab. literature we have השג יד (*Mishnah, Arachin* iv. 1). The Gl. מלוה יוי וג' is preserved in the Syr. Cf. Prov. xix. 33.

11. Cf. Jer. li. 59 and Ps. lxxix. 12.

12[a], 12[c]. Cf. Deut. x. 17. See also Is. i. 11 and Prov. xvi. 8. See also Ecclus. xxxiv. 19, 20. [משוא פנים] 2 Chron. xix. 7.

13. [לא י פ' אל דל] Cf. Lev. xix. 15. [תהנונים מצוק] Gl. Cf. Dan. ix. 25 and Ps. cxviii. 5. Gr. עשוק, or מוצק, cf. above, iv. 9.

14. [תרבה שיח] Cf. 1 Sam. i. 12, 16. [תחבט] Gl. The root חבט is sometimes used in Rab. literature in connection with prayer, Gen. *Rabbah* L. 6 שנתהבט עליו אותו זקן. See Rab. Dict. *s. v.*

15. [הלא דמעה...מרודיה] Cf. Lam. i. 2, 7, iii. 19.

CH. **35**] NOTES ON THE TEXT. 59

16. הנהה] Esther ii. 18. Here perhaps as much as גיחוח, Jer. T. *Peah* 15 c
הנחת רוחו של אביו. חשתה] from חשה "hastened." Cf. Siegfried-Stade's
Heb. Wb. s. v. חָשָׁה 11. The verse gives no good sense. I am therefore inclined
to emend in the first clause רצוץ for רצון (see above, xxxii. 13[1] text and Gl. for a
similar confusion) and to read in the second clause 'צעקת עני ענן ח (cf. the Syr.).
For the metaphor in this verse and the next cf. Lam. iii. 44. Cf. also Ecclus. xxi. 6.

18ᵃ. וכגבור לא יתמהמה] Cf. Is. xlii. 13 and lxiv. 12. Gl. וגבור is
preserved in some MSS. of the Gr. Cf. Fr.

18ᶜ. Cf. Deut. xxxiii. 11 and xxxii. 43.

18ᵉ. ומטה רשע] Ez. vii. 11. שבט הרשע] Ps. cxxv. 3 שבט זדון
Gl. רשעים is preserved in the Gr. גרוע '] Cf. Ps. lxxv. 11.

19ᵃ. עד ישוב, etc.] Cf. Jer. xxv. 14, li. 57 and Prov. xxiv. 12 and xii. 14.

19ᶜ. עד יריב ריב עמו] Cf. Is. li. 22. ושמחתם ב'] Cf. Is. xxv. 9.

20. רחמים, etc.] The reading is very doubtful, the paper being mostly
torn off. The supplied letters are suggested by the Gr. Syr. suggests ויחפיר
איביו. חזיזים] Zech. x. 1. Cf. also O. H. xl. 13.

20⁽¹⁾. Only the ך is certain. The rest is entirely destroyed except the ב
the פ and the פ, of which faint signs remain. "The Persian note is (except for
one letter) entire. It may be read این فاسوق از نُسختهای دیگر واید زا هشت[ه]
بود وپی نشته. Its import is rendered obscure by the difficulty of the words
واید زا هشت[ه]. Literally it might be rendered 'This verse from other copies and
here was omitted and written,' which probably means that it was omitted from
other copies; and that in the present copy it was either written or erased. The
writer's Persian is in any case peculiar; and though ای may be used with the
participle (Vullers, *Institut. linguae Persicae,* § 147) it seems more likely that בי
stands here for the preposition "without," which may be compounded with *sub-
stantives* in the sense of *un-*. נא apparently is an accented form of the preposition
j which is not prefixed to verbs by Persian writers. בור is inaccurately used for
שד, somewhat as in a document in the Bodleian כט מאן נבישתה היסת
means 'our signature is subscribed.' Finally, the arrangement of the words
seems contorted." (D. S. M.)

XXXVI.

1. אלהי הכל] Cf. Num. xvi. 22, cf. O. H. lxv. 23ᶜ.

2. והרים פחדך] Cf. 1 Chr. xiv. 17. The *Yod* and the *Mim* of והרים are
fairly certain.

3. יד] Gl., as in Gr. and Syr. Cf. Is. x. 32 and Zech. ii. 13. See also the
הביננו prayer (B. T. *Berachoth* 29ᵃ, cf. Dalman *Die Worte Jesu* p. 304) ועל
הרשעים תניף ידך. גבורתיך] Cf. Jer. xvi. 21.

4. הכבד בם] Gl., as in Gr. and Syr. Cf. Ez. xxviii. 22 and xxxviii. 23.

5. כי אין אל זולתך] Cf. 1 Chr. xvii. 20.

8—2

חכמת בן סירא [CH. 36

6. [חדש אות..ומופת] Cf. Deut. vi. 22, see also Lam. v. 18 and Ps. lxxiv. 9. GL [תמה] Cf. Dan. iii. 33 and vi. 28. [האדר יד ואמץ זרוע וימין] Cf. Exod. xv. 6, Prov. xxxi. 17 and Ps. xliv. 4, and lxxiv. 11. [חרין] Gl. Aram. See Rab. Dict. *s. v.* [ימים] Gl. read ימין.

7. [העיר אף וש׳ ח׳] Cf. Jer. x. 25 and Ps. lxxix. 6. [צר..אויב] Cf. Ps. lxxiv. 10. [והדוף] Cf. Ps. lxviii. 2. The reading of the Gl. is extremely doubtful.

8. [קין..מועד] Cf. Dan. xi. 27 and 35.

8[(1)]. [כי מי י׳ ל׳ מה ח׳] To be found only in the Syr. Cf. Job ix. 12 and Eccles. viii. 4.

10. [השבת ראש]. The parallel in Ps. lxxiv. 13 suggests שברת, but see also Ps. viii. 3. [פ׳ מואב] Num. xxiv. 17. Gl. אויב. Cf. Gr. and Syr. [האומר א׳ ד׳] Cf. Is. xlvii. 8 and 10.

11. [שבטי יעקב] Is. xlix. 6.

12. [נקרא בשמך] Cf. Deut. xxviii. 10 and O. H. xlvii. 11. ישראל [ב׳ כ׳] Exod. iv. 22. Cf. also O. H. xliv. 23[b] Gl. and Syr.

13. [מכון שבתך] Cf. Exod. xv. 17 and 2 Chr. vi. 30. See also Ps. lxxiv. 3 and 6.

14. [ומכבודך את היכלך] Gl. הדריך. Cf. Lam. i. 6. [מ׳ ציון א׳ הודך] Cf. 1 Kings viii. 11, Haggai ii. 7 and 2 Chr. v. 14 and vii. 1.

15. [למראש מעשיך] Cf. Ps. lxxiv. 2 [תן עדות] Cf. Is. lv. 4 and xliii. 9. זכור עדתך קנית קדם, from which verse the Rabbis infer that Israel is one of the six things which God created (or thought of creating) before the creation of the world (Gen: *Rabbah* I. 4). [והקם..דבר] Cf. 1 Sam. i. 23, 1 Kings viii. 20.

16. [פעלת קוויך] Cf. Job vii. 2. [יאמינו] Gen. xlii. 20.

17[a]. [תשמע ת׳ ע׳] Cf. 1 Kings viii. 30, Dan. ix. 17. [ברצונך] etc. Gl. ברצונך. Cf. Ps. cvi. 4.

17[b]. [וידעו כל א׳ א׳] Gl. ויראו. Cf. Is. lii. 10. [כי אתה אל...] 1 Kings viii. 60. To students of Jewish liturgy it will be interesting to compare the prayer beginning רבון העולמים (incorporated in the Daily Prayer Book from the *Tanna Debê Eliyahu*) with the last 17 verses. The paragraphs in the former commencing אבל אנחנו עמך...אתה הוא עד שלא נברא...אתה הוא ה׳ seem only a paraphrase of our Text. The first paragraphs of the *Amidah* to Rosh Hashanah וּבְכֵן תֵּן פַּחְדְּךָ, etc. seem also to have been influenced by this psalm of Ben Sira.

18. [גרגרת] Prov. i. 9 and elsewhere. Cf. Heb. and Rab. Dict. The Gloss is much faded but תָּמוּר and תַּנְעַם are certain.

XXXVII.

27. [בחמר] Gl. Perhaps corruption of בחסר.

28. [זן] Ps. cxliv. 13. Cf. also O. H. xlix. 8 and Driver's Glossary, *s. v.*

CH. 37]   NOTES ON THE TEXT.   61

29. תִזְרַע לְ] Cf. Jer. iv. 3.   וְאַל תִּשְׁפֹּךְ] Cf. above, xxx. 18 טוּבָה
שְׁפוּכָה.   תִּתְחַנֵּג א' מטמים] Gl. *hithp.* of חנג "to dance." See Levy *Ch. Wb. s. v.* Perhaps we should read תִּתְעַנֵּג whilst מט may be a corruption of מִמְתַקִּים Cf. Prov. xxv. 16.

30. יִקָּנֵן] Cf. Ps. civ. 17.   זָרָא] Num. xi. 20.

31. וְתָעוּ] Cf. רוּחַ עוֹעִים Is. xix. 14. See also Gesenius (ed. Buhl) *s.* עוה.

XXXVIII.

1. רֵעַ] in the sense of "cultivate," "honour." This recalls, as was suggested to me, the Arab. رعى, which means also "to pasture," and figuratively "to rule," "to honour." For the Rab. quotation both in Heb. and in Aram. see *Jewish Quarterly Review*, III. pp. 694 and 702.   חֵלֶק אֵל] Cf. above, vii. 15. The Gl. כִּי is preserved in the versions.   לְפִי צָרְכָּךְ] Cf. the Gr.

2. מַשּׂוּאוֹת] Cf. Gen. xliii. 34 and II. Sam. xi. 8.

3. תָּרִים רֹאשׁ] Cf. Ps. iii. 4, cx. 7.   וְלִפְנֵי נְדִיבִים יִתְיַצָּב]וּל מלכים Gl. which is preserved in the Syr. Cf. Prov. xxii. 29.

4. בֹּרֵא שָׁמַיִם] Gl., which is preserved in the Syr. and in the Rab. quotation. Cf. *Jewish Quarterly Review*, III. 693 and 702.

5. Cf. Exod. xv. 25.   בוחם] Gl., which is preserved in the Vet. Lat., see Fr.

7ª. The Rab. quotation (*Jewish Quarterly Review*, III. 693) agrees more with the Gr.

8ᵇ. וְיִשְׁבֹּת] Gl. יִשְׁבַּח. For a similar variant cf. O. H. xlv. 26ᶜ, Heb. and Gr., and Lévi's note on it.   מִפְּנֵי אָרְצוֹ] Gl. is represented by the versions.

9. בח' אל תתעבר] Cf. above, vii. 10.   פלל] Gl. Cf. Ps. cvi. 30.

10. וּמַהְבִּיר פָּנִים] Prov. xxiv. 23, xxviii. 21.

11. נִיחוֹחַ אַזְכָּרָה] only the ח is fairly certain. Perhaps we should read וְאַזְכָּרָה. Cf. O. H. lx. 16ᶜ. Gl. אַזְכַּרְתָּהּ. Cf. Lev. ii. 2. This would suggest מִנְחָה instead of נִיחוֹחַ.   בְּכַנְפֵי הוֹנְךָ] Perhaps we should read כְּכַנְפֵי and take it as a noun derived from the v. כָּנַף, meaning "the gatherings." Cf. Levy and *Aruch Hashalem, s. v.* and see also commentaries to Is. xxx. 20 (יְכַנֵּף). See also B. T. *Shabbath* 73 b מַאן דבניף מלחא. We should then translate this clause "And prepare a fat offering according to the savings of thy substance." Cf. Prov. iii. 8 and 9. It would be worth considering whether the כנף שקוצים Dan. ix. 27 has not the same meaning. The Gr. כְּפִי אֵינְךָ or כְּאַפַּס הוֹנְךָ (?).

12. יִשְׁמַשׁ מֵאָה] Gl. Read יָמוּשׁ מֵאִתְּךָ; cf. the Gr.

13. The 'מ in the Gl. is much faded. Perhaps the copyist wanted to write מָזוֹר (cf. the Syr.) but got confused by the מֵץ' in the text.

14ᵇ. פִּשְׁרָה] "interpretation," "solution." Cf. Dan. ii. 4, iv. 2 and Eccles. viii. 1. It is however possible that this term is connected with the כּוֹס שֶׁל פּוֹשְׁרִים of the Talmud (cf. Kohut and Levy, *s. v.* חרש פשר). The פִּשְׁרָה would then correspond with the שִׁקּוּי of Prov. iii. 8. Cf. also Blau, *Das Altjüdische Zauberwesen*, p. 157, note 2, "Gemeint ist irgend eine Lösung." וְרִפְאוּת] Prov. iii. 8.   יְמַנֶּה] Gl.; cf. Jonah ii. 1 (וַיְמַן).

15. [יתגבר] Probably in the same sense as Job xv. 25 "to behave proudly."
א״ד לוי מתלא [יסתונר על ידי] Gl. So Gr. and Syr. Cf. *Cant. Rabbah* vi. 11
אמר תרעא דלא פתיח למצוותה יהא פתוח לאסיא. *Pesikta Rabbathi* 42[b]
(ed. Friedmann) this *mashal* is given in Hebrew.
16[a]. [ונהה] Ez. xxxii. 18.
16[c]. בראשנה היתה הוצאת המת [ואל תתעלם] Cf. B. T. *Moed Katon* 27 b
קשה לקרוביו יותר ממיתתו עד שהיו קרוביו מניחין אותו ובורחין. Gl.
תתהר. Cf. Ps. xxxvii. 1.
17[a]. [והמר] Zech. xii. 10. [והום הספר] Gl. Read והחם. Cf. B. T.
Shabbath 153 a אחים הספידא and see *Aruch Hashalem* III. p. 423. Cf. also
O. H. xlii. 3 and 18 where dots are found on the words וארח and חקר.
[כיוצא בו] "in a similar manner," "like him." This is a regular Rab. preposition, Mishnah *Zebachim* v. 7 כיוצא בהם מהם. Cf. Geiger (as above,
xxx. 12[a]), p. 53, and Strack (as above, *ibid.*), p. 60.
17[c]. [יום ושנים בעבור רמעה] Cf. B. T. *Moed Katon*
ב' רבה. See also Ecclus. xxii. 7. Gr. and Syr. perhaps ימים להספר
ב' יגון.
18. [מדין] Gr. and Syr. מדון. Cf. above, xxx. 21. [יבנה עצבה] Gr.
יכרע עצמה. Cf. O. H. xli. 2 and xlvi. 9.
20. [פרע] "dissolve," "dismiss," etc. See Heb. and Rab. Dict. *s. v.* The
first clause agrees more with the Syr.
22. [זכור חקו] Cf. O. H. xli. 3.
23. [מושבת מתו, etc.] Cf. O. H. xliv. 9.
24. קנאת סופרים [ח' סופר תרבה חכמה] See B. T. *Baba Bathra* 21[a]
בדקדוק חברים...במיעוט [וחסר עסק] *Perek Rabbi Meir* § 6 תרבה חכמה
סחורה.
25[a]. [תומך מלמד] Cf. Jud. iii. 31, and see also Amos i. 5 and Prov. xv. 32
and xxxi. 19. עורד [בחנית מהעיר] Read ב' מעורר. Cf. 2 Sam. xxiii. 18
את חניתו. Cf. also 1 Chr. xi. 11 and 20.
25[c]. [באלוף] Cf. Ps. cxliv. 14 (אלופינו), and see Heb. Dict. *s. v.* אלוף and
אלף. [וישובב] Cf. Ez. xxxviii. 4 and elsewhere. [לשדד] Gl. Cf. Is.
xxviii. 24. [ושעיותיו] Aram. Cf. Levy, *Ch. Wb. s. v.* שעיתא "conversation,"
"talk."
26. [לכלות מרבכ] which is confirmed by the Syr. (למנמרו), but it can
hardly be doubted that it is a corruption of לבלות meaning "to give provender."
Cf. Judg. xix. 21 (ויבול לחמורים) (*Kethib* ויבול) and Moore's Critical Commentary
(p. 417) to this verse. [תלמים] Only the *Mem* is fairly certain, whilst of the
Lamed only a faint sign of the upper stroke is visible.
27. [טמ...] Perhaps we should supply [עצי ש]טמ and emend שטמים.
More probably the *Nun* was by mistake connected with the *Yod* following it.
We have thus the rest of אבנים. The space permits also of the word בעצים.

Cf. the Gr. In the second clause the versions suggest the addition of בימים ישים. Cf. B. T. *Moed Katon* 25ᵇ.

XLIX.

12. Cf. 1 Kings ix. 3.

13ᵇ. [וירפא את הריסתינו] 1 Kings xviii. 30. [ויצב דלתים ובריח] Deut. iii. 5 דלתים ובריח, Joshua vi. 26 יציב דלתיה: See also 1 Kings xvi. 34.

14. [מעט] Syr. זעורין "few." [כהניך] Read with the versions בתנוך Cf. O. H. lxiv. 16. [נלקח פנים] Perhaps as much as לפנים or פנימה "taken within (the heaven)." The Cabbalists speak of an angel who is שר הפנים, but this is too late a notion for Sirach. This clause is omitted in the Syriac.

15. [כיוסף אם נולד גבר] "If there ever was born another man like Joseph," whilst the Syr. misread אם. This clause is a mere paraphrase of Gen. xli. 38 and 39 הנמצא כזה איש etc. and thus in no way proves that Daniel was unknown to B. S. [וגם נ' נפקדה] See Gen. l. 25 and 26.

16. See 1 Chr. i. 1 שת אנוש אדם, but *Shem* being the ancestor of the Hebrews takes the place of honour with B. S. [נפקרו] Syr. נבראו. Perhaps we ought to read נכבדו (cf. the Gr. ἐδοξάσθησαν and O. H. xliv. 7 Gl.), which would give a better parallelism to the second clause תפארת אדם, for which cf. Is. xliv. 13.

L.

1ᵃ. The first clause om. in the Gr., whilst the Syr. seems to have read עטרת (for ותפארת). Note the יחנן in the second clause.

1ᵇᶜ. [נפקד] Perhaps we should read נברך, though only לברוך occurs in *Kal* (2 Chr. xxxiv. 10). The Syr. read נבנה. [חזק היכל] Cf. 1 Maccabees vi. 7.

3. [אשיח בם בהמונו] "I will speak of them in his multitude," which gives no sense. The Greek χαλκὸς ὡσεὶ θαλάσσης τὸ περίμετρον is corrupt and suggests something like כים נחשת (cf. O. H. xlviii. 17ᶜ). Codex A, however, reads λάκκος (for χαλκός). 2 Chr. xxvi. 10 וחצב ברות ἐλατόμησε λάκκους. In Ps. lvi. 7 כרו לפני שיחה, Field gives from one Cod. λάκκον for שיחה. I am, therefore, inclined to read שיחה כים בהמונו "A pit (or reservoir) like the sea in its abundance." The comparison with the sea may have been suggested by Gen. i. 10 ולמקוה המים קרא ימים. See Heb. Dict. s.v. שוחה and שיחה as well as *Aruch Hashalem*, s.v. חרץ, שח and שווה, and Levy's *Ch. Wb.* s.v. שווה. Cf. also Gesenius (ed. Buhl) s. ll. שׁוּחַ (p. 779) "*Nebenf.* שחה, שחח Vgl. moab. אשחת *Grube, Teich?*" We shall then emend אשוח. Cf. *Jewish Quarterly Review*, x. p. 206.

2. [מעון] Perhaps a corruption of מעין.

4. [מחתף] Cf. Prov. xxiii. 28 and above, xxxii. 21. [ומחזק] etc. Cf. O. H. xlviii. 17.

5. [מה נהדר] O. H. xlvi. 2. Cf. the Paitanic description (in the עבודה to the Day of Atonement) of the glory of the high priest when he left the sanctuary on the day of Atonement. אמת מה נהדר היה כהן גדול בצאתו מבית

64   חכמת בן סירא   [CH. 50

קדשי הקדשים. See Landshut, *Amude Haabodah*, p. 274, and Rapoport, *Bikkure Haittim*, ix. 116. בהגיחו or בניחו [בהשניחו מאהל] Perhaps we should read (see Job xxxviii. 8 and xl. 23) for בהשגיחו. Syr. מהיכל. The Gr. had also probably מהיכל and translated ναοῦ, which was corrupted into λαοῦ, cf. Bretschneider, as quoted by Edersheim in the *Speaker's Commentary*. A similar mistake in the Gr. is pointed out above, xxxvi. 14.

6. מבין מלא [וכירח מבין] Probably a clerical error, having come in from the first clause. [בימי מועד] Cf. below, v. 8ª, from which it is clear that by ימי מועד is meant ניסן. See also commentaries on Hos. xii. 10.

7. [משרקת] Prof. Israel Lévi of Paris says, "this word is an Arabism meaning as much as 'to shine.' Cf. the marginal reading of the O. H. xliii. 9 b, which gives משריק for מזהיר in the text."

8ª. [בנין בענפי] Perhaps we should read בענפים or בענף. Cf. *Berachoth* 43 b [וכשושן]. האי מאן דנפיק ביומי דניסן וחזי אילנות דקא מלבלבי. Ecclus. xxxix. 13.

8ᶜ. [כפרח לבנון בימי קיץ] Cf. Nahum i. 4, see Fr.

9ª. [לבונה על המנחה] See Lev. ii. 1 and vi. 8. Perhaps אש is a corruption of אשי, see Fr. The Gr. read ולבונה, whilst both the Gr. and the Syr. had מנחתה.

9ᵇᶜ. [בכלי זהב....א..יל] Only these letters are legible. The rest of the clause (indicated by the dots) is partly faded and partly torn. [הנאחז] Esther i. 6 אחח, 2 Chr. ix. 18 מאחזים. [אבני חפץ] Isaiah liv. 12, O. H. xlv. 11 b.

10. [כזית רענן מלא גרגר] Cf. Jer. xi. 16 and Is. xvii. 6. [וכען שמן] Neh. viii. 15 עלי זית ועלי עץ שמן.

11ª. [בגדי כבוד..תפארת] Exod. xxviii. 40. Cf. also above, vi. 31. The Gr. had probably כליל ת'. Cf. Ez. xxviii. 12.

12ª. [והוא נצב על מערכות] *Tamid*, ii. 3 אש המערכה, and *ibid*. 5 המערכה השנייה לקטורת...הציתו שתי המערכות באש. Maimonides in chap. ii. of הלכות תמידין § 2 בראש המזבח עורכים עצים עורכין בבוקר בזמן שכה"ג רוצה. Cf. also *Mishnah Tamid*, vii. 3 מערכה גדולה של אש להקטיר היה עולה בכבש והסגן בימינו הגיע למחצית הכבש אחז הסגן בימינו והעלהו הושיט לו הראשון הראש והרגל...וכך היו מושטין לו כל שאר האיברים והוא סומך עליהן חרקן.

12ᶜ. [ויקיפוהו כערבי נחל] Job xl. 22 יסבהו ערבי נחל.

14. [ולנסדר] Note that v. 15 regarding the libation (נסכים) is omitted in the Hebrew. One is inclined to think that it was overlooked by the copyist through homoeoteleuton (the Gr. version suggesting that it also finished with אל עליון); see, however, 2 Chr. xxix. 27 ובעת החל העולה החל שיר ה' והחצצרות, no mention being made there of the libations, cf. Herzfeld's *Geschichte*, ii. pp. 163—166.

16ᶜ. [להזכיר] Read להזכיר. Cf. Num. x. 10 and Ps. xxxviii. 1.

CH. 50]   NOTES ON THE TEXT.   65

18. וְעַל הֲמוֹן הֱעֱרִיבוֹ. וְהָשִׁיר מְשׁוֹרָר 2 Chr. xxix. 28 [וְיִתֵּן הַשִּׁיר קוֹלוֹ
נֵרוֹ] Perhaps the lighting of the נֵר מַעֲרָבִי (see *Tamid*, v. 1) is meant by it. The Gr. seems, as was suggested to me, to have read וְעַל הֲמוֹן הֶעֱרִיבוֹ רָנַן. O. H. xlvii. 9 would suggest reading here וְקוֹל הָמוֹן instead of וְעַל ה׳; see also Gl. *ibid*.

19ᵃ. וִירְנוּ etc.] Cf. Lev. ix. 24.

19ᶜ. וּמִשְׁפָּטוֹ] Probably the נְסָכִים and the מִנְחָה are meant by it, see Num. xv. 24 and elsewhere וּמִנְחָתָם וְנִסְכֵּיהֶם כַּמִּשְׁפָּט.

21. [ל...מְפָנָיו] The rest is illegible, but the faint signs still discernible suggest הָעָם כֻּלּוֹ.

22ᵃ. עַתָּה בָּרְכוּ] etc. Cf. 1 Sam. xxv. 32, Ps. xxxi. 21 and O. H. xxxix. 35, xlv. 25ᶜ.   הַמַּפְלִיא לַעֲשׂוֹת] See above, xxxi. 9.

23. יִתֵּן] etc. O. H. xlv. 26. בְּשָׁלוֹם] Gr. and Syr. שָׁלוֹם.

24. יֵאָמֵן...חַסְדּוֹ etc.] Cf. 1 Chr. xvii. 23, 24, also Ecclus. i. 15, Gr. and Syr., and see also commentaries. בְּרִית פִּנְחָס] Num. xxv. 12. Cf. 1 Maccabees ii. 54. This clause agrees with none of the versions.

24⁽ᶠ⁾. Cf. O. H. xlv. 15ᶜ. See Syr.

25. אֵינֶנּוּ עָם] Cf. Deut. xxxii. 21.

26. וּבְגוֹי נָבָל] O. H. *alia*. 5, Deut. *ibid*. See Comm. on the Gr.

27ᵃ. [אוֹפַנִּים] Cf. Prov. xxv. 11. לְשִׁמְעוֹן בֶּן יֵשׁוּעַ בֶּן אֶלְעָזָר בֶּן סִירָא Cf. below, *vv.* 30⁽ᶠ⁾ and 30⁽ᵖ⁾. Saadyah (as above) p. 18 gives the pedigree of the ancestors of Ben Sira. Harkavy, *ibid*. and p. 200, thinks it to be a mere clerical error and emends the passage on the authority of the Syr. and certain Gr. MSS. (cf. Fr.) into יֵשׁוּעַ בֶּן שִׁמְעוֹן בֶּן אֶלְעָזָר בֶּן סִירָא. Dr Blau (*Revue des Etudes Juives*, xxxv. p. 20) agrees with Harkavy, thinking "que les deux traditions, celle du grec et celle du syriaque, se complètent mutuellement." Our MS., however, repeating the same order three times, makes it clear that it cannot be a mere mistake of the scribe. It is more probable that the name of our author was שִׁמְעוֹן. Probably he was called so after the high priest שִׁמְעוֹן whose younger contemporary he was,—a custom usual enough among the Jews at a very early period. The retention of the name יֵשׁוּעַ or Jesus after the disappearance of the name שִׁמְעוֹן may easily be attributed to the popularity of this name at a later age.

27ᶜ. אֲשֶׁר נִבַּע בְּפִתּוּר לִבֵּן] The *Beth* of בְּפִתּוּר and the *Nun* of לִבֵּן are rather doubtful. The former may also be taken for a *Kaph*, whilst the leg of the latter is too short for a final *Nun* and might represent a *Waw* (לִבּוֹ). But in either case the clause as it stands is unintelligible. Prov. x. 31 פִּי צַדִּיק יָנוּב חָכְמָה would suggest the emendation אֲשֶׁר נָב בְּפִיו חָכְמָה. The נִיבַּע probably came in from the second clause (הִבִּיעַ) as well as the לִבּוֹ which is now missing there, but is guaranteed by the Gr. We should then have here the same parallelism as in Ps. xlix. 4 פִּי יְדַבֵּר חָכְמוֹת וְהָגוּת לִבִּי תְבוּנוֹת. Of course פִּתְרוֹן = בְּפִתְרוֹן is also possible but this would not give a real parallelism. The Gr. (ἐχάραξα ἐν τῷ βιβλίῳ τούτῳ) suggests נָב בַּסֵּפֶר הַלֹּז or נִיב "engraved in this book." Cf. Exod. xxvii. 8 (נְבוּב לֻחֹת).

9

66   חכמת בן סירא   [CH. 50

28. אשרי etc.] Cf. Prov. iii. 13. See also Ps. i. 1, 2, xxxvii. 30 and above xiv. 20. [ונתן על ל׳ Perhaps we should read אל ל׳ (cf. Neh. ii. 12, vii. 5 and Eccles. viii. 1), though על is not impossible.
29[b]. Cf. Prov. xiv. 27 and xix. 23.

LI.

1[a]. [אודיך The hardly legible letters may perhaps also be read שמך.
1[b]. Cf. 2 Sam. xxii. 47 and Ps. xviii. 47.
1[c]. אספרה etc.] Cf. Ps. xxii. 23 and xxvii. 1.
2[a]. Cf. Ps. xxxiv. 23 and lxxi. 23.
2[b]. Cf. Job xxxiii. 18.
2[b(1)]. Cf. Ps. lxxxvi. 13. See Syr.
2[c]. [מדבת עם Ez. xxxvi. 3. משוט etc.] Cf. Job v. 21. The דבת probably came in wrongly from the first clause. [שטי כזב Ps. xl. 5.
2[e]. [נגד קמי Cf. Ps. xxiii. 5.
3[a]. [ברוב חסדך Neh. xiii. 22.
3[b]. [צופי סלע Read צלע. Cf. Jer. xx. 10 שמרי צלעי.
4[a]. Supply as the Gr. suggests מסביב.
4[b]. [מבבות Read מלבות. Cf. Exod. iii. 2. [לאין פחה Read לא נפחו. Cf. Job xx. 26.
5[a]. [מרחם ת׳ Cf. Ps. lxxi. 20 and Jonah ii. 3 (מבטן שאול. [לאמי Perhaps corruption of לאורה.
5[d]. [וטפלי שקר Job xiii. 4. Cf. also Ps. cxix. 69.
6. ותנע etc.] Cf. Ps. lxxxviii. 4. [לשאול תחתיות Cf. Ps. lxxxvi. 13 and lxxxviii. 7.
8[a]. וחסדיו etc.] Cf. Ps. xxv. 6.
8[c]. וינאלם etc.] Cf. Gen. xlviii. 6.
9. [ו' מארין קולי Cf. Is. xxix. 4. [ומשערי שאול שועתי Cf. Jonah ii. 3.
10[a]. Cf. Exod. xv. 2.
10[b]. [אל תרפני etc. Cf. Prov. xxiv. 10. [ביום שואה ומשואה Zephaniah i. 15.
11[a]. [אהללה שמך Ps. cxlv. 2.
12[a]. ימלטני etc.] Cf. Ps. xli. 2 and Job vi. 23.
12[c]. [ואברכה Cf. Ps. cxlv. 1 etc.
12[c(1)]. הודו etc.] Ps. cxxxvi. The next 15 verses are not to be found in any version, but they have left their impress on the Jewish Prayer Book, especially the (שמונה עשרה).
12[c(2)]. Cf. Ps. cxxi. 4.
12[d(1)]. [ליוצר הכל Cf. Jer. x. 16.
12[c(1)]. Cf. Is. xlix. 7.

NOTES ON THE TEXT.

12c(6,7). Cf. Ps. cxlvii. 2. See also Is. xii. 11 and xliv. 28.

12c(7). [עירו ומקדשו] Cf. Dan. ix. 26.

12c(8). [למצמיח] etc.] Cf. Ps. cxxxii. 17.

12c(9). For this and the preceding verse cf. 1 Chr. xxix. 22 (וימשחו...ולצדוק). Cf. also Ez. xl. 46, xliv. 15 and xlviii. 11.

12c(10). Cf. Gen. xv. 1.

12c(19). Cf. Gen. xlix. 24 and elsewhere.

12c(13). Cf. Ps. cxxxii. 13.

12c(14). [למלך מלכי מ׳] For this way of naming God see Rab. Dict. s. מלך. See also E. Landau's *Synonyma für Gott* (Zürich 1888) p. 9 Anm. 2. Usually מ׳ מ׳ המלכים.

12c(15). Ps. cxlviii. 14.

13. [אני נער etc.] Cf. Ps. lxxi. 17 and cxix. 9 (במה יזכה נער). The second clause is only to be found in the Syr. (cf. also Gr. 15b). Note the traces of the alphabetic acrostic, of which the following letters remain: א, ב, ג, ה, ו, י, מ, ס, ת, (v. 28 begins with שמעו) ש, ר, ק, צ, פ, ע, (v. 23 begins with סכלים). Cf. Bickell, *Zeitschrift für Kath. Theol.* 1882, pp. 326—332, and see Dr Taylor's Appendix.

*13(1). [באמתה etc.] Cf. Ps. xxv. 5 and cxix. 35; cf. Gr. 15b and Ps. xxvi. 12. אלהים למדתני מנעורי Cf. Ps. lxxi. 17 אדני מנעורי חכמה למדתי suggesting the reading למדתני for למדתי. Syr. מרי. Cf. Gr. 15c for the rest of the clause.

14. The verse agrees with the Syr., though traces of it are discernible in the Gr. 13b.

17. [עלה etc.] Cf. above, vi. 30, and below, v. 26ª. This clause agrees with the Syr., see Ed. as to the Gr. [אתן הודאה] Mishnah *Berachoth* iv. 3 אני נותן הודאה (var. הודיה). Probably we ought also to read in O. H. xlvii. 8 הודיות or נ׳ הוראות.

*18. [חשבתי] Cf. Ps. cxix. 59. [ולא אהפך] Gr. 18c אבוש. The parallel from the Ps. suggests however the emendation אשוב ולה. The אהפך probably came in from the next verse.

*18b(1). [חשקה etc.] See Gen. xxxiv. 8. Cf. also the Rab. expression חשקה נפשי בתורה (B. T. *Jebamoth* 63 b). Syr. דבקה. Gr. perhaps אָבְקָה, cf. Gen. xxxii. 25. See also Ed.

20ª. [נפשי נתתי] Cf. 1 Chr. xxii. 19, see also below, v. 26ª and above vii. 20.

20ª(1). ,, אט] The Syr. would suggest to supply אטעה, but the faint signs remaining of the missing letters do not admit of an *Ain*. They rather suggest a *He*, reading thus אטה ממנה. Both this clause and the next verse are omitted in the Gr.

20ª(2). ,, ולה אח] The signs left of which the top is lost are too small to permit of אחרור (cf. the Syr.). Of course אחור may be a corruption of the word suggested. [ואי ב]תוכה or בה. Cf. Syr. and below, v. 21.

---
* See Addendum, p. 68.

20bcd. וּבְטֶרֶם] Cf. Exod. xxiv. 10. Probably allusion to Ps. xix. 10 יִרְאַת ה' טְהוֹרָה. The Rabbis alluding to the same verse interpret it to mean the man הלומד תורה בטהרה (B. T. *Yoma* 72 b), which however refers to the purity of the person. At the end of the last clause supply with Gr. and Syr. לא אעזבה or אעזב.

21. מֵעֵי יֶהֱמוּ] Jer. xxxi. 20, but כתנור suggests the reading יהמו for 'יה. [קנין Cf. Prov. iv. 7 and viii. 21. See also *Perek R. Meir* (and parallels) תורה קנין אחד.

23. בית מדרש] See Rab. Dict.

24. עד מתי] Cf. Prov. i. 22 and Ps. xciv. 9. אילו ואילו] Syr. הלין. Bib. Hebrew אֵלֶּה. Cf. Strack (as above), p. 30. The ואילו is probably a dittography. צמאה] Cf. Is. lv. 1. See Fr. *ad loc.*

25. Cf. Is. *ibid.*

26ᵃ. Cf. above, *v.* 17.

26ᶜ. קרובה היא למבקשיה] Cf. Deut. xxx. 14, see also *Aboth d'R. Nathan*, II. ch. xxxv. ואל תלמוד מחצה למחצה והיא גדולה למבקשיה. The second clause is omitted in the Gr.

27. ועמדתי] Read with Syr. ועמלתי. Cf. B. T. *Megillah* 6ᵇ the expression יגעתי ומצאתי with regard to the Torah.

28. רבים] which word is omitted in the Syr. לִמּוּדֵי] *plur.* of לִמּוּד (in the sense of teachings, lessons). Cf. Rab. Dict.

29. בישיבתי] Read בשבתי. For this and the preceding verse, cf. Ps. lxxi. 17 and 18. Cf. also Ecclus. vi. 18 and xxv. 3. Syr. בתשובתי, Gr. בישועתו.

30. בצדקה] Versions עת בוא בטרם or בזמנה שלא.

30⁽¹⁾. Cf. Ps. lxxxix. 53 and cxlv. 4. See the Syr. of this verse and Fr. above, l. 29 (Gr.).

30⁽²⁾. Cf. above, l. 27. See also the Syr.

30⁽³⁾. Cf. Fr. as to the subscription of some Gr. MSS.

30⁽⁴⁾. Ps. cxiii. 2.

ADDENDUM.

Text, p. 23. Against the verse beginning באמתה put the number 15ᵇᶜ instead of 13⁽¹⁾. Against the verse beginning חשבתי put the number 18ᵃᵇ; the second clause perhaps represents 18ᶜ. Against the verse beginning חשקה put the number 19ᵃ instead of 18ᵇ⁽¹⁾; see notes.

²¹ מעי יהמו כתנור לה להביט בה   בעבור כן קניתיה קנין טוב :
²² נתן יי לי שכר שפתותי   ובלשוני אהודנו :
²³ פנו אלי סכלים   ולינו בבית מדרשי :
²⁴ עד מתי תחסרון מן אילו ואילו   ונפשכם צמאה מאד תהיה :
²⁵ פי פתחתי ודברתי בה קנו לכם חכמה בלא כסף :
²⁶ᵃ וצואריכם בעלה הביאו   ומשאה תשא נפשכם :
²⁶ᵇ קרובה היא למבקשיה   ונותן נפשו מוצא אתה :
²⁷ ראו בעיניכם כי קטן הייתי   ועמדתי בה ומצאתיה :
²⁸ רבים שמעו למודי בנערותי   וכסף וזהב תקנו בי :
²⁹ תשמח נפשי בישיבתי   ולא תבושו בשירתי :
³⁰ מעשיכם עשו בצדקה   והוא נותן לכם שכרכם בעתו :
³⁰⁽¹⁾ ברוך יי לעולם   ומשובח שמו לדר ודר :
³⁰⁽²⁾ עד הנה דברי שמעון בן ישוע שנקרא בן סירא :
³⁰⁽³⁾ חכמת שמעון בן ישוע בן אלעזר בן סירא :
³⁰⁽⁴⁾ יהי שם יי מבורך מעתה ועד עולם :

51. 12ᶜ—20ᵈ]

⁽ᵃ⁾¹² הודו למצמיח קרן לבית דוד	כי לעולם חסדו :
⁽⁹⁾ הודו לבוחר בבני צדוק לכהן	כי לעולם חסדו :
⁽¹⁰⁾ הודו למגן אברהם	כי לעולם חסדו :
⁽¹¹⁾ הודו לצור יצחק	כי לעולם חסדו :
⁽¹²⁾ הודו לאביר יעקב	כי לעולם חסדו :
⁽¹³⁾ הודו לבוחר בציון	כי לעולם חסדו :
⁽¹⁴⁾ הודו למלך מלכי מלכים	כי לעולם חסדו :
⁽¹⁵⁾ וירם קרן לעמו תהלה לכל חסידיו לבני ישראל עם קרבו הללויה :	

¹³ אני נער הייתי	וחפצתי בה ובקשתיה :
⁽¹³⁾ באמתה דרכה רגלי	אדני מנעורי חכמה למדתי :
¹⁴ ואתפלל תפלה בנערותי	¹⁶ והרבה מצאתי דעה :
¹⁷ עלה היה לי לכבוד	ולמלמדי אתן הודאה :
¹⁸ חשבתי להיטיב	ולא אהפך כי אמצאנו :
⁽¹⁸⁾¹⁴ חשקה נפשי בה	ופני לא אהפך ממנה :
²⁰ נפשי נתתי אחריה	⁽¹⁾²⁰ ולנצח נצחים לא אטה... :
⁽²⁾²⁰⁼ ידי פתחה שעריה	ולה אהוז ואביט ב[תוכה] :
²⁰⁼ᵇ,ᶜ,ᵈ ובטהרה מצאתיה ולב קניתי לה מתחלתה בעבור כ... :	

ותגע למות נפשי	⁶והייתי לשאול תחתיות :
⁷ואפנה סביב ואין עוזר לי	ואצפה סומך ואין :
⁸ואזכרה את רחמי יייִ	וחסדיו אשר מעולם :
⁸ᵃהמציל את חוסי בו	ויגאלם מכל רע :
⁹וארים מארץ קולי	ומשערי שאול שועתי :
¹⁰וארומם ייִי אבי אתה	⁽¹⁾¹⁰ᵃכי אתה גבור ישע :
¹⁰ᵃאל תרפני ביום צרה	ביום שואה ומשואה :
¹¹אהללה שמך תמיד	ואזכרך בתפלה :
¹²אז שמע קולי ייִי	⁽¹⁾¹²ᵃויאזין אל תחנוני :
¹²ᵃויפדני מכל רע	וימלטני ביום צרה :
¹²ᵇעל כן הודיתי ואהללה	ואברכה את שם ייִי :
⁽¹⁾¹²ᶜהודו לייִי כי טוב	כי לעולם חסדו :
⁽²⁾ הודו לאל התשבחות	כי לעולם חסדו :
⁽³⁾ הודו לשומר ישראל	כי לעולם חסדו :
⁽⁴⁾ הודו ליוצר הכל	כי לעולם חסדו :
⁽⁵⁾ [הוד]ו לגואל ישראל	כי לעולם חסדו :
⁽⁶⁾ [הו]דו למקבץ נדחי ישראל	כי לעולם חסדו :
⁽⁷⁾ הודו לבונה עירו ומקדשו ·	כי לעולם חסדו :

ויעשהו כרצונו :	⁵⁰המגדל אדם מרחם
ויהי בשלום ביניכם :	⁵³יתן לכם חכמת לבב
ויקם לו ברית פינחס :	⁵⁴יאמן עם שמעון חסדו
כימי שמים :	⁽¹⁾⁵⁴אשר לא יכרת לו ולזרעו
והשלישית איננו עם :	²⁵בשני גוים קצה נפשי
וגוי נבל הדר בשכם :	²⁶יושבי שעיר ופלשת
לשמעון בן ישוע בן אלעזר בן סירא :	²⁷מוסר שכל ומושל אופנים
ואשר הביע בתבונות :	²⁷אשר ניבע בפתור לבן
ונתן על לבו יחכם :	²⁸אשרי איש באלה יהגה
⁽¹⁾אודך אלהי אבי : ¹אהללך אלהי ישעי	²⁹כי יראת ייי חיים
¹כי פדית ממות נפשי :	¹אספרה שמך מעוז חיי
⁽¹⁾ומיד שאול הצלת רגלי :	²חשכת בשרי משחת
משוט רבת לשון ומשפת שטי כזב :	²פציתני מרבת עם
³עזרתני כרוב חסדך :	³נגד קמי הייתה לי
ומיד מבקשי נפשי :	³ממוקש צופי סלע
⁴וכמצוקות שלהבת... :	⁴מרבות צרות הושעתני
⁵מרחם [תה]ום לאמ[י] .. :	⁵מכבות אש לאין פחה
⁵והצי לשון מרמה :	⁵משפתי זמה וטפלי שקר

ⁱⁱᵃבעטותו בגדי כבוד	והתלבשו בגדי תפארת :
ⁱⁱᵇבעלותו על מזבח הוד	ויהדר עזרת מקדש :
¹²ᵃבקבלו נתחים מיד אחיו	והוא נצב על מערכות :
¹²ᵇסביב לו עטרת בנים	כשתילי ארזים בלבנון :
¹²ᶜויקיפותו כערבי נחל	¹³ᵃכל בני אהרן בכבודם :
¹³ᵇואשי יי׳ בידם	נגד כל קהל ישראל :
¹⁴עד כלותו לשרת מזבח	ולסדר מערכות עליון :
¹⁶ᵃאז ירעו בני אהרן הכהנים	בהצצרות מקשה :
¹⁶ᵇויריעו וישמיעו קול אדיר	להזכיר לפני עליון :
¹⁷ᵃכל בשר יחדו נמהרו	ויפלו על פניהם ארצה :
¹⁷ᵇלהשתחות לפני עליון	לפני קדוש ישראל :
¹⁸ויתן השיר קולו	ועל המון העריכו נרו :
¹⁹ᵃוירנו כל עם הארץ	בתפלה לפני רחום :
¹⁹ᵇעד כלותו לשרת מזבח	ומשפטיו הגיע אליו :
²⁰ᵃאז ירד ונשא ידיו	על כל קהל ישראל :
²⁰ᵇוברכת יי׳ בשפתיו	ובשם יי׳ התפאר :
²¹וישנו לנפל שנית	העם כלו מפניו :
²²עתה ברכו נא את יי׳ אלהי ישראל המפלא לעשות בארץ :

¹²ויריםו היכל קדש	המכונן לכבוד עולם :	**49.** 12
¹³נחמיה יאדר זכרו	המקים את חרבתינו :
¹³וירפא את הריסתינו	ויצב דלתים ובריח :
¹⁴מעט נוצר על הא‫ר‬ץ כהניך	וגם הוא נלקח פנים :
¹⁵כיוסף אם נולד גבר	וגם גויתו נפקדה :
¹⁶ושם ושת ואנוש נפקדו	ועל כל חי תפארת אדם :
¹גדול אחיו ותפארת עמו	שמעון בן יוחנן הכהן :	**50.** 1
¹אשר בדורו נפקד הבית	ובימיו חזק היכל :
²אשר בדורו נכרה מקוה	אשיח בם בהמונו :
²אשר בימיו נבנה קיר	פנות מעון בהיכל מלך :
⁴הדואג לעמו מחתף	ומחזק עירו מצר :
⁵מה נהדר בהשגיחו מאהל	ובצאתו מבית הפרכת :
⁶ככוכב אור מבין עבים	וכירח מלא מבן בימי מועד :
⁷וכשמש משרקת אל היכל המלך	וכקשת נראתה בענן :
⁸כנץ בענפי בימי מועד	וכשושן על יבלי מים :
⁹כפרח לבנן בימי קיץ	¹⁰וכאש לבונה על המנחה :
⁹ᵇבכלי זהב ... א .. יל	הנאחז על אבני חפץ :
¹⁰כזית רענן מלא גרגר	וכעץ שמן מרוה ענף :

[38. 13—27]

פ̇

	¹³כי יש עת אשר בידו מצלחת	¹³כי גם הוא אל אל יעתיר:	
ימנה	¹⁴אשר יצלח לו פשרה	ורפאות למען מחיה:	
	¹⁵אשר חוטא לפני עושהו	יתגבר לפני רופא:	יסתוגר
	¹⁶בני על המת הזיב דמעה	התמרר ונהה קינה:	התמרמר ונהי
כמשפט א' שארם	¹⁶ᵇכמשפטו ⁰אסוף ⁰שארו	ואל תתעלם בגויעתם:	תתחד בגויעם
בכי וההם	¹⁷המר בכי ⁰והתם מספר	ושית אבלו כיוצא בו:	
	¹⁷ᵇיום ושנים בעבור דמעה	והנחם בעבור עון:	
	¹⁸מדין יוצא אסון	כן רע לבב יבנה עצבה:	
תשית עליו	²⁰אל תשיב אליו לב עוד	פרע זכרו וזכור אחרית:	וחכר
כן	²²זכור חקו כי הוא חקך	לו אתמול ולך היום:	
	²¹אל תזכרהו כי אין לו תקוה	מה תעיל ולך תריע:	
בשבות מת ישבות ז'	²³מושבת ⁰מתוושבת זכרו	והנחם עם צאת נפשו:	

	²⁴חכמת סופר תרבה חכמה	וחסר עסק הוא יתחכם:	
	²⁵מה יתחכם תומך מלמד	ומתפאר בחנית מהעיר:	
וישובב בשיר	²⁵ᵇבאלוף ינהג לשבר יושבב בשור	ושעיותיו עם בני [ב]ק̇ר:	
	²⁶ושקידתו לכלות מרבק	לב ישית לשד̇ר בת]לוס[ם:	
	²⁷אף עשה . . . . . טם	אשר לילה . . . . :	ינהג

. . . .

בחמר 37. 27	²⁷בני בחייך נס נפשך	וראה מה רע לה אל תתן לה:	אל תמסר
כי לב טוב	²⁸כי לא הכל לכל טוב	לא כל נפש כל זן תבחר	אל לנפש
תזר ל	²⁹אל תזרע לכל תענוג	ואל תשפך על כל מטעמים:	
אוכל ירון	³⁰כי ברוב תענוג יקנן חולי	והמרבה יגיע אל זרא:	והמזיע ובהישמר
גועו	³¹בלא מוסר רבים יגועו ועוע	ונשמר יוסיף חיים:	אל לפט חכם פן אתה שונא אדם מנב
רעה צרכך 38. 1	¹רעי רופא לפני צרכו	גם אתו חלק אל:	כי
	²מאת אל יחכם רופא	ומאת מלך ישא משאות:	מלכים
	³דעת רופא תרים ראשו ולפני נדיבים יתיצב:		
ברא שמים	⁴אל מארץ מוציא תרופות	וגבר מבין אל ימאס בם:	כוחם :
מעץ	⁵הלא בעץ המתיקו מים	בעבור להודיע כל אנוש כחו :	בגבורתם :
	⁶ויתן לאנוש בינה	להתפאר בגבורתו :	קרח
	⁷בהם רופא יניח מכאוב	וכן רוקח עשה מרקחת :	מצבי ארצי
ישבת	⁸למען לא ישבתו מעשהו	ותושיה מבני אדם :	פלא
במחלה	⁹בני בחולי אל תתעבר	התפלל אל אל כי הוא ירפא :	ערך
נפש ס׳ והחט׳	¹⁰[נו]ש מעול ומהכר פנים	ומכל פשעים טהר לב :	הוגד
אזרתה	¹¹ה[נ]גש ניח[ו]ח אזכרה	ודשן ערוך בכנפי הוניך :	ואל ישמש מאח נגב צרכיך :
	¹²וגם לרופא תן מקום	ולא ימוש כי גם בו צורך :	

[36. 1—21

פּ

יד	36. ₁ הושיענו אלהי הכל	²ֿ(וֿ)[הר]יֿםֿ פחדך על כל הגוים:	
	₃ הניף °על עם נכר	ויראו את גבורתיך:	
בם	₄ כאשר נקדשת לעינהם בנו	כן לעינינו הכבד בנו:	בם :
	₅ וידעו כאשר ידענו	כי אין אלהים זולתך:	
	₆ חדש אות ושנה מופת	האדיר יד ואמץ זרוע וימין:	
	₇ העיר אף ושפוך חמה	והכניע צר והדוף אויב:	וחנדוף
מצער	₈ החיש קץ ופקוד מועֿד	⁹(י)כי מי יאמר לך מה תעשה:	תפעל.
אויב	₁₀ השבת ראש פאתי מואב	האומר אין זולתי:	
	₁₁ אסוף כל שבטי יעקב	ויתנחלו כימי קדם:	
	₁₂ רחם על עם נקרא בשמך	ישראל בכור כיניתה:	
	₁₃ רחם על קרית קדשך	ירושלם מכון שבתיך:	
מהדריך	₁₄ מלא ציון את־הודך	ומכבודך את היכלך:	
	₁₅ תן עדות למראש מעשיך	והקם חזון דבר בשמך:	
	₁₆ תן את פעלת קוייך	ונביאיך יאמנו:	
עבדך	₁₇ᵃ תשמע תפלת עבדיך	כרצונך על עמך:	ברצונך
ויראו	₁₇ᶜ וידעו כל אפסי ארץ	כי אתה אלה(נו) לעו(ל)ם:	
פּ	₁₈ כל מאכל אוכל גרגרת	אך יש אוכל נ(חמ)ד לע(ינ)ים:	אל יש מאכל ...
	¹⁹[כ]ל זכֿר תקבל אשׁה	אך . . . . :	חמד ...
		אך יש אשה יפה:	כי יש מאכל מאכל ומאכל

* * * * * * *

35. 9—20]

מעשׂיך	ובששון הקדש מעשׂר :	⁹ בכל מעשׂיך האר פנים	35.9
מבשׂיך	בטוב עין ובהשׂגת יד :	¹⁰ תן לאל כמתנתו לך	כמתתו
וּבֿהנשׂת וּבֿהניש	ושבעתים ישׁיב לך :	¹¹ כי אלוה תשלומות הוא	
ישלם	ואל תבטח על זבח מעשק :	¹² אל תשחד כי לא יקח	
	ואין עמו משוא פנים :	¹³ כי אלהי משפט הוא	
ותחנונים	ותחנוני מצוק ישמע :	¹⁴ לא ישא פנים אל דל	
תחבט	ואלמנה כי תרבה שיח :	¹⁵ לא יטש צעקת יתום	אנקת
	ואנחה על מרודיה :	¹⁶ הלא דמעה על לחי תרד	
צעקתה	וְצַעֲקָה ענן השתה :	¹⁶ תמרורי רצון הנחה	
וצעקתיה	ועד תגיעׂ לא תנוח :	¹⁷ שועת דל ענן חל עם	עבים חלפה
בי	ושופט צדק יעשה משפט :	¹⁷ לא תמוש עד יפקוד אל	
עושה	וכגבור לא יתאפק :	¹⁸ גם אל לא יתמהמה	ארון
סה	ולגוים ישיב נקם :	¹⁸ עד ימחץ מתני אכזרי	מפני
רשׂעים	ומטה רשע גדוע יגדע :	¹⁸ עד יוריש שבט זדון	יבטי
	וגמול אדם כמזמתו :	¹⁹ עד ישיב לאנוש פעלו	
ויבׂמחם	וְשִׂמְחָתָם בִּישׁוּעָתוֹ	¹⁹ עד יריבׂ ריב עמו	
אין פסוק אז	כעת חזיזים בעת בצורת :	²⁰ [רחמ]ם מׁיׄיׄיׄ זׁמן מצוקה	
נוסבתחא יריעֹ	בׂ . . . מׁ . . פׂ . . ך :	²⁰⁽¹⁾	
ואידר זא הישותהו			
בור ובי נבישתה			

[32. 14—33. 3]

	ומשחרהו ישיג מענה :	¹⁴דורש אל יקח מוסר	ישׂא
	ויענהו בתפלתו :	¹⁴⁽¹⁾דורש חפצי אל יקח לקח	
	ומתלחלה יוקש בה :	¹⁵דורש תורה יפיקנה	
	ותחבולות מנשף יוציא :	¹⁶ירא יייׄ יבין משפט	
וחכמות	וכחׄמות רבות יוציאו מלבם :	¹⁶⁽¹⁾יראי יייׄ יבינו משפטו	
ויאׄר למסור	ואחר צרכו ימשׁך תוחה :	¹⁷איש חכם יטה תוכחות	חסם
	ולץ לא ישמר לשׁונו :	¹⁷⁽¹⁾איש חכם לא יכסה כחׄמה	חכמה
	זד ולץ לא ישמר תורה :	¹⁸ᵃאיש חכם לא יקח שחד	
	ואחר מעשׁיך אל תתקצף :	¹⁹בלא עצה אל תפעל דבר	רשעים
	ואל תתקל בנגף פעמים :	²⁰בדרך מוקשת אל תלך	
הזהר	ובאחריתך השמר :	²¹אל תבטח בדרך מחתף	
	ובארחתיך הזהר :	²¹⁽¹⁾אל תבטח בדרך רשעים	
מצות מצותן	כי כל עושה אלה שומר מצוׄה :	²²בכל דרכיך שמור נפשך	
	כי עושה זה שומר מצוה :	²³בכל מעשיך שמור נפשך	
	ובוטח בייי לא יבוש :	²⁴נוצר תורה שומר נפשו	
שב במסער	כי אם בניסוי שׁ]ב ומ[ל[ט]	¹ירא יייׄ לא יפגע רע	33.
	ומתמוטט בםׄסׄ	²לא יחכם שונא תורה	
	ותורתו כאׄ . . ן̇ . .	³איש נבון יבין דבר	
	∗ ∗ ∗ ∗ ∗ ∗ ∗		

32. 1—13]

אין גי... אבא	¹ ׳׳היה להם כאחד מהם	דאג להם ואחר תסוב יזהכין צרכם ואחר תרבין׳:	
אן מפסוק איסת	² ׳׳למען תשמח בכבודם	ועל מוסר תשא שכל:	
נ וסכהא			
דינר			
סבכי	³ מלל שב֜ כי֜ הוא לך	והצנע֜ שכל ואל תמנע שיר:	לבת
אבא אעל	⁴ במקום הין אל תשפך שיח ובלא מזמר מה תשפך שיח ובל עת מה תתחכם:		
	⁵׳׳כחותם על כים זהב	שיר אל על משתה הין:	שירת
נוב זיד	⁵ כומז אורם על נֹוב זהב	משפט שיר על משתה הין:	
נהפך ספיר	⁶ ׳׳כרביד זהב ובו נפך֜ וספיר כך נאים דברים יפים על משתה הין		
מלא	⁶ ׳׳מליאות פז וחותם ברקת	קול מזמור על נועם תירוש:	
אתך	⁷ דבר נער אם צריך אתה בחזק פעמים ושלש אם ישאלך:		ישא לך
	⁸ כל לאמר ומעט הרבה	ודמה לידע ומחריש יהדו:	
	⁹ בין זקנים אל תקומם	ושרים אל תרב למרד:	
	¹⁰׳׳לפני ברד ינצח ברק	ולפני דכא ינצח הן:	
בדד ינצח ברד	¹⁰ לפני ברד ינצח ברק	ולפני בושי הן:	
ברד ינצח בדד			
	¹¹ בעת מפקד אל תתאחר	פטר לביתך ושלם רצון:	
	¹¹׳׳בעת שלחן אל תרבה דברים	ואם עלה על לבך דבר:	
	¹² ...[כ]ל[בב]ך֜ ושלם רצון	ביראת אל ולא בחסר כל:	
	¹³ [וע]ל [כ]ל [א]לה ברך עושך	המרוך מטובתו:	
דריש אל חי	¹³ דו֜רש א[ל] י[קנ]ו֜ה֜ רצון	ומתהלה יוקש בו:	
וקוה רצון			

	ומאכלו יעלה עליו:	²⁵שנות לב טוב תחת מטעמים	30. ²⁵
תפריג	דאגת מחיה תפריע נומה:	¹שֶׁקֶר עשיר ימחה שארו	31. ¹ שקר
ומחלה חז' תפריג	ומחלי חזק תפריע נומה:	²דאגת מחיה תפריג נומה	
	ומסתיר סוד אוהב כנפש:	²⁽¹⁾רע נאמן תנוד חרפה	תנוד
עמל:	ואם ינוח לקבל תענוג:	³עמלי עשיר לקבל הון	עמל
	ואם ינוח יהיה צריך:	⁴יגע עני לחסר ביתו	
	ואם ינוח לא נחה לו:	⁴⁽¹⁾עמל עני לחסר כחו	
במח'	ואוהב מחיר בו ישנה:	⁵רודף חרון לא ינקה	חריץ
	והבוטח על פנינים:	⁶רבים היו חבולי זהב	חללי
	וגם להושיע ביום עברה:	⁶⁽¹⁾ולא מצאו להנצל מרעה	
פתח	וכל פותה יוקש בו:	⁷כי תקלה הוא לאויל	מצוא
	ואחר ממון לא נלח:	⁸אשרי איש נמצא תמים	
	כי הפליא לעשות בעמו:	⁹מי הוא זה ונאשרנו	
	והיה לו שלום והיה לו תפארת: לתפארה תפארת	¹⁰מי הוא זה שנדבק בו	הנדבק
	אהיה לך לתפארת:	¹⁰⁽¹⁾כי ברבות שלום חייו	
	היא לך לתפארת: אהיה לך להתפאר:	¹⁰⁽²⁾מי ברכו וישלם חייו	
	ולהרע רע ולא אבה:	¹⁰ᶜ מי יוכל לסור ולא סר	
	יתהללתו יספר קהל:	¹¹על כן חזק טובו	

* * * * * * * *

30. 11—24]

	ואל תשא לשחיתותיו :	¹¹אל תמשילהו בנעוריו	30. 11
מט'	רציץ מתניו שעורנו נער :	¹¹ᵃכפתן על חי תפגע	(¹¹)
	ובקע מתניו כשהוא קטן :	¹²כיף ראשו בנעורותו	
ולוד מסך	ונולד ממנו מפח נפש :	¹²ᵃלמה ישׂקה ומרה בך	יקשיח
ולך			ישקיה
יתעל	פן באולתו יתלע בך :	¹³יסר בנך והכבד עולו	
	מעשיר וננע בבשרו :	¹⁴טוב מסכן וחי בעצמו	
	ורוח טובה מפנינים :	¹⁵חיי שר אויתי מפז	עשר
			שאר
שאר :	ואין טובה על טוב לבב :	¹⁶אין עושר על עושר שׂר עצם	
מחיים רעים :	ונחת עולם מכאב נאמן :	¹⁷טוב למות מחיי שוא	
ולוד ושׂא	וירד שאול מכאב עומד :	¹⁷ᵃטוב למות מחיים רעים	(¹⁷)
מצנת נלול :	תנופה מצנת לפני גלול :	¹⁸טובה שפוכה על פה סתום	פום
בגזל		¹⁹ᵃᵃכאשר סירים יחבק נערה ומתאנח ⁽¹⁹ᵃ⁾כן עושה באונס משפט :	
בידן :	ויי מבקש מידו :	⁽¹⁹ᵇ⁾כן נאמן לן עם בתולה	
בעצתך :	ואל תכשל בעונך :	²⁰אל תתן לדין נפשך	
	וגיל אדם האריך אפו :	²²שמחת לבב הם חיי איש	
	וקצפון הרחק ממך :	²²פוג נפשך ופיג לבך	
	ואין תעלה בקצפון :	²³כי רבים דרג דין	
	ובלא עת תזקין דאנה :	²⁴קנאה ודין יקצרו ימים	

והו יכיר על כל מפעל איש : ²⁰ לא צוה אנוש לחטא ולא החלים
אנש כזב : ⁽¹⁾²⁰ ולא מרחם על עושה שוא ועל מגלה סוד : ¹ אל
תתאוה תואר נערי שוא ואל תשמח בבני עולה : ² וגם אם פרו אל
תבע בם אם אין אתם יראת יי· ³ אל תאמין בחייהם ואל תבטח
בעקבותם : ⁽¹⁾³ª כי לא תהיה להם אחרית טובה . ⁴ כי טוב אחד
עושה רצון מאלף ומת ערירי ממי שהיו לו בנים רבים ..לה :
ומאחרית זדון : ⁵ מאחד ערירי ירא יי ישב עיר וממשפחת
בגדים תחרב : ⁵ רבות כאלה ראתה עיני ועצמות כאלה שמעה
אזני : ⁶ בעדת רשעים יוקדת אש ובגוי חנף נצתה חמה :
⁷ אשר לא נשא לנסיכי קדם המורים עולם בגבורתם : ⁸ ולא
ע[ל] חמל על מגורי לוט המתעברים בגאותם : ⁹ ולא חמל
על גוי חרם הנודשים בעונם : ¹⁰ כן שש מאות אלף רגלי
הנאספים בזדון לבם : ¹¹ ואף כי אחו[ד] מקשה ערף תמה זה אם
ינקה : ¹¹ כי רחמים ואף עמו ונשא וסולח ועל רשעים
יניח רגזו : ¹² כרב רחמיו כן תוכחתו איש כמפעליו ישפט :
¹³ אל ימלט בגזל עול ולא ישבית תאות צדיק לעולם : ¹⁴ כל
העושה צדקה יש לו שכר וכל אדם כמעשיו יצא לפניו :
¹⁵ יי הקשה את לב פרעה אשר לא ידעו : שמעשיו
מגולין תחת השמים ¹⁶ רחמיו : יראו לכל בריותיו ואורו
ושבחו חלק לבני אדם : ¹⁷ª אל תאמר מאל נסתרתי ובמרום מי
יזכרני : ¹⁷ᵇ בעם כבד לא אודע ומה נפשי בקצות רוחות כל בני
אדם : ¹⁸ הן השמים ושמי השמים ותהום וארץ : ברדתו
עליהם עֹמוֹדים בפקדו וכרגשו : ¹⁹ אף קצבי הרים ויסודי
תבל בהביטו אליהם רעש ירעשו : ²⁰ גם עלי לא ישים לב
ובדרכי מי יתבונן : ⁽¹⁾²¹ אם חטאתי לא תראני עין או אם אכזב
בכל סתר מי יודע : ²² מה צדק מי יגידנו ותקות מה כי אצוק
חוק : ²³ חסרי לב יבינו אלה וגבר ע[ר] תה יחשב זאת : ²⁴ שמעו
אלי וקחו [מש]לי ועל דברי שימו לב : ²⁵ אביעה במשקל רוחי
ובהצנע אחוה דעי· ²⁶ כברא אל מעשיו מראש על חיידם

14. 12—15. 19]

ידך הדשן: 12זכור כי לא 'בשאול תענוג ולא בות יתמהמה:
וחוק לשאול לא הגד לך 13בטרם תמית היטב לאוהב:
והשינת ידך תן לו 14אל תמנע מטובת יום: ובהלקה אח
אל תעבר וחמוד רע אל תחמוד: 15הלא לאחר תעזב חילך
ויגיעך לידי גורל: 16תן לאח וָתָּן ופנק נפשך כי אין בשאול
לבקש תענוג (15)16וכל דבר שיפה: לעשוֹת לכפי אלהים עשה 17כל הבשר
כבגד יבלה וחוק עולם גוע יגועו: 18כפרח עלה על עץ רענן
שזה נובל ואחר גֹמֵל: 19כל מעשיו רקוב ירקבו ופעל ידיו
ימשך אחריו: 20אשרי אנוש בחכמה יהגה ובתבונה ישעה:
21השם על דרכיה לבו ובתבונתיה יתבונן: 22לצאת אחריה
בחקר וכל מבואיה ירצד: 23המשקיף בעד החלונה ועל
פתחיה יצותת: 24החונה סביבות ביתה והביא יתריו בקירה:
25ונטה אהלו על ידה ושכן שכן טוב: 26וישים קנו בעופיה
ובענפיה יתלונן: 27וחוסה בצלה מחרב ובמעונותיה ישכן:

15. 1כי ירא יי יעשה זאת ותופש תורה ידריכנה: 2וקדמתהו
כאם וכאשת נעורים תקבלנו: 3והאכלתהו לחם שכל ומי
תבואה תשקנו: 4ונשען עליה ולא ימוט ובה יבטח ולא
יבוש: 5ורוממתהו מרעהו ובתוך קהל תפתח פיו: 6ששון
ושמחה ימצא ושם עולם תורישנו: 7לא ידריכוה מתי
שוא ואנשי זדון לא יראוה: 8רחוקה היא מלצים ואנשי
9לא נאמר תהלה בפי רשע כי לא מא׳ נחלקה לו:
כזב לא יזכרוה: 10בפה חכם תאמר תהלה ומשל בה ילמדנה:
11אל תאמר מא׳ פשעי כי את אשר שנא לא עשה: 12פן
תאמר הוא התקילני כי אין צורך באנשי חמס: 13רעה
ותעבה שנא יי ולא יאננה ליראיו: 14אלהים מבראשית
ברא אָדם וישתדהו ביד חותפו ויתנהו ביד יצרו: 15אם
תחפץ תשמר מצוה ותבונה לעשות רצונו: (15)אם תאמין
בו גם אתה תחיה 16מוצק לפניך אש ומים באשר תחפץ שלח
ידיך: 17לפני אדם חיים ומות אשר יחפץ ינתן לו: 18ספקה
חכמת יי אמץ גבורות וחוזה כל: 19עיני אל יראו מעשיו

⁷עַד אֲשֶׁר יוֹעִיל יְהָתֵל בָּךְ · פְּעָמִים שָׁלֹשׁ יַעֲרִיצְךָ וּבְכֵן יִרְאֲךָ
וְהִתְעַבֵּר בָּךְ וּבְרֹאשׁוֹ יָנִיעַ אֵלֶיךָ · ⁸הִשָּׁמֶר אַל תַּרְחִיב מְאֹד
וְאַל תִּדְמֶה בַּחֲסִירֵי מַדָּע : ⁹קָרֵב נָדִיב הָיָה רָחוֹק וּכְדֵי כֵן
יַגִּישְׁךָ : ¹⁰אַל תִּתְקָרֵב פֶּן תַּרְחִיק וְאַל תִּתְרַחֵק פֶּן תִּשָּׂנֵא : ¹¹אַל
תִּבְטַח לַחְפּשׁ עִמּוֹ וְאַל תַּאֲמִין לְרֹב שִׂיחוֹ : ¹²כִּי מֵרֹבוֹת שִׂיחוֹ
נִסְיוֹן וְשִׂחֵק לְךָ וַחֲקָרְךָ : ¹²אַכְזָרִי יִתֵּן מוֹשֵׁל וְלֹא יַחְמֹל עַל
נֶפֶשׁ רַבִּים קוֹשֵׁר קֶשֶׁר : ¹³הִשָּׁמֶר וֶהֱיֵה זָהִיר וְאַל תֵּלֵךְ
עִם אַנְשֵׁי חָמָס : ¹⁵כָּל הַבָּשָׂר יֶאֱהַב מִינוֹ וְכָל אָדָם אֶת
הַדּוֹמֶה לוֹ : ¹⁶מִין כָּל בָּשָׂר אֶצְלוֹ וְאֶל מִינוֹ · יְחוּבַּר אָדָם ·
¹⁷מַה יְחוּבַּר זְאֵב אֶל כֶּבֶשׂ כָּךְ רָשָׁע לְצַדִּיק · ⁽¹⁷⁾ᵇוְכֵן עָשִׁיר אֶל אִישׁ נֶאֱצָל
¹⁸מֵאִישׁ שְׁלוֹם צָבוּעַ : אַל כֶּלֶב מֵאַיִן שְׁלוֹם עָשִׁיר אֶל רָשׁ :
¹⁹מַאֲכַל אֲרִי פִּרְאֵי מִדְבָּר כֵּן מַרְעִית עָשִׁיר דַּלִּים : ²⁰תּוֹעֲבַת
גַּאֲוָה עֲנָוָה וְתוֹעֲבַת עָשִׁיר אֶבְיוֹן : ²¹עָשִׁיר מָט בְּסֶמֶךְ
מֵרֵעַ וְדַל נִמְט נִדְחֶה מֵרֵעַ אֶל רַע : ²²עָשִׁיר מְדַבֵּר וְעוֹזְרָיו
רַבִּים וּדְבָרָיו מְכוֹעָרִין מוֹפִין : ²²ᶜדַּל נִמְט גַּע גַּע וְנָשָׂא וְדָבָר
מַשְׂכִּיל וְאֵין לוֹ מָקוֹם : ²³עָשִׁיר דּוֹבֵר הַכֹּל נִסְכְּתוּ וְאֶת
שִׂכְלוֹ עַד עָב יַגִּיעוּ : ²³ᵇדַּל דּוֹבֵר מִי זֶה יֹאמְרוּ וְאִם נִתְקַל
גַּם הֵם יֶהְדְּפוּהוּ : ²⁴טוֹב הָעוֹשֶׁר אִם אֵין עָוֹן וְרַע הָעֹנִי עַל
פִּי זָדוֹן : ²⁵לֵב אֱנוֹשׁ יְשַׁנֶּה פָּנָיו אִם לְטוֹב וְאִם לְרָע : ²⁶עִקְּבַת
לֵב טוֹב פָּנִים אוֹרִים וְשִׂיג וָשִׂיחַ מַחְשֶׁבֶת עָמָל : ¹⁴·¹אַשְׁרֵי
אֱנוֹשׁ לֹא עֲצָבוּ פִּיהוּ וְלֹא אָבָה עָלָיו דִּין לִבּוֹ : ²אַשְׁרֵי אִישׁ
לֹא חֲסָרַתּוּ נַפְשׁוֹ וְלֹא שָׁבְתָה תּוֹחַלְתּוֹ : ³לְלֵב קָטָן לֹא
נָאוָה עוֹשֶׁר וּלְאִישׁ רַע עַיִן לֹא נָאוֶה חָרוּץ : ⁴מוֹנֵעַ נַפְשׁוֹ
יִקְבֹּץ לְאַחֵר וּבְטוֹבָתוֹ יִתְבַּעֲבַע זָר : ⁵רַע לְנַפְשׁוֹ לְמִי יֵיטִיב
וְלֹא יִקְרֶה בְטוֹבָתוֹ : ⁶רַע לְנַפְשׁוֹ אֵין רַע מִמֶּנּוּ וְעִמּוֹ תַּשְׁלוֹמַת
רָעָתוֹ : ⁷בְּעַיִן כּוֹשֵׁל מְעַט הֲנֵה חֶלְקוֹ וְלוֹקֵחַ חֵלֶק רֵעֵהוּ מְאַבֵּד
חֶלְקוֹ : ¹⁰עַיִן רַע עַיִן תָּעוּט עַל לֶחֶם וּמְהוּמָה עַל שֻׁלְחָנוֹ :
⁽¹¹⁾עַיִן טוֹבָה מַרְבָּה הַלֶּחֶם וּמַעְיָן יָבֵשׁ יִזַּל מַיִם עַל הַשֻּׁלְחָן :
¹¹בְּנִי אִם יֶשׁ לְךָ שָׁרֵת נַפְשֶׁךָ וְאִם יֶשׁ לְךָ הֵיטִיב לְךָ וְלֹא

[11. 34ᵇ—13. 6

11. 34ᵇ וינכרך במחמדיך: ⁵היטב לצדיק ומצא תשלומת אם
12. 2 לא ממנו מיי: ³אין טובה למנוח רשע וגם צדקה לא
עשה: ⁴פי שנים רע תשיג בעת צורך בכל טובה תגיע
אליו: ⁵כלי לחם אל תתן לו למה בם יקביל אליך: ⁶כי גם אל
שונא רעים ולרשעים ישיב נקם: ⁷תן לטוב ומנע מרע
⁸הקיר סך ואל תתן לוד: ⁹לא יודע בטובה אוהב ולא
יכוסה ברעה שונא: ¹בטובת איש גם שונא ריע וברעתו
גם ריע בודד: ¹⁰אל תאמין בשונא לעד כי כנחשת רועו יחליא:
¹¹וגם אם ישמע לך ויהלך בנחת: תן לבך להתירא ממנו
¹²היה לו כמגלה רז: ולא ימצא להשחיתך ודע אחרית
קנאה: ¹³אל תעמידהו אצלך למה יהדפך ויעמד תחתיך:
¹⁴אל תושיבהו לימינך למה יבקש מושבך: ¹⁵ולאחור תשיג
אמרי ולאנחתי תתאגה: ¹⁶מה יוחן חובר נשוך וכל
הקרב אל חת שן: ¹⁷כן חובר אל אשת זדון ומתגלל
בעונתיו ⁽¹⁸⁾לא יעבר: עד תבער בו אש. ¹⁹כאשר יבוא
עליך‘ לא יתגלה לך ואם תפול לא יפול להצילך ²⁰עד עת
עמד לא יופיע ואם נמוט לא יתכלכל‘ ²¹בשפתיו יתמהמה
צר ובלבו יחשוב מרמרות עמוקות: ²²וגם אם בעיניו
ידמיע אויב אם מצא עת לא ישבע דם ²³אם רע
קראך נמצא שם כאיש סומך יחפש עקב: ²⁴ראש
יניע ותניף ידו ולרובה לחש ישנא פנים: 13. 1 נוגע בזפת
תדבק ידו וחובר אל לץ ילמד דרכו.

²כבד ממך ᵐᵉᵍᵃ תשא ואל עשיר ממך מה תתחבר:
³מה יחבר פרור אל סיר אשר הוא נוקש בו והוא נשבר:
⁴אן מה יחבר עשיר אל דל· ⁵עשיר יענה הוא יתנוה
ועל דל נעוה הוא יתחנן: ⁶אם תכשר לו יעבד בך ואם
תכרע יחמל עליך: ⁷אם שלך ייטב דבריו עמך וירששך
ולא יכאב לו· ⁸צרך לו עמך והשיע לך ושוחק לך ובטיחך

31 בני כבוד תלבשנה ועטרת תפארת תעטרנה: 32 אם
תחפוץ בני תתחכם ואם תשים לבך תערם: 33 אם תובא
לשמע הט אזנך תוסר: 35 כל שיחה. חפוץ לשמע ומשל
בינה אל יצאך: 36 ראה מה יבין ומהריהו ותשחוק בסיפי
רגלך: 37 והתבוננת ביראת עליון ובמצותו והגה תמיד:

7.1 38 והוא יבין לבך ואשר איתה יחכמך: 1 אל תעש לך רעה
ואל ישינך רעה 2הרחק מעון ויט ממך: 3 אל תדע הדושי על
אח פן תקצרדו שבעתים: 4 אל תבקש מאל ממשלת וכן ממלך
מושב כבוד 5 אל תצטדק לפני מלך ופני מלך אל תתבונן:
6 אל תבקש להיות מושל אם אין לך חיל להשבית זדון:
7פן תגור מפני נדיב ונתונה בצע בתמימך: 7 אל תרשיעך
בעדת שערי ואל תפילך בקהלה: 8 אל תקשור לשנות הט
כי באחת לא תנקה: 9 אל תאין בצבא מלאכת עברה הי
כא נחלקה: 10 אל תתקצר בתפלה ובצדקה אל תתעבר:
11 אל תבז לאנוש במר רוח זכר כי יש מרים ומשפיל:
12 אל תחרוש חמס על אח וכן על רע והבר יחדו: 13 אל תחפץ
לכחש על כחש כי תקותו לא תנעם: 14 אל תסוד בעדת
שרים ואל תישן דבר בתפלה: 16 אל תחשיבך במתי עם
זכור עכרון לא יתעבר: 17 מאד מאד השפיל גאוה כי תקות
אנוש רמה: (17) אל תאין לאמר לפריץ גל אל אל ורצה דרכו:
18 אל תמיר אוהב במחיר ואה תלוי בזהב אופיר: 19 אל
תמאס אשה משכלת וטובת הן מפנינים: 20 אל תדע
באמת עבד אמת וכן שוכר נותן נפש: 21 עבד משכיל
הבב כנפש אל תמנע ממנו חפש: 22 בהמה לך ראה עיניך
ואם אמגה היא העמידה: 23 בנים לך יסיר אותם ושא
להם נשים בנעוריהם: 24 בנות לך נצור שארם ואל תאיר
אהם פנים: 25 הוצא בת ויצא עסק ואל נבון גבר חברה:
26 אשה לך אל תתעבה ושנואה אל תאמן בה: 27 בכל לבך פחד

* * * * * *

ואחר יהי דברך: ¹¹היה כמהר להאזין ובארך רוח השב פתגם:
¹²אם יש אתך ענה רעך ואם אין ידך על פיך: ¹³כבוד וקלון
ביד בוטא ולשון אדם מפלתו: ¹⁴אל תקרא בעל שתים
ובלשנך אל תרגל רע: ¹⁵כי על גנב נבראה בשת חרפה רעהו
בעל שתים: ¹⁵מעט והרבה אל תשחת ⁶ותחת אוהב אל תהי שנא
שם רע וקלון תוריש חרפה כן איש רע בעל שתים: ²אל
תפול ביד נפשך ותעבה חילך עליך: ³עליך תאכל ופריך
תשרש: והניחתך כעץ יבש ⁴כי נפש עזה תשחת בעליה
ושמחת שונא תשיגם: ⁵חיך ערב ירבה אוהב ושפתי חן
שואל שלום: ⁶אנשי שלומך יהיו רבים ובעל סודך אחד מאלף.
⁷קנית אוהב בנסיון קנהו ואל תמהר לבטח עליו: ⁸כי יש אוהב
כפי עת ולא יעמוד ביום צרה: ⁹יש אוהב נהפך לשנא ואת
ריב חרפתך יחשוף: ¹⁰יש אוהב חבר שלחן ולא ימצא
ביום רעה: ¹¹בטובתך הא כמוך . וברעתך יתנדה ממך:
¹²אם תשיגך רעה יהפך בך ומפניך יסתר: ¹³משנאיך הבדל
ומאהביך השמר: ¹⁴אוהב אמונה אוהב תקוף ומוצאו מצא
הון: ¹⁵לאוהב אמונה אין מחיר ואין משקל לטובתו: ¹⁶צרור
חיים אוהב אמונה ירא אל ישיגם. ¹⁷כי כמוהו כן רעהו
¹⁷וכשמו כן מעשיו. ¹⁸כחורש וכקוצר קרב איה וקוה לרב
תבואתה: ¹⁹כי בעבדתה מעט תעבוד ולמחר תאכל פריה:
²⁰עקובה היא לאויל ולא יכלכלנה חסר לב: ²¹כאבן משא
תהיה עליו ולא יאחר להשליכה: ²²כי המוסר כשמה כן
הוא ולא לרבים היא נכוחה: ²³כלי יוצר לבער כבשן וכמהו
איש על חשבונו: ²⁴על עבדת עץ יהי פרי כן חשבון על
יצר אחד: ²⁵הט שכמך ושאה ואל תקץ בתחבולתיה:
²⁶דרש וחקר בקש ומצא והחזקתה ואל תרפה: ²⁷כי לאחור
תמצא מנוחתה ונהפך לך לתענוג: ²⁸והיתה לך רשתה
מכון עז וחבלתה בגדי כתם: ²⁹עלי זהב עלה ומוסרתיה
פתיל תכלת:

[4. 10ᶜ—5. 10]

¹⁰וגֿ יקראך בן ויחנך ויצילך משחת · ¹¹חכמות למדה
בניה ותעיד לכל מבינים בה : ¹²ארביה אהבו חיים ומבקשיה
יפיקו רצון מיֿי : ¹³ותמכיה ימצאו כבוד מיֿי וחנו בברכת יֿי
¹⁴משרתי קדש · משרתיה ואלהו במא ויהא ¹⁵שומע לי ישפט אמת
ומאזין לי ייחן בחדרי מבית : ¹⁶כי בהתנכר אלך עמו ¹⁷ולפנים
יבחרנו בנסיונות : ¹⁷ᵃועד עת ימלא לבו בי ¹⁸אשוב ואאשרנו
וגליתי לו מסתרי : ¹⁹ אם יסור ונטותידו ויסרתידו באסורים :
¹⁹(¹)אם יסור מאחרי אשליכנו ואסגירנו לשדדים : ²⁰בני עת
המון שמר ופחד מרע וגֿ נפשך אֿל תבוש : ²¹כי יש בֿשאֿת
משאת עון ויש בשת כבוד וחן : ²²אל תשא פניך על נפשך
ואל תכשל למכשוליך : ²³אֿל תמנע דבר בעולם אֿל תצפין
את חכמתך : ²⁴כי באומר נודעת חכמה ותבונה במענה לשון :
²⁵אֿל תסרב עם האֿ וגֿ אלהים היכנע : ²⁶אֿל תבוש לשוב מעון
וגֿ תעמוד לפני שבלת : ²⁷אֿל תצע לנבל נפשך וגֿ תמאן לפני
מושלים : ²⁷(¹)אֿל תשב עם שופט עול כי כאשר כרצונו תשפט
עמו ²⁸עד המות היעצה על הצדק וגֿי נלחם לך · ²⁹אֿל תקרא
בעל שתים וגֿ לשונך אֿל תרגל : ³⁰אֿל תהי גבהן בלשניך ורפי
ורשש במלאכתך : ³⁰אֿל תהי ככלב בביתך ומוזר ומתירא
במלאכתך : ³¹אֿל תהי ידך פתוחה לקחת וקפוצה בתוך מתן :

⁵·¹אֿל תשען על חילך וגֿ תאמר יש לאֿ ידי · ¹(¹)אֿל תשען על כוחך
ללכת אחר תאות נפשך : ²אֿל תלך אחרי לבך ועיניך ללכת
בחמדות רעה : ³אֿל תאמר מי יוכל כחו כי יֿי מבקש נרדפים :
⁴אֿל תאמר חטאתי ומה יעשה לי מאומה כי אֿל ארך אפים הוא :
⁴אֿל תאמר רחום יֿי וכל עונותי ימחה : ⁵אֿל סליחה אֿל תבטח
להוסיף עון על עון : ⁶ואמרת רחמיו רבים לרוב עונותי יסלח :
⁶כי רחמים ואף עמֿ[ו] וגֿ רשעים ינוח רגזו : ⁷אֿל תאחר לשוב
אליו וגֿ תתעבר מיום אֿל יום : ⁷כי פתאום יצא זעמו וביום נקם
תספה : ⁸אֿל תבטח על נכסי שקר כי לא יועילו ביום עברה :
⁹אֿל תהיה זורה לכל רוח ופונה דרך שבולת : ¹⁰היה סמוך לֿדעתך

3.6 מכבד אמו : ⁶בני במאמר ובמעשה כבד אביך עבור ישיגוך
כל ברכות : ⁹ברכת אב תיסד שרש וקללת אם תנתש נטע :
¹⁰אל תתכבד בקלון אביך כי לא כבוד הוא לך : ¹¹כבוד איש כבוד
אביו ומרבה חטא מקלל אמו : ¹²בני התחזק בכבור אביך ואל
תעזבהו כל ימי חייך : ¹³וגם אם יחסר מדעו עזוב לו ואל תכלים
אותו כל ימי חייו : ¹⁴צדקת אב לא תמחה ותמור חטאת היא
תנטע : ¹⁵ביום צרה תזכר לך כחם על כפור להשבית עוניך : ¹⁶כי
מזיד בוזה אביו ומכעיס בוראו מקלל אמו : ¹⁷בני בעשרך
התהלך בענוה ותאהב מנותן מתנות ¹⁸מעט נפשך מכל
גדולת עולם ולפני אל תמצא רחמים : ²⁰כי רבים רחמי אהים
¹⁹ולענוים יגלה סודו ⋅ ²¹פלאות ממך אל תדרוש ומכוסה
ממך אל תחקור : ²²במה שהורשית התבונן ואין לך עסק
בנסתרות : ²³וביותר ממך אל תמר כי רב ממך הראית : ²⁴כי
רבים עשתוני בני אדם ודמיונות דעות מתעות : ²⁵לב כבד
תבאש אחריתו ואוהב טובות ינהג בהם : ²⁷לב כבד ירבו
מכאביו ומתהולל מוסיף עון על עון : ²⁸באין אישון יחסר
אור ובאין דעת תחסר חכמה : ²⁸אל תרוץ לרפאות מכת לץ
כי אין לה רפואה כי מנטע רע נטעו : ²⁹לב חכם יבין משלי
חכמים ואזן מקשבת לחכמה תשמח : ³⁰אש לוהטת יכבו מים
כן צדקה תכפר חטאת : ³¹פועל טוב יקראנו בדרכיו ובעת
4.1 מוטו ימצא משען : ¹בני אל תלענ לחיי עני ואל תדאיב נפש
עני ומר נפש : ²דוה נפש חסידה אל תפוח ואל תתעלם ממדכדי
נפש : ³אל תחמיר מעי דך וקרב עני אל תכאיב : ⁴אל תמנע מתן
ממסכינך ⁵ולא תבזה שאלות דל ⁶ולא תתן לו מקום לקללך :
⁶צועק מר רוח בכאב נפשו ובקול צעקתו ישמע צורו :
⁷האהב לנפשך לעדה ולשלטון עוד הכאף ראש : ⁸הט לעני
אונך והשיבהו שלום בענוה : ⁹הושע מוצק ממציקיו ואל
תקוץ רוחך במשפט יושר : ¹⁰היה כאב ליתומים ותמור בעל
לאלמנות :

www.ingramcontent.com/pod-product-compliance
Lightning Source LLC
Chambersburg PA
CBHW020252170426
43202CB00008B/329